RELIGIONS AS BRANDS

T0330491

Ashgate AHRC/ESRC Religion and Society Series

Series Editors:

Linda Woodhead, University of Lancaster, UK
Rebecca Catto, University of Coventry, UK

This book series emanates from the largest research programme on religion in Europe today – the AHRC/ESRC Religion and Society Programme which has invested in over seventy-five research projects. Thirty-two separate disciplines are represented looking at religion across the world, many with a contemporary and some with an historical focus. This international, multi-disciplinary and interdisciplinary book series will include monographs, paperback textbooks and edited research collections drawn from this leading research programme.

Other titles in the series:

Everyday Lived Islam in Europe
Edited by Nathal M. Dessing, Nadia Jeldtoft, Jørgen S. Nielsen
and Linda Woodhead

Media Portrayals of Religion and the Secular Sacred
Representation and Change
Kim Knott, Elizabeth Poole and Teemu Taira

Varieties of Religious Establishment
Edited by Winnifred Fallers Sullivan and Lori G. Beaman

Understanding Muslim Chaplaincy
Sophie Gilliat-Ray, Mansur Ali and Stephen Pattison

Ageing, Ritual and Social Change
Comparing the Secular and Religious in Eastern and Western Europe
Edited by Peter Coleman, Daniela Koleva and Joanna Bornat

Social Identities Between the Sacred and the Secular
Abby Day, Giselle Vincett and Christopher R. Cotter

Religions as Brands

New Perspectives on the Marketization of Religion and Spirituality

Edited by

JEAN-CLAUDE USUNIER
Université de Lausanne, Switzerland

JÖRG STOLZ
Université de Lausanne, Switzerland

Routledge
Taylor & Francis Group

LONDON AND NEW YORK

Religions as Brands

During the twentieth century, religion has gone on the market place. Churches and religious groups are forced to "sell god" in order to be attractive to "religious consumers." More and more, religions are seen as "brands" that have to be recognizable to their members and the general public. What does this do to religion? How do religious groups and believers react? What is the consequence for society as a whole?

This book brings together some of the best international specialists from marketing, sociology and economics in order to answer these and similar questions. The interdisciplinary book treats new developments in three fields that have hitherto evolved rather independently: (1) the commoditization of religion, (2) the link between religion and consumer behavior, and (3) the economics of religion. By combining and cross-fertilizing these three fields, the book shows just what happens when religions become brands.

First published 2014 by Ashgate publishing

2 Park Square, Milton Park, Abingdon, Oxfordshire OX14 4RN
711 Third Avenue, New York, NY 10017

Routledge is an imprint of the Taylor & Francis Group, an informa business

First issued in paperback 2018

British Library Cataloguing in Publication Data
A catalogue record for this book is available from the British Library

The Library of Congress has cataloged the printed edition as follows:
Religion as brands : new perspectives on the marketization of religion and spirituality / edited by Jean-Claude Usunier and Jörg Stolz.
    pages cm.—(Ashgate AHRC/ESRC religion and society series)
  Includes index.
  ISBN 978-1-4094-6755-7 (hardcover)
1. Religion—Economic aspects. 2. Branding (Marketing)
3. Consumption (Economics) I. Usunier, Jean-Claude, editor of compilation.
  HB72.R4515 2013
  206—dc23

                                                            2013015410

ISBN 978-1-4094-6755-7 (hbk)
ISBN 978-1-138-54624-0 (pbk)

Contents

List of Figures

List of Tables

Notes on Contributors

Steve Bruce has been Professor of Sociology at the University of Aberdeen since 1991. He was born in Edinburgh in 1954 and schooled at the Queen Victoria School Dunblane, Perthshire. He studied sociology and religious studies at the University of Stirling (MA 1976; PhD 1980) and taught at The Queen's University, Belfast, from 1978 to 1991. He was elected a Fellow of the British Academy in 2003 and a Fellow of the Royal Society of Edinburgh in 2005. He has written extensively on the nature of religion in the modern world and on the links between religion and politics. His two most recent works are *Secularization* (Oxford University Press, 2011) and *Politics and Religion in the United Kingdom* (Routledge, 2011).

Jason Dean is an American-born academic who has taught in universities in Africa and in Europe. He is currently an associate researcher at the Center for the Sociology of Religions and Social Ethics (CSRES) at the University of Strasbourg, France. He is the author of numerous publications on Islamic hermeneutics and medical ethics, the social organization of religious groups, and the institutionalization of Islam in France, which have appeared, in English and in French, in scientific journals and collective publications.

Olivier Favre, PhD, is affiliated with the Observatory of religions of the University of Lausanne. His main researches focus on evangelism. His publications, including *Evangelical churches in Switzerland*, are based on both quantitative data and qualitative interviews. He also participates in the synthesis of a large research program on religious phenomena in Switzerland and worked on religious official data of the Federal Office of Statistics. Besides that, he is involved in a pastoral ministry in an evangelical church.

Roger Finke is professor of Sociology and Religious Studies at Pennsylvania State University. He studied sociology at the University of Washington in Seattle. Prior to joining PennState in 2000, he was professor of sociology at the Loyola University of Chicago and at Purdue University in West Lafayette. His research projects are looking at cross-national variation in religious regulation, persecution, and violence. He is also interested and involved in studying religious organizations and the diverse religious market in the US. He also serves as the director of the Association of Religion Data Archives. His publications include *Acts of Faith. Explaining the Human Side of Religion* (with Rodney Stark) and *The Churching of America, 1776–1990: Winners and Losers in Our Religious Economy* (with Rodney Stark).

Markus Hero, PhD, teaches and conducts research at the Center for Religious Studies (CERES) at Ruhr University in Bochum, Germany. The sociologist and economist mainly focuses on the societal and economic aspects of contemporary changes in religion. Hero's areas of research primarily concern the field of new and alternative religiosity, as well as the impacts of religious plurality. He is the author of *Die neuen Formen des religiösen Lebens. Eine institutionentheoretische Analyse neuer Religiosität* and co-editor of a volume dealing with religious pluralization in Germany. In his articles, he mainly writes about the substance and institutional aspects of contemporary spirituality.

Jochen Hirschle is a research assistant at the Department of Sociology at the University of Innsbruck, Austria. He has studied Sociology at the University of Cologne and achieved a PhD at the Chair for Empirical Social and Economic Research. He worked as a project manager in market research in Frankfurt/M, Aachen and Cologne, and from 2007 to 2011 as a Post-Doc researcher at the FernUniversität in Hagen. His research interests lie in the fields of economic and religious change. Specifically, he studies the development of capitalism under conditions of affluence and its impact on social and religious practices of individuals. He has published, among others, in the *Socio-Economic Review*, the *Journal for the Scientific Study of Religion*, and *European Societies*. His most recent book is *Die Entstehung des transzendenten Kapitalismus* (UVK, 2012).

Christopher P. Scheitle is Senior Research Associate at Penn State University and Adjunct Assistant Professor of Sociology at the College of St. Benedict-St. John's University. He is author of *Places of Faith: A Road Trip Across America's Religious Landscape* (Oxford, 2012; with Roger Finke) and *Beyond the Congregation: The World of Religious Nonprofits* (Oxford, 2010). His primary research area involves the organizational structure and dynamics of religion in the United States.

Haytham Siala is Senior Lecturer at Roehampton University Business School, Roehampton University. His current research interests include the influence of religion on consumer behavior, the impact of culture on consumer interactions in e-Commerce, and user acceptance models for Information Technologies.

Philippe Simonnot was a professor of law and economics at the Universities of Paris X Nanterre and Versailles. He is the author of numerous books in economic history and sociology of religious institutions, including *Les Papes, l'Église et l'argent, Histoire économique du christianisme des origines à nos jours, and Le Marché de Dieu*. He authors economic chronics in the French newspapers, including *Le Monde* and *Le Figaro*. In 2007, he launched the *Observatoire des Religions*online, in order to study religion in a scientific—mainly economic—way.

Elizabeth Stickel-Minton is affiliated with Lundquist College of Business, University of Oregon, 1208 University of Oregon, Eugene. She received her

MBA from Idaho State University and her BBA from the University of Alaska Southeast in marketing. Before starting the doctoral program, she conducted tourism development reviews for a rural tourism development agency and worked in marketing and accounting for an aviation tourism company in Alaska. Her research interests are public policy, services marketing, and religion as a determinant of consumer behavior. Her current research projects include "Religion as an individual difference variable affecting sustainable consumption" and "How religious affiliation grouping influences consumer behavior findings."

Jörg Stolz is Professor of Sociology of Religion at the University of Lausanne. His research focuses on the explanation of secularization, the competition between the religious and the secular, evangelicalism, stereotypes, and religious pluralism with the theory of social mechanisms (analytical sociology). Concerning methods, he is especially interested in mixed methods research. He is president-elect of the International Society for the Sociology of Religion. He is the author of *Soziologie der Fremdenfeindlichkeit. Theoretische und empirische Analysen* of *L'avenir des Réformés. Les Eglises face aux changements sociaux* (with Edmée Ballif) and has edited the book *Salvation goods and religious markets. Theory and Applications*. He has published in various international journals such as the British Journal of Sociology, Sociology of Religion, or Review of Religious Research.

Hanifa Touag graduated from the Institut d'Etudes Politiques (IEP) in Paris in 2010, She is an active member of the Centre for Interdisciplinary Research on Islam in the Contemporary World (CISCOW). She is now preparing a doctoral thesis on salafists movements in Brussels under the direction of Professor Brigitte Maréchal (Université catholique de Louvain) and Professor Catherine Wihtol de Wenden (I.E.P de Paris). She is notably the author of a master's memoir on islamists women in Morocco and she has also written several articles on Islamic consumption (in J-P. Delville (ed.), *Mutations des religions et des identités religieuses*, 2012) and on the new muslim healers (in Brigitte Maréchal and Farid El Asri (eds) *Islam belge au pluriel*, 2012).

Jean-Claude Usunier is professor at the University of Lausanne, Switzerland, in the Faculty of Business and Economics (HEC). His research interests are cross-cultural consumer behavior, cultural and linguistic aspects of international marketing, with special interest for commoditization processes in international trade. He serves on the editorial board of several international business journals. His books include *International and Cross-Cultural Management Research* (Sage, 1998), *International Business Negotiations* (Elsevier, 2003) and *Marketing Across Cultures* (Pearson, 2012).

David Voas is Professor of Population Studies in the Institute for Social and Economic Research at the University of Essex. He previously worked at the University of Manchester. He is the national programme director in Great Britain for the European Values Study and co-director of British Religion in Numbers (www.brin.ac.uk). He serves on the editorial boards of the *British Journal of Sociology* and the *Journal for the Scientific Study of Religion.* His research is focused on the causes and consequences of value change and ethno-religious change in modern society, typically using large international survey datasets.

Thomas Wagner is a PhD candidate in Ethnomusicology at Royal Holloway, University of London. His dissertation explores the relationship between worship music, marketing and transcendence in consumer cultures. His work on this subject has recently appeared as an article in the Australian Journal of Communication co-authored with Tanya Riches. Tom is currently co-editing a volume for Ashgate Publishing entitled *Christian Congregational Musics: Performance, Identity, Experience* (2013).

Preface

David Voas

In the beginning, research on religion was the domain of theology. And then secular scholars saw that the scriptures could be studied as literary texts, that archaeology and historical records provided additional information, and ultimately that psychology and sociology offered insights into the formation and transmission of faith. They did not rest there, because the creation of knowledge is never complete. In the age of the market, the term "religious service" came to sound less like worship and more like something that a producer supplies to a consumer.

Two consequences have followed. One is the deliberate application of the tools of modern marketing to religion. The other is the deliberate application of the tools of microeconomics to the analysis of the "religious market," now to be discussed in terms of firms, products, competition, and so on. By the turn of the millennium, these practical and theoretical strands were both well developed, though the people involved saw little overlap between them.

This volume grows out of an attempt to address that communication gap. It does so with specific reference to a topic that has so far received less attention than it deserves: the concept of brands in the market for religion. The editors are leaders in the two domains: Usunier is an expert on marketing and culture, and one of few scholars to have studied this area closely; Stolz is a sociologist of religion who has done more than anyone else to show the extent to which religious organizations must compete with secular providers as well as amongst themselves.

A brand is a set of associations that people have with a product, service, or firm. The notion can be extended to individuals—celebrities may become brands and so attach their personalities to perfume, sunglasses, diets, and so on—and also to abstractions like social movements ("Occupy"). The category of religion is arguably a brand, alongside more concrete entities such as the Catholic Church, Lourdes, or the sacrament of baptism.

"Religion" as a concept brand is under pressure. Religious leaders face the sort of challenge familiar to cigarette manufacturers. It is not enough to show that the product is good of its kind; the brand manager must overcome some resistance to the kind of thing it is. Fairly or unfairly, religion has come to be associated with a number of unpopular things: American politicians, preachy morality, hypocrisy, child abuse, Islamist extremism, immigrants. Deinstitutionalized spirituality might be seen as an attempt to rebrand religious experience by cutting it free of the negative connotations of "religion."

xviii Religions as Brands

By its nature religion is something that provokes contention, and religious providers are always in danger of weakening their brands by attracting unfavorable as well as favorable publicity. Religious professionals also face the temptation of being free-riders on the reputation of their brands, letting quality and service standards drop without suffering any immediate loss. In the long (and increasingly the short) term, however, consumers do notice. Rival suppliers respond by offering religious renewal, a process of rebranding, or new brand creation.

As even these few reflections show, there is little difficulty in applying the terminology of brands to religion. The question is whether it is wise or illuminating to do so. How far are we willing to allow the empire of markets to extend? And are we speaking in metaphors, or is it really the case that religious belief and practice are most usefully analyzed with the tools of microeconomics?

From the standpoint of marketing, the situation is paradoxical. Religious leaders could not be *religious* leaders if they made image a priority. No doubt "Mother Theresa" became a brand, and that brand was successfully deployed for charitable purposes, but many people would be offended by the suggestion that there was anything conscious about the way her name and image became trademarks for altruism. Marketing must be relabeled mission in this context, for the irony is that few things are as bad for a religious brand as public signs of brand management.

For social scientists, the proof of the pudding is in the eating. Contrasting views are well represented in this volume; Roger Finke is one of the main proponents of applying a supply-side economic perspective to religion; Steve Bruce is a leader of the opposition. My own view is that analyzing religions as brands can be fruitful, though we must expect the model to break down if pushed too far. It does not seem very helpful, for example, to discuss antipathy towards Islam and Muslims in these terms. It can be done, but the exercise seems unlikely to produce any real insights.

As a better instance of where these concepts could be deployed, take the case of religion in Europe and the United States. National churches are typically strong brands: the Church of Denmark, the Swiss Reformed Church, the Catholic Church in Italy, and so on, are associated to varying degrees with identity and culture in their respective homelands. Most European countries have weak religious markets, but state regulation is rarely to blame (contrary to the claims of many American scholars). Suppressing competition is unnecessary: European have little enthusiasm for new suppliers in part because they have attachments to strong brands. Brands are about identity, and the stronger religious identities are the less they are threatened by rival kinds of belief and practice.

By contrast, denominationalism has been in long-term decline in the United States. The old Protestant brands (Lutheran, Methodist, Presbyterian, Baptist, etc.) are no longer as important to most people as other more local characteristics of the churches available. Even the super-brands of *Protestant, Catholic, Jew* that for Will Herberg in 1955 were the enduring social divides in American life are now regularly breached in marriage. The brands that matter are more ephemeral:

the Toronto blessing, *The Purpose-Driven Life*, John Paul II, and a host of others that 20 years later become largely irrelevant. The most competitive markets are commodity markets, where brands do not exist at all.

Students of marketing and sociology of religion can learn from each other, and both may have something to say to religious organizations. With apologies for taking an example close to home, consider the Church of England. Consistency is generally seen as part of the brand promise: the consumer can be confident that a McDonald's hamburger will taste the same in Moscow and Atlanta. Such reliability is not found in Anglican churches, which offer worship styles ranging from hyper-ritualistic to guitars-and-video, combined with theologies from radical orthodoxy to religionless Christianity. Does this diversity undermine the brand, or has it cleverly been stretched to colonize all market niches? In trying to answer this question and a host of others like it, the dialogue the editors have begun is invaluable.

PART I
Introduction

Chapter 1

Religions as Brands:
New Perspectives on the Marketization
of Religion and Spirituality

Jörg Stolz and Jean-Claude Usunier

The church cannot engage in marketing. The church cannot put itself on a pedestal, create itself, praise itself. One cannot serve God while at the same time covering oneself by serving the devil and the world.[1]

Karl Barth

We shouldn't be surprised then that religion—whether in the form of a film or a church—is being marketed in the current commercialized culture. In order to be heard above the noise of the rest of society, religion, too, must participate in order to survive.

Mara Einstein

There can be no doubt: marketing and branding have started to transform religions.[2] Despite ferocious critiques, we have seen the emergence of televangelists (e.g. Oral Roberts, Jim Bakker), celebrity pastors (e.g. Rick Warren), stars of compassion (e.g. Mother Teresa), church commercials, religious "product lines," mega-churches, branded religious sites (e.g. Lourdes), religious best-sellers (e.g. *the Left Behind* series), and blockbusters (e.g. *The Passion of the Christ*). Marketing and branding have not spared non-Christian religions. Think of the success of the Kabbalah centers, veiled Barbie dolls, Mecca cola, the Buddha as a decorative item, or the marketing of the Dalai Lama. At the same time, observers have noted that shopping and consuming may take on religious traits. After all, branding makes products into something "out of the ordinary," "mythical," and sometimes even "sacred." Brand communities have formed around such products as Jeep, Star Trek, or Harley Davidson. And Apple fans have not only venerated their Macs, they have also deeply believed in the transformative power of the

---

[1] The translation is ours. The original text is: "Die Kirche kann nicht Propaganda treiben. Die Kirche kann sich nicht selber wollen, bauen, rühmen wie alle anderen … Man kann nicht Gott dienen und mit dem Teufel und der Welt solche Rückversicherungen eingehen" Barth (1930).
[2] We thank David Voas and Vincent Vandersluis for excellent remarks and David Voas, Vincent Vandersluis, and Christine Rhone for help with the English at different stages of this text.

savior of their brand: Steve Jobs. Are then religions becoming brands while brands are becoming religions?

In this introduction, we lay out the different questions to ask and survey the relevant literature. It is interesting to note that various disciplines—sociology, economics, marketing, theology, history, and anthropology—have contributed to our current knowledge about "religions as brands." However, these disciplines have not always taken their respective insights into common consideration. One of the aims of this book is therefore to bring these strands of research into closer contact and to suggest promising directions for future research.

The plan of our introduction is as follows. We first describe the *historical antecedents* of religious consumer society. By this term we mean a society in which religious organizations see themselves as offering "products" and "services" on a "market," while individuals see themselves as "consumers" choosing these "products" and "services." We show that modernization processes, the transformation of forms of religious groups, and generalized competition between religious and secular goods have led to a situation that makes both religious consuming and religious marketing increasingly probable. In a second part, we look at the *individual effects* of the above-mentioned historical antecedents. We analyze changing expectations of individuals towards religious organizations and an increase in choosing and combining different forms of religion and spirituality. We also discuss recent claims that shopping and consuming might be modern forms of religion and spirituality. In a third part, we describe the *organizational effects* of the historical antecedents. We look at both general and specific forms of religious branding and marketing and also discuss the influence of societal and cultural context. Part four describes the contributions to this volume, giving a sense of how they open up new perspectives concerning the question of "religions as brands."

Antecedents: Causes of the Religious Consumer Society

A substantial part of the literature describes historical causes that are said to have led to a "religious consumer society."[3] We look at modernization processes, a change in the form of religious groups and the emergence of a generalized religious-secular competition.

---

[3]   While most authors would probably agree with some kind of story of a modernization process leading to the religious consumer society, there is a debate as to *when* it happened. Some scholars think that the major turning point was the 1960s. They speak of a rather sudden "cultural revolution" (Einstein, 2008; McLeod, 2007; Stolz, Könemann, Schneuwly Purdie, Englberger, and Krüggeler, 2012)). Other scholars, however, believe that the important change came about only in the 1980s (Gauthier, Martikainen, and Woodhead, 2011). Our own view clearly gives preference to the argument concerning the 1960s. We base this judgment on the quantitative, qualitative and historical data produced by scholars such as McLeod (2007) and Brown (2001).

Modernization processes

While the specific theoretical preferences and terms vary, most authors seem to agree that some sort of *"modernization process"* is responsible for the emergence of the current religious consumer society (Altermatt, 1981; Beck, 1992; Dawson, 2011; Gauthier *et al.*, 2011; Norris and Inglehart, 2004; Wallis and Bruce, 1995). This process entails (among many others):

- *A breakdown of religious norms.* Before the 1960s, there was general pressure on individuals to be members of a religion, and to have the same religion as their parents. Depending on various context variables, there could also be pressure to believe and practise.
- *An increased individual freedom to choose*, emphasizing the freedom and duty of individuals to decide for themselves in all matters important to them—including religious identity, practice, and belief.
- *A change in values.* Traditional values linked to authority and duty are replaced by self-realization and individualistic values. In the religious field this can be seen as a replacement of the semantic of "religiosity" by "spirituality."
- Increases in *disposable income*. This gives individuals a wider range of options, especially concerning secular leisure, which may compete with religious options.
- An increase in *individual security*. The invention of welfare schemes, various types of insurance, improved biomedical services, etc. give individuals a level of security unprecedented in history. This in turn competes with the reassuring function of religious beliefs and practices.
- An *increased exposure to mass media* (TV, radio, later the internet). Individuals spend more and more time exposing themselves to and interacting with mass media. This increases the possibility of getting information about all kinds of religions, but equally about all kinds of secular matters.
- *Increased individual mobility.* Individuals travel increasingly long distances and start to think of their world (and possibly their religious and spiritual involvement) in terms of options that have a price, that may be consumed and that have to be chosen according to individual preferences.

Interestingly, these modernizing processes have led both to extended *religious markets* and to *less religiosity*. On the one hand, there has indeed been an increasing number of individuals choosing religious "products" that were specifically marketed by religious entrepreneurs. Alternative spirituality, a form of "consumer religion," has shown important growth. And it is no accident that the number of megachurches rose dramatically from the 1960s on (Chaves, 2006). On the other hand, there has been a clear tendency towards *less religiosity* for many individuals. Since religion was not prescribed anymore and since individuals were now "free to choose," they were also free to choose no religion, no belief, no practice. This led to a rise in "fuzzy religiosity" (Storm, 2009; Voas, 2009) and to a rise in the number of secular individuals. Due to this increased freedom, religion also lost its former importance in the choice of a spouse, leading to a marked rise in the number of religiously mixed couples as well as in couples with only one partner having a religion (Voas, 2003). Summing up, we thus observe a *simultaneous* process of marketization, individualization, and secularization. Much of the literature sees these processes as mutually exclusive, which is misleading. Rather, they are part of one single social process that has to be explained with a more general theory (Stolz, 2008, 2009a).

The change of religious groups from institutions to non-profit organizations

A second large-scale cause for the emergence of religious consumer society can be seen in the changing *form* of religious groups. In many countries they seem to evolve from institutions to kinds of non-profit organizations. While, in the nineteenth century and well into the twentieth century, they were institutions to which individuals often belonged by tradition and which were linked multi-functionally to many other societal institutions (the power structure, schools, hospitals, media etc.), religious groups have increasingly been transformed into voluntary associations such as sports clubs or philanthropic societies. Like all other voluntary associations, religious groups now have to compete for memberships and for their members' time, donations, and energy. And like all other voluntary associations, they are therefore forced to engage in some form of marketing and branding. Thus, religious organizations should not be seen as incorporated "religious companies" with a commercial object and limited liability, but rather as non-profit organizations (NPOs) or voluntary (membership) organizations. In several important respects, non-profit organizations are distinguishable from firms orientated to profit (Mottner, 2007; Schwarz, 1986; Stolz, 2009):

1. They have members and their main goal lies not in the profit making but in the satisfaction of the needs of their members or other specified social groups.
2. They do not produce private goods (like cars), but a number of services for their members or for the general public (or both).
3. They have several important publics that all have to be cared for: members, prospective members, staff, volunteers, and the general public.
4. They do not finance themselves principally by the sale of products, but by members' contributions or donations.
5. They compete on various levels with various other organizations and institutions. In modern societies, the main competition often stems not so much from other religious institutions as from secular organizations.

This has important practical consequences for the marketing activities in which religious organizations may engage (see below).

Religious-secular competition

A third large-scale process that has made the religious consumer society possible is the emergence of a *generalized religious-secular competition*. This process is well established in the marketing literature (Einstein, 2011; Mottner, 2007), but has not yet been given the attention it deserves in the sociology of religion and economics of religion literature (see, however, Gruber and Hungerman, 2008; Stolz, 2009b). Since individuals are now free to choose, all organizations and institutions that want to stay "in business" have to compete for the attention, the time and the donations of individuals (Einstein, 2008). This is just as true for religious organizations and groups as for any other secular institutions.

The religious-secular competition is a very serious matter for religious organizations. In fact, the traditional and institutionally based "motivators" that led to religious activity have been destroyed or at least seriously damaged by the modernization process. Christian practice in the nineteenth century was often motivated by the fact that non-practice was socially stigmatized, or that practice was prescribed by employers, or that the church was a place where spouses, friends and business partners could be found, or that the congregation was a place where social status could be displayed (among other things by appearing in one's "Sunday best"), or that individuals were concerned with their lives hereafter (Brown, 2001; Bruce, 2002). Since these motivators have faded away and an array of secular alternatives is available for finding spouses and showing status, Christian Churches have to engage in marketing in order to renew individual interest in their "products."[4]

Individual Effects: Religious and Spiritual Shopping and Consuming

The societal changes mentioned have had various *effects on individuals* that are characteristic of "religious consumer society." We discuss four such effects: changing expectations towards religious organizations, an increase in choosing and combining religious/secular elements, a tendency to shop and consume religion/spirituality, and the possibility that consumption (of all kinds of products) may itself become a form of religion in modernity.

Changing expectations of individuals towards religious organizations

A first effect resides in significant changes in individual expectations towards religion. In consumer society, individuals learn that products and services should be attuned to their every need. It is therefore no wonder that they also expect

---

[4] The socioeconomic literature concerned with religion has focused almost exclusively on the competition between different religious groups. In contrast, we argue that the competition between the religious and the secular is much more important than intra-religious competition.

such behavior from religious organizations and their products and services. A substantial number of publications show that individuals increasingly expect:

1. *"High quality" services* (Bruhn, 1999; Santos and Mathews, 2001; Stolz and Ballif, 2010). Several studies show that members of Christian churches increasingly expect high quality religious services, high quality music, good speakers and convenient access to places of worship. One way of reacting to the rising costs this entails has been the trend towards megachurches (Chaves, 2006; Fath, 2008).
2. *Entertainment.* In religious services, writes Mara Einstein (2008: 8) "consumers have a heightened expectation of being entertained, which is usually met with music and dramatic presentations." Religious groups will increasingly copy successful entertainment formats from the secular sphere or invent new forms, in order to let individuals "have a good time" during their rituals and religious services (Favre, in this volume).
3. *Freedom to choose.* Individuals are increasingly concerned that religious groups will not restrict their choices and will respect their absolute freedom to believe and practise according to their individual preferences (Stolz and Ballif, 2010). Just as in the world of shopping and consuming, they want to be able to choose what they like instead of being told what to do.

An increase in individualized religion and religious shopping

In religious consumer society, individuals increasingly *choose* what to believe, how to practice and what norms to obey (if any). Different disciplinary approaches—individualization theorists, consumer society theorists, economists of religion, marketing theorists and even secularization theorists—agree on this point (Iannaccone, 1992; Roof, 1999). The agreement stops, however, when it comes to the question of what this increasing choice does to individual religiosity.

One position, often found in religious economics or the rational choice approach to religion, is that increasing religious freedom leads to increased religious shopping and a generalized religious market (Finke and Iannaccone, 1993; Iannaccone, 1991, 1992, 1998; Stark, 1999; Stark and Finke, 2000).[5] These authors normally see any kind of society as a potential religious market that is more or less regulated. Individuals are seen as "naturally religious" and will behave as religious and spiritual shoppers, if only they are allowed to do so. They choose religious beliefs and practices according to their preferences—much as they choose cars or toothpaste. For example, Stark and Iannaccone (1994) argued that it was wrong to believe that Europe in the second half of the twentieth century

---

[5] This approach is often called the "supply-side approach," because it argues that demand of religion across all societies is essentially stable and that differences in aggregated religiosity must therefore be explained by variation in the supply of religion.

underwent a process of "secularization" and, on the contrary, that increasing individual freedom would eventually lead to a religious revival.[6]

A second position sees the effect of increasing religious freedom not so much in increases in "shopping" and "consuming," but rather in the fact that individuals believe and practise in an increasingly syncretistic and individualized way. Various terms have been created and used in order to highlight this phenomenon: bricolage, à la carte religion, do-it-yourself religion, recomposition, Sheilaism, or patchwork-religion (Bailey, 1990; Bellah, 1985; Dobbelaere, 2002: 173; Hervieu-Léger, 2001; Luckmann, 1967). The overall message of this literature is that more religious freedom does not lead to less religiosity, but to a change in the *form of religiosity*. Since individuals are no longer controlled by institutions, they become religious in ways that often do not look religious to the unsuspecting observer (hence the talk of "invisible" or "implicit" religion) or that are increasingly "spiritual" (Bloch, 1998; Heelas and Woodhead, 2004). Since each individual becomes a "special case," qualitative research in particular seems to be a good method to investigate these new forms of religiosity and spirituality.

A third position also acknowledges increasing individual religious freedom, but sees various possible individual reactions to such a state of affairs (Gruber and Hungerman, 2006; Need and De Graaf, 1996; Stolz, 2009b). Individuals may, according to this position, become religious shoppers, but they may also choose not to be religious or entertain a kind of "fuzzy fidelity" (Storm, 2009; Voas, 2009). It depends on the context just what kind of reaction should be expected of a given individual or social group. In contexts where there are strong norms that the individual should be religious in some way, where there are few secular alternatives, where there is freedom as to the kind of religious products that may be chosen and where individuals have a certain income, they are very likely to become "religious shoppers." Good examples are the Halal markets, the markets for Islamic fashion (Sandikzi and Ger, 2010), or the market for Christian music in the evangelical milieu. In contexts, on the other hand, where there are few norms sanctioning religious behavior and where there are many secular alternatives, we should expect more fuzzy fidelity and secularity.[7]

---

[6]   See for general overviews and assessments: Warner (1993), Young (1997), De Graaf (2012), Jelen (2002), Stolz (2007). See for critical views Bruce (1999), Bryant (2000). The mainstream version of the rational choice approach to religion has been strongly challenged on empirical grounds. Some of the most influential articles and books have been Chaves/Gorski (2001), Voas/Olson/Crockett (2002), and Norris/Inglehart (2004).

[7]   In this way, some of the differences between the USA and most European states can be (partly) explained. In the US, there has been a strong societal expectation that individuals should be "religious" and a generally held belief that religion is a "good thing" even after the 1960s (Lipset, 1991). In such a situation, religious freedom will lead to a religious market. In many European countries, after the 1960s, individuals were not expected to be religious anymore. The result was, therefore, more fuzzy fidelity and secularism. Other variables that strongly influence the reactions of individuals to religious freedom are gender, age,

Shopping and consuming as a new religion

Some authors have argued that one of the important life domains where individuals can experience sacredness these days is *shopping* and *consuming* (Belk, Wallendorf, and Sherry, 1989). Baggini (2005), writing about the opening of a new branch of Ikea, suggests that "shopping is the new religion and Mammon our new God." This is because "The kind of 'must have' mania that infects some shoppers as they close in on a good deal is more akin to the imperatives of religious devotion than those of personal finance." Belk *et al.* (1989) show various ways in which individuals may "sacralize" the experience of consuming. Other authors describe how individuals may engage in various forms of "brand fandom": they venerate the product, feel an emotional bond to other brand users, fantasize about enemies of the brand and begin to engage in "evangelistic" behavior. In extreme cases, "cult brands" may be so strongly venerated that fans create "brand communities" (Muniz and O'Guinn, 2001). This has happened, *inter alia*, with Macintosh, the Apple Newton, Harley Davidson, Star Trek, Jeep, or Saab (Muniz and Jensen-Schau, 2005).[8]

While it may be tempting to see shopping as the new religion of consumer society and shopping malls as the temples of our society, we should be wary of accepting these theories too quickly. For the research started off by the famous article by Belk *et al.* (Belk *et al.*, 1989) may be seen as one example of a much larger research tradition concerned with seeing the sacred in all kinds of domains of modern life.[9] The phenomenon has been given various names: invisible religion, surrogate religion, quasi-religion, implicit religion, or secular religion (Bailey, 1990; Greil and Robbins, 1994; Luckmann, 1967).

While the specifics differ, the argument is always that elements and/or functions that once characterized religion can now be found in seemingly secular domains of life. Formerly it was religion that gave meaning, integrated the social group, legitimated the social structure, allowed individuals to accept misfortune and distress, and let them experience times of frenzy and enthusiasm. Today, these attributes and functions may be found in other social situations. Frenzy and enthusiasm, for example, can be found in the collective excitement at a pop concert or a football game. The problem with this line of research, evidently, is that the definition of "religion" (or implicit, or quasi-religion etc.) used is so broad that it is difficult to conceive of phenomena that could not—at least in principle—also

---

religious socialization, religious tradition and the level of development of their country of residence (Norris and Inglehart, 2004; Ruiter and Graaf, 2006).

[8]   Shachar *et al.* (2011) provide one of the few articles that uses experimental evidence in order to argue that "religiosity and brand reliance are negatively related, at least in part, because both allow individuals to express aspects of themselves to others."

[9]   Belk *et al.* already acknowledge this in their article.

become "implicitly religious."[10] In order to make a convincing case for a growing "implicit religion," it does not suffice just to enumerate "religious" or "sacred" traits and functions in various social phenomena. Rather, it is important to give a clear, operationalizable, definition allowing for the measurement of religious change.[11]

Our own view is that one may indeed find some "religious" or "spiritual" elements in the world of consumption, but that most authors in marketing and sociology seriously overstate their case. In order to get a balanced view, it may be useful to look at Table 1.1. Here, we order a number of "candidates" for religious and quasi-religious phenomena both on a "likeness to religion and/or spirituality" and a "formal organization" continuum (Brinkerhoff and Jacob, 1999). Likeness to religion and spirituality is a construct that measures the number of traits that are similar to the attributes normally thought to characterize transcendence-orientated religions and spiritualities. We then distinguish four degrees of likeness to religion and spirituality and call them zero-religions/spiritualities, secular religions/ spiritualities, hybrid religions/spiritualities, and religions/spiritualities.

Zero-religions and spiritualities have no or almost no resemblance to transcendence-orientated religions or spiritualities. Of course, virtually all social practices may give "meaning" to individuals or may in some fashion or other "structure" the life of individuals. In so far as religions and spiritualities also give meaning and structure, even here we find a likeness to religion. However, most attributes normally found in transcendence-orientated religions and spiritualities are lacking. Phenomena found in this category are, for example, school, police, construction companies (high formal organization), or watching television, cleaning (low formal organization). Shopping in most cases would clearly fall under the heading of zero-spirituality.

Secular religions and spiritualities have somewhat more likeness to transcendence-orientated religions and spiritualities. They may, for example, show similar functions—such as the capacity to integrate, give meaning, give identity, compensate, and legitimate. However, they normally lack the criteria of transcendence. While we may find "specialists," a "founder," certain "ethics," "myths," "veneration," and emotions of awe, these elements are not linked to some sort of god, supernatural entity or transcendent principle. It is the political leader, the founder of the ideology, the inventor of the brand, the pop star who

---

[10] Here are some phenomena that have in fact been written about as "implicit religion" or "quasi religion": sports, pop music, television, sex, one's own home, art, psychotherapy, mindfulness, self-help groups, medicine, vegetarianism, science (Babik, 2006; Brinkerhoff and Jacob, 1999; Hamilton, 2000; Lam, 2001; Rudy and Greil, 1988).

[11] In the (few) cases where this has been done, several hypotheses of the proponents of this line of argument have been falsified. Thus, there does not seem to be a trend towards "believing without belonging" or "vicarious religion" (Bruce and Voas, 2010; Voas and Crockett, 2005). Nor can we speak of a "spiritual revolution" in western societies (Voas and Bruce, 2007).

Table 1.1   A typology ordering phenomena according to their "likeness" to religions/spiritualities

| | | Degree of "likeness" to transcendent religions/spiritualities | | | |
		none	low	medium	high
Formal Organization	high	**Zero-Religions** • Police • School • Construction company	**Secular Religions** • Nazism • Marxism • Psychotherapy	**Hybrid Religions** • Scientology • Transcendent Meditation • Alcoholics Anonymous • Synanon	**Religions** • Islam • Christianity • Judaism • Buddhism • Christian Science • Raelianism
	low	**Zero-Spiritualities** • Shopping • Television • Cleaning	**Secular Spiritualities** • Brand fandom • Identity shopping • Pop fandom • Soccer fandom • Extreme sports • Wellness • Conspiracy theories • Positive thinking • Intensive pub culture • Sports yoga	**Hybrid Spiritualities** • Extreme brand fandom • Dianetics • Sacred sex • Rave culture • Mindfulness • Alien research groups • Star Wars religion • Astrology • Reiki • Hybrid yoga	**Spiritualities** • New Age • Esotericism • Channelling • Spiritual yoga

is venerated—but not a supernatural invisible or incarnated God. It is obvious that brand fandom and shopping products that serve to define individual identity (clothing, accessories, cars, etc.) may be seen as secular spiritualities.[12]

Hybrid religions and spiritualities are phenomena that have many attributes in common with religions and spiritualities—but as their name suggests, they also seem to be something else—para-sciences, therapies, musical cultures, fan-cultures, businesses, etc. As Greil and Rudy (1990) explain, often these phenomena actively seek an ambiguous status concerning their "religious" nature. This is because a "religious" label gives certain advantages (e.g. respectability, tax exemption, non-falsifiability), but also disadvantages (e.g. being seen as "not serious" or "not scientific"). Good examples of such hybrid phenomena are

---

[12]   Interestingly, even economics has been called a "religion." In his book on "Economics as Religion," Robert Nelson (2001: i). writes: "Economists think of themselves as scientists, but as I will be arguing in this book, they are more like theologians." See also Piore (2006: 19). In our terminology, we are faced with a "secular religion."

Scientology, Transcendental Meditation, Alcoholics Anonymous, or Synanon on the formally organized side, as well as rave culture, astrology, sacred sex, or Reiki on the less organized side. Extreme brand fandom such as the brand communities that have formed around Mac, Saab, or Harley Davidson have indeed produced transcendental elements built into millenarian ideas, myths, rituals, and ethics (Belk, 2005; Lam, 2001; Muniz and O'Guinn, 2001).[13]

While this analysis shows that it is conceivable that consumption phenomena include religious and spiritual elements, it is clearly exaggerated to say that shopping, brand fandom or even extreme brand fandom are the "new religion" of our times.

Organizational Effects: Marketing and Branding Religion and Spirituality

We now turn to the organizational side of "religious consumer society." The historical antecedents mentioned above (modernization, change from institution to voluntary association, religious-secular competition) have put religious organizations and entrepreneurs in a completely new situation, leading to an increased need to market and brand their products and services. Let us first say what we mean by marketing and branding.

Marketing may be defined as "the performance of business activities that direct the flow of goods and services from the producer to the consumer, to satisfy the needs and desires of the consumer and the goals and objectives of the producer" (Barna, 1990: 41). Marketing should be understood in a broad way not just as advertising and publicizing, but as including any means that furthers a mutually satisfying exchange between the organization and the customer. This includes the design of the product or service, the choice of the target market, the screening of the main competitors, the organization of the means of distribution, as well as the publicizing and branding of the product (Kotler and Levy, 1969).

A *brand* can be defined as the idea or image of a specific product or service that consumers connect with by identifying the name, logo, slogan, or design of the company that owns the idea or image. The *branding process* occurs when that idea or image is marketed so that it is recognizable by more and more people, and identified with a certain service or product when there are many other companies offering the same service or product. As outlined by Keller (1993: 10), "the semantic meaning of a suggestive brand name may enable consumers to infer certain attributes and benefits" and "facilitates marketing activity designed to link certain associations to the brand." Advertising professionals work on branding

---

[13]   In Mac devotees' communities, Belk (2005: 205) finds "a creation myth, a messianic myth, a satanic myth, and a resurrection myth." Such brand communities may therefore be seen as hybrid spiritualities. It has to be noted, though, that these cases of extreme brand fandom are rather rare and that the studies investigating them have concentrated on the most extreme cases.

not only to build brand recognition, but also to build good reputations and a set of standards that the company should strive to maintain or surpass. Branding is identity-generating storytelling and therefore involves not only the alphanumeric content of a brand name, but also logos, slogans, and celebrity endorsers who officially speak for the brand.[14]

According to Mottner (2007), branding language helps to identify some of the tools and strategies that may be used. These include: 1) brand name, 2) brand personality, 3) brand equity, 4) brand positioning, 5) brand image, 6) brand campaign, and 7) brand promise.

Changing acceptance and use of religious marketing and branding by organizations

Researchers in general seem to agree that both acceptance and use of religious marketing and branding have increased in western countries since the 1950s for "suppliers" of various religions (Cutler and Winans, 1999; Einstein, 2008; McDaniel, 1986; Twitchell, 2005; Webb, Joseph, Schimmel, and Moberg, 1998). According to these authors, religious groups increasingly investigate consumer needs, design forms of worship and product lines, engage in advertising, image campaigns, and branding. Such claims are made especially concerning Christian churches, be they mainline, evangelical or fundamentalist (Chen, 2012; Einstein, 2011), but also for non-Christian religions. Prominent examples in Islam are the transformation of the veil from a "stigmatized practice to a fashionable object" (Sandikzi and Ger, 2010), or the booming Halal Industry (Fischer, 2009).[15] A good example of marketing by a religious group rooted in Jewish mysticism can be seen in the Kabbalah Center established by Philip S. Berg (Einstein, 2008: 147 ff.). A Buddhist example is the huge success of Buddhist books even in mainstream bookstores (Jones, 2007); a Hindu example is the successful marketing of Yoga in the domain of "wellness" (Deshpande, Herman, and Lobb, 2011). New religious movements like Scientology, the Moonies, or the Raelians have also been known to engage in important efforts of marketing (Barker, 1984; Einstein, 2011; Palmer, 2004). In all traditions, we see a growing importance of religious tourism (Finney,

---

[14] The economic institutionalization of branding and legal protection based on property rights against potential infringers is a relatively recent phenomenon. The early attempts at legalizing property rights on names and inventions, about two hundred years ago, were accompanied by debates as well as legislative trial and error processes. The French Revolution dismantled the nascent intellectual and industrial property rights and was obliged to reintroduce them after some years. Benjamin Franklin was among the strongest opponents of property rights, because he valued innovations (and the public good through their broad diffusion) over profits (and their private appropriation).

[15] Haenni (2009) mentions a great number of Muslim consumer products and brands that have emerged, for example: Muslim drinks (Muslim-Up, Arab-Cola), Muslim dolls (Muslim Barbies Razanne and Full), Muslim fast food (Halal Fried Chicken, Beurger King), or "green leisure."

Orwig, and Spake, 2012). While almost everybody seems to agree that both the acceptance and the use of religious marketing by organizations have grown—and the claim seems plausible overall—there is a clear lack of quantitative longitudinal data to prove the point.[16] An important parameter influencing public acceptance and the use of religious marketing and branding is the overall legal framework (see Usunier in this volume).

Specific religious marketing and branding techniques

Marketing has a strong normative stance and uses a combination of action strategies. We discuss publics/markets and strategies (marketing mix) of religious organizations.

Publics and markets   A number of publications highlight the fact that religious groups face different publics. If they want to survive in a society where individuals have choices, they are well advised to distinguish these different publics or various types of markets (market segmentation) in order to engage in a positive exchange with each of them (Schwarz, 1986). Mottner (2007) distinguishes input publics, internal publics, partner or intermediary publics, and consuming publics. Input publics provide resources and constraints to the organization, including donors and various stakeholders; internal publics consist of staff and volunteers; partner or intermediary publics are marketing agencies, consultants or other entities that help the organization to fulfill its objectives; consuming publics are its members, prospective members, people who are served in a general way, or even the general public. Webb, Joseph, Schimmel, and Moberg (1998) advise distinguishing prospective members, present members and former members in order to plan a church's strategy. The central idea in public or market segmentation is that different publics/markets have different needs that can only be met separately. A special marketing policy can be implemented for every public. For example, the very successful megachurch ICF in Switzerland has created specifically designed worship services for different age groups (Favre, in this volume). The Alpha Course was created in order to meet the needs of a population with a certain interest in spirituality or "life questions," but who would not normally enter a church (Hunt, 2003; Sengers, 2009). Both the Christian music industry and the Islamic fashion, toys and halal industry are targeting devout middle-class populations in the respective religious traditions. The Catholic and reformed churches in Germany and Switzerland have tried to use the marketing tool of "life-style milieus" in order to find targetable publics for their services (MDG, 2005; Meier, 2006; Stolz and Ballif, 2010).

---

[16]   Cutler and Winans (1999), for example, point to the career of George Barna who has specialized in teaching church marketing to churches; they also show that publications about church marketing have clearly increased in recent decades. Webb (1998: 4) locates the first attempts at formal church marketing back in the late 1950s, when James Culliton proposed that churches should use the "'4 P's' of product, price, place, and promotion."

As Mottner (2007: 93) explains, when religious organizations use marketing, they often do so not to make individuals "buy a product." Rather, they try to influence a whole range of behaviors in their target publics. These include:

"a. joining an organized religious group, either from another religion (conversion) or from having no religion;
b. maintaining or increasing "loyalty" to a certain type of religion;
c. increasing the level of "religiosity" and conformity to a specific religion's norms;
d. increasing one's depth of belief or faith in a religion; and
e. financial support of religious organizations."

Branding   In the scholarly literature on "religious branding," there is, paradoxically, little overlap between territorial boundaries of disciplines. As a general rule, the religious branding literature uses the term "brand" interchangeably with "name," or sometimes "slogan" or "catch phrase." Few authors cite classical references in the branding literature (Keller, 1993). Few references in Science of Religion articles or Economics of Religion papers, even when they explicitly mention religious branding, come from the marketing, branding, and consumer research literature.

There can be no doubt that *branding as a concept* is applicable to religious phenomena. Religions may be considered to have *brand names*: Christianity, Islam, Judaism, or Christian Science. They normally have signs that may well be interpreted as easily recognizable *brand logos*: the cross or fish for Christianity, the Yin-Yang sign for Taoism, the star and crescent for Islam, the Lotus flower for Buddhism, the star of David for Judaism. They have "brand stories" (myths) that are embodied in rituals, objects, works of art, buildings and clothing. Their places of worship are often built in a branded, i.e. recognizable, way representing churches, mosques or temples. Registering the name of world religions, however, is generally impossible, because the label is considered a generic name, not acceptable for registration. As a consequence, generic religious names and symbols may be seen as "half-brands," with a full capacity to support a wide range of religious marketing, advertising, and sales objectives (Einstein, 2011), but with legal limitations as regards brand name protection.[17]

In contrast, new religions or religious organizations included in larger religious traditions may find it easier to register their trademark. Thus, Scientology has been

---

[17]   If we think of religious brand names (e.g. names of holy books, names of holy places, sacraments and rituals, pilgrimages, etc.) as pre-industrial property rights, they are non-economic and non-institutionalized exclusion rights, which include the moral, but not the commercial aspects of property rights. By institutionalization, we mean the legal framework of property rights which has been elevated to a global scale by the adoption in 1995 of the TRIPS (Trade Related Industrial Property Rights) agreement by member states of the World Trade Organization.

able to protect its names, logos, and products by trademark rights.[18] Likewise, the Alpha Course, Transcendental Meditation, and "Purpose Driven" products are registered trademarks. Of course, consumer brands that try to become "religious" also have the full set of branding tools, both marketing and legal (Muniz and Jensen-Schau, 2005).

As in branding in general, religious or spiritual brands may be used in order to market and possibly sell a whole line of products. A good example is the "Purpose Driven" brand by Rick Warren. Here, the brand is used to symbolize both the "purpose-driven" man, pastor and author Rick Warren, the bestselling books "The Purpose Driven Life," the Saddleback church which is presented as the first model of a "Purpose Driven Church," the various CDs and videos presenting the "Purpose Driven" concept, etc. We find similar lines of products for the Nicky Gumbel Alpha Course (Hunt, 2003).

Strategy The famous 4 Ps of marketing (Product, Price, Promotion, Place) may be applied to religions and spiritualities (see Usunier, in this volume).[19] The specific choices in these domains form what marketers call the "marketing mix." In what follows we give various examples, highlighting specifics for religious and spiritual organizations and products.

Product or service offering Religious organizations and entrepreneurs offer a wide variety of products and services that often claim to have some sort of transcendent utility. Max Weber called them "salvation goods" (Stolz, 2006; Weber, 1978 (1920)). A number of publications treat the question of how religious and spiritual entrepreneurs change their products or services in order to compete successfully with other religious or secular providers. Among the strategies employed we find:

- using *market research* in order to better understand the religious and spiritual or other needs of a given population.
- *gearing the product to a special kind of public or audience.* Religious organizations create special religious services for different age groups, social milieus, groups with various interests, etc. (Stolz and Ballif, 2010).
- making the product more *entertaining.* Religious groups increasingly include music and humor in their services (Einstein, 2008).
- using *economies of scale* in order to guarantee a very high *quality* product. By becoming a *megachurch,* the organization can offer first class entertainment, music, facilities and the diversity of small groups to customers (Chaves, 2006; Fath, 2008).

---

[18] See for example: http://www.rtc.org/guarant/pg006.html.
[19] Mottner (2007) extends the list to 7 P's, adding Physical evidence, People and Process.

- *adapting the product quickly to changing needs of the population.*
  Alternative healers in particular have been found to adapt very quickly to
  the perceived needs of customers, by changing the number and types of
  healing techniques offered (Mayer, 2007).
- *reducing the demands on the customer in terms of lifestyle, commitment, or
  belief,* in order to reach a greater number of possible customers (Einstein,
  2008).

Price   Some products on religious and spiritual markets do have a monetary
price that can be adjusted. These goods may be called religious or spiritual
consumer goods (Stolz, 2006). Examples are the prices of religious books,
religious films, spiritual healing sessions, meditation courses, entrance fees for
spiritual concerts and the like.

Many religious and spiritual goods, however, do not have direct prices but
shadow prices (Stolz, 2010). This often means that the individual pays a church
tax or membership fee, or makes a donation and can then enjoy the benefits of
products produced by the group either freely or at a much reduced price. A question
for religious groups is then how to set their church tax rate, membership fees and/
or how strongly they should insist on donations. The fact that, in religion, we often
have a group in which members contribute to produce religious goods together
leads to the interesting fact that religious groups will often give out religious
consumer goods and services *for free or clearly under the market price even to
nonmembers.* Jehovah's Witnesses give away their brochures for free (although
the individual members have to pay for them); Christian religious services are
normally open to all; and many films or theatrical events organized by religious
organizations are free or priced inexpensively. The theological reason might often
be that the gift is seen either as "good works" or as a means of evangelization.

One cost of the religious product is the *time* used when taking part in the ritual,
since time has a shadow price (Becker, 1990 (1976); Iannaccone, 1990). One
market adaptation may lie in reducing the length of religious services in order
to make them more attractive since they become less time-consuming. Another
strategy is to organize large religious events. With these, the individual only has to
show up once and is sure to have an extraordinary experience, but does not have to
commit to a recurring and fixed ritual. A third strategy is used by megachurches:
when going to a religious service, individuals may also be able to fulfill other
needs (i.e. going to the gym, eating out), thus saving time. A fourth strategy is to
use modern media (internet, television, radio) in order to allow individuals to take
part while not being physically present.

Another cost possibly linked to the religious product may be seen in that
individuals may hold a negative view of the fact that they have to *believe
implausible things or act in ways that seem unnatural to them.* One way to lower
these costs is to devise special formats for individuals who are not yet believers
or who are "doubting." Recent decades have seen various examples, such as the

Alpha course, seeker services, the Thomas mass and others (Hunt, 2003; Kotila, 1999; Sengers, 2009).

An important literature following Kelley (1986 (1972)) and Iannaccone (1994) argues that various religious groups use an explicit or implicit strategy not to lower but to *raise* the cost of membership in order to screen out free riders and thus increase the quality of the group atmosphere and level of belief. This in turn is thought to increase the attractiveness of the group, making it grow in the medium and long term. It is true that in western countries and among Christian churches, conservative churches have fared better than liberal ones. There is no consensus, however, on whether this finding can satisfactorily be explained by the free-rider mechanism (Bruce, 1999; Olson, 2001, 2005).

Promotion   A growing literature analyses promotional activities by religious organizations. Several points can be made.

- Religious organizations may use the *whole range of promotional tools* available to secular organizations. These range from commercials on television or radio, ads in newspapers, billboard advertising, internet sites to door-to-door evangelization. Einstein (2011) analyses TV ads by Scientology and the Methodists; Chen (2012) looks at a very successful use of search engine optimization by the Latter Day Saints.
- There does *not seem to be one main promotional tool* for religious organizations that is sure to be most successful. Rather, religious organizations normally use a whole range of promotional tools, while unsuccessful organizations often do not use any or only at a very low level (Vokurka, McDaniel, and Cooper, 2002). When it comes to organizational growth, one of the most important tools seems nevertheless to be communication through friendship networks and word of mouth (Carrick Coleman, 2008).
- Since religious organizations normally do "*good works*," these activities are especially useful in order to create a positive image. If they can be publicized and if the religious leaders can be shown to lead these good works in the media, the religious organization has a powerful tool at hand.
- Since religions are often ritual based (and ritual being, in essence, repetitive), they may find problems in "creating news" that could be used for publicity. One way around this problem is to organize special "*religious events*" that are newsworthy and may therefore be used to get the religious organization into the media (Salzbrunn, 2004). Examples are yearly religious festivals, Catholic world youth days, Lutheran "church days," evangelization rallies, and the like. Such events may become especially newsworthy if they seem to have a wider, not only religious importance. The Saddleback Church Forum, for example, was able to host a meeting between Barack Obama and John McCain when they were running for president in 2008. Religious organizations may also gain much publicity

when they conduct the ceremonies associated with nationally important events (such as major funerals, services following natural catastrophes like earthquakes or tsunamis, or when a national event is celebrated or remembered).

- Although rather rare, some religious organizations may use *scandal* and *humor* in order to get publicity. For example when the Raelians claimed that they had cloned a human being (Palmer, 2004), the payoff was very inexpensive, worldwide media coverage and a boost to organizational growth. Bhagwan Shree Rashneesh was also known to use unusual, confusing and sometimes humorous statements and actions in order to attract attention and media coverage (Gordon, 1987). Even mainline churches in Europe can obtain a lot of publicity when they defy the state and offer "church asylum" to asylum seekers who are supposed to leave the country in question (Just and Sträter, 2003).
- An extremely useful promotional tool is the *"brand personality"* and *"celebrity endorser."* When religious organizations have a "religious star" available to them, this individual's life, opinions, successes, failures, etc. become newsworthy and can get the religious organization into the media. Examples for brand personalities are the Pope, the Dalai Lama, Sister Emmanuelle, or Mother Theresa. Widely known examples of celebrity endorsers are Tom Cruise (Scientology) and Madonna (Kabbalah). As is the case for brand personalities or celebrity endorsers in general, religious organizations are extremely vulnerable if the individuals that stand for the organization are seen to fall short of public expectations.

Place (distribution)   Some authors discuss questions of the "place" for the optimal distribution of the products of religious organizations in religious consumer society. Again, some general points can be made:

- In countries with established churches, these churches have often used the *parish system*, trying to offer a comprehensive supply with a church in the center of every village. With growing mobility, increasing secularization and growing religious diversity, such a system often cannot be sustained in religious consumer society. The small churches are not sufficiently attractive to compete with all the other secular possibilities for spending one's time. The parish system therefore seems to break down, giving way to a system in which larger churches try to attract individuals from larger areas (Stolz and Ballif, 2010).
- Historical Christian churches in inner cities may capitalize on their location by transforming themselves into *"city churches,"* that is, churches that are not the home of a congregation, but that are geared to the needs of larger audiences. Such city churches try to attract passers-by, offer religious concerts, theater, meditation and meeting spaces (Sigrist, 2000).

- In contrast, *megachurches* often seek out places in the suburbs, easily accessible by car, where land is relatively cheap, and where enough parking is readily available.
- New kinds of places are emerging that give more flexibility to a variety of religious and spiritual providers: *Spiritual meeting centers* and *esoteric fairs* have the advantage of not being centered on just one or two types of supply, and of acting as an open space in which many different suppliers may engage with various publics.
- An increasingly important location for religious and spiritual supply is *bookstores*. Here, the competition between various religious and spiritual goods and between secular and religious/spiritual products becomes completely obvious.
- An interesting phenomenon is the continuing success of *"house churches,"* where individuals try to create the "religious supply" themselves, renouncing the services of an institutionalized church.
- Overall, in an increasingly globalized world, we note the growing importance of religious and spiritual *place-brands*. Lourdes, Santiago de Compostela, Jerusalem, Mecca, Bethlehem, and Stonehenge are sites that can be successfully branded and then become very attractive both for religious and secular tourists (Finney *et al.*, 2012).
- Surveying the major new developments in places of distribution of religious products, we can observe the downfall of the formerly institutionalized distribution of religious goods and an upswing of more consumer-orientated, flexible, and readily branded channels of distribution.

Effects of marketing and branding

It is clear that some religious organizations have been effective at marketing and branding and that this has helped them to *grow* considerably—good examples are megachurches (see in this volume). It is not the case, however, that marketing always leads to growth. In fact, most churches in the western world—despite applying certain types of marketing—have *difficulty keeping their members*. The reason is precisely the fierce secular competition these religious groups face.

Many observers have noted that the increasing use of marketing and branding in the religious sphere has led to a considerable *blurring of genres* and to the fact that it may become increasingly difficult to distinguish the religious from the secular. Often, religious organizations will seek to copy successful secular products in order to become more attractive both to religious and secular audiences. The religious service becomes a pop-music "celebration"; the sermon is turned into an entertaining "message" full of humor, movement, and theater. Many televangelists have copied the "amiable style" of secular talk show hosts like Johnny Carson or Jay Leno (Moore, 1994). Many successful megachurches, like ICF (International Christian Fellowship), Vineyard, or Hillsong use high quality pop bands and choirs (see the chapter by Olivier Favre and Thomas Wagner in this volume). Some forms of yoga have been completely incorporated into the wellness programmes of fitness clubs. In another dimension, many esoteric producers copy elements of science by making their organizations "institutes" conducting "seminars" and "conferences" (Greil and Rudy, 1990; Hero, 2010: 147 ff.). When the copying is successful, we may witness cross-over phenomena, that is, religious products may enjoy success in the secular market (e.g. the *"Left Behind"* series, holidays in the cloister) or secular products may do so in the religious sphere (e.g. rap music in Black Churches (Barnes, 2008)).[20] We should not forget, however, that while there is blurring in some cases, we also find a *refocusing of boundaries* in other cases, namely when religious products are sharply branded in order to convey one and only one important message.

Limits of religious marketing and branding

When religious organizations try to market and brand their products, they meet interesting problems.

- *Vulnerability of transcendent claims.* Religious and spiritual products are linked to some sort of transcendent claim. Explicitly or implicitly, they promise some sort of "salvation good." Problems may arise when religious organizations try to be too specific in their claims, opening themselves up to criticism. Thus, Jehovah's Witnesses have been criticized for their erroneous predictions of the end of the world, Scientology and various spiritual techniques have been under attack concerning the effectiveness of their therapies, and young world creationists are ridiculed for their beliefs. These problems occur when the claims of religious organizations concerning salvation goods are too specific and thus falsifiable; it does not occur when the claims are general and non-falsifiable. In the latter case, religious organizations find themselves in the company of secular organizations that also market and brand their products with all kinds of rather far-fetched unverifiable promises and claims (the luxury perfume will make you irresistible, the branded computer will show that you're "hip," the new coffee brand will improve your relationship with your parents-in-law ...).
- *Difficulties in controlling product stability and quality.* Since religious organizations are mostly non-profit organizations or voluntary associations, it is often very difficult to control the stability and quality of the "product." The way a religious service in the reformed church is performed in one village may differ greatly from the way it is performed in another. Denominational names may be stable, but the "product" underneath may

---

[20]   As a reaction to this blurring of genres, some have reprimanded religious organizations for the "shallowness" or "lightness" of their audience-tuned products (Carrette and King, 2005).

differ drastically. While it may be possible to promote the denomination with ads or internet sites, such marketing is inefficient if the claims cannot be followed up when people actually see the product (Einstein, 2008).

- *Lack of acceptability by the general public.* Another obstacle is related to limited acceptance by the general public due to a number of converging reasons. First, religious organizations are considered non-profit organizations relying chiefly on donations; the public may therefore adopt a critical view if the donated funds are used to promote the "public image" of the organization. Second, religious goods, especially salvation goods, are perceived as non-sellable; promoting them can therefore be seen as a form of desacralization, of breaking a taboo (McGraw, Schwartz, and Tetlock, 2012). Third, the public is increasingly critical when organizations are seen to be trying to "manipulate" people. Any type of evangelizing strategy is therefore easily seen as going against the principle of religious freedom (Wrenn, 1994). On a completely different note, some religious groups reject brands and branding as symbols of a negatively perceived capitalist society, this being especially true for Muslims (Izberk-Bilgin, 39). In general, we can say that the acceptability of marketing and branding is strongly dependent on the cultural context, making it mandatory for international organizations to adapt their marketing efforts to the respective local cultures (Usunier and Lee, 2009).
- *Lack of acceptability by the group members themselves.* A great many religious organizations also face internal opposition to marketing and branding. Members and staff of churches may see marketing as the exact opposite of their beliefs and religious practice. Marketing may be thought to go against the central religious message, or to soften or alter it (Barth, 1930; Kunz, 2006; Wrenn, 1994).
- *Lack of skills.* A further limit to religious marketing and branding lies in the fact that religious organizations may lack the necessary skills to do the marketing. Marketing is normally not taught in theological seminaries or in other religious group schools and universities (Kuzma, Kuzma, and Kuzma, 2009).

The Contributions in This Volume

As a second introductory chapter in this volume, *Jean-Claude Usunier* explores how the General Agreement on Trade in Services (GATS, 1995, one of the 18 trade agreements in the World Trade Organization) promotes the global commoditization of religions. GATS legally opens the way for free trade in religious services worldwide. Usunier further questions in detail whether marketing concepts and practices apply to religion and gives a positive, though nuanced, answer.

Marketing and branding religion and spirituality

A first group of chapters investigates the supply side, i.e. the applicability of marketing/branding concepts and practices to religious organizations.

Olivier Favre studies the ICF (International Christian Fellowship), a Swiss evangelical movement established as a church since 1996, as an important example of religious marketing consistent with a modern urban environment. From its start, the organization has aimed to attract young adults by developing appropriate marketing tools, sustained by a radical growth strategy. Favre shows that the insistence on marketing by ICF leads to interesting "blurring" phenomena.

Thomas Wagner analyses the musical worship experiences of congregation members of the Australian and London branches of Hillsong Church, an Australia based inter- and trans-national Pentecostal church that brands itself through its distinctive musical offerings. Through interviews with the musicians and technicians as well as "lay" members of the church, Wagner seeks to comprehend the complex interplay of pragmatic production decisions, the understandings of locality among the musicians and members of Hillsong, and how these understandings inform the experience of the Hillsong brand.

Markus Hero shows that the concept of entrepreneurship applies extremely well to the field of alternative spirituality. Drawing in an original way on neo institutionalist theory, Hero focuses on spiritual small businesses that tailor their health services by propagating religious connections to human identity, the body and its health as a discursive way of generating trust. Hero's article is mainly conceptual and suggests many possibilities for further research.

The contribution by *Jason Dean* on "non-fortuitous limits to the brand metaphor in the popularizing of 'justly balanced Islam'" also looks at social, political, symbolic, and legal rivalries in the competition among churches. Dean shows that a Bourdieusian, sociological model of rivalry is more appropriate for describing religious competition than a Beckerian, economic model.

Hanifa Touag investigates traditional Muslim healing rites—*roqya*—by Salafists in France and Belgium. Drawing on ethnographic research and interviews with both practitioners and patients, Touag describes how the *roqya* rite has been able to impose itself on a "market of healing." The adoption of the rite is shown to combine secular and spiritual attributes and functions.

Religious and spiritual consuming

A second group of chapters looks at the demand-side of religious and spiritual consuming or the influence of religiosity on demand.

Jochen Hirschle argues that consumption competes on both the level of imaginations and the level of social action with religious institutions. In the empirical part of his chapter, he tests this hypothesis by analyzing the development of income, consumption-related leisure activities and church attendance using a sample of young German Catholics. According to Hirschle, it is precisely in these confines, on the borderline between economic/secular and non-economic/sacred realities, that late-modern spiritual consumers try to reconfigure meaning.

Haytham Siala investigates the impact that religious factors have on a consumer's perception of brand loyalty. Specifically, the study focuses on the attitudinal and affective form of brand loyalty and how the concept of Takaful can become a 'catalyst' to inducing religious brand loyalty in devout religious customers. An empirical investigation conducted on a sample of Muslim consumers tests whether the extent of religious commitment can instill attitudinal brand loyalty towards a car insurer selling religiously-conforming insurance services. The results confirm that there is a positive relationship between the exogenous religious constructs and the endogenous attitudinal brand loyalty, price tolerance and word-of-mouth constructs.

Elizabeth Stickel-Minton examines how religious affiliation grouping influences consumer behavior. She assesses the predictive ability of three different religious grouping systems supported in the literature: simple (Catholic, Protestant, Jew, none), fundamental (liberal, moderate, fundamentalist), and denominational. Her findings suggest that the segmentation of religious affiliation may be to blame for non-significant results in previous studies.

Economic analyses of religious phenomena

Roger Finke and *Christopher P. Scheitle* show that the pluralism of religious suppliers is a product of the pluralism of religious preferences and the number of potential adherents within an environment. This pluralism of suppliers, in turn, produces a pluralism of religious consumers. They then distinguish between expected pluralism and observed pluralism, and argue that a relationship between pluralism and participation will be expected only when a meaningful gap between these two variables exists.

Steve Bruce presents a critique of the market-of-religions paradigm and explains why he rejects the rational choice theory of religion, before outlining in an original way the circumstances in which such an economic approach to religion would be viable. As we read Bruce, his view on secularization is in no way incompatible with the religious marketing and branding that is presented in other chapters in this book.

Finally, *Philippe Simonnot*, in his contribution on the Temple of Jerusalem discusses the "business model" of Jewish monotheism as a Unique Selling Proposition, a classical advertising copy strategy. Simonnot shows that, despite a shared tendency of all religions to want to be sole and exclusive suppliers, monotheism is better placed than polytheism because, as a matter of principle, it gives to a single God.

All chapters in the book show new perspectives on the marketization of religion and spirituality. We hope that they will—in their combination—help to encourage future research and thinking in our overlapping disciplinary fields.

Chapter 2

"9591": The Global Commoditization of Religions through GATS, WTO, and Marketing Practices

Jean-Claude Usunier

When I submitted this mysterious title to my colleague Jörg Stolz, he googled for "9591 marketing religion" and found: "Yoga, Meditation, *Meditationsreisen* [meditation travels], Ayurveda." In fact, "9591" is the code number of the (product) category "religious services" in the large (almost 900 pages) Central Product Classification (CPC), which serves as a basis for multilateral trade negotiations in the World Trade Organization (WTO). Product category "9591" contains subcodes such as "religious baptismal services," or "religious marriage services." If religion is mostly about delivering religious services, its commoditization becomes natural, obvious, and self-evident. This contribution shows how the paradigm of Markets of Religion (MoR) is enforced by making it progressively legitimate. I will focus on the assumptions and processes underlying the opening of religious markets worldwide through the GATS (General Agreement on Trade in Services, 1995), its legitimization by both academic discourse on the market of religion, and the application of marketing tools to religion and religious services.

The first part describes how the GATS paves the way for the commoditization of virtually every service, including those delivered by religion through Churches and Congregations (which are considered "Membership Organizations" by CPC code 95). This leads in a second part to define commoditization, its underlying assumptions and its processing, taking illustrations in religion to make the matter more concrete. The legitimacy of commoditizing a previously non-merchant item such as religion is reinforced by commercial practices that are subsumed as a body of knowledge under the term "marketing." The third part investigates the applicability of marketing concepts, tools, and practices to religious organizations and to their services and assesses the degree of fit between religion and marketing. The issue of the commoditization of religion being surrounded by semantics, rhetoric, and discourse, the fourth part is dedicated to branding, the most sophisticated part of marketing. The economic value related to brand names value is based on meaning developed in the minds of consumers over years by advertising and marketing communications. Religions like branding are meaning-based activities. We show that, while branding may apply to religion, it generates symbolic rivalry between commoditization and religion which can be dangerous for spiritual meaning *per se.*

The GATS and the Opening of the Global Religious Market

Legalization and enforcement of commoditization have been progressively organized over time. It started at the end of WWII as a relatively soft process, organized by the General Agreement on Tariffs and Trade (GATT, 1947). Since 1995, global commoditization has been enforced by the WTO and its 18 commerce-related agreements, especially through the General Agreement on Trade in Services (GATS, 1995). The GATS covers all services in 12 main sectors (e.g. financial, communication, environment, and education services). Only services rendered in the exercise of governmental activities are not covered by the GATS. Few services indeed are not partly delivered on a commercial basis (e.g. public transportation) or without competition (e.g. public hospitals being in competition with private clinics for healthcare). Religious services are outside the realm of services rendered in the exercise of governmental activities,[1] which are limited to kingly missions *stricto sensu.*[2] As a consequence, religious services are covered by the GATS and its provisions on the Most-Favoured Nation (MFN) clause, market access, and national treatment. These provisions are designed to facilitate the global opening of services markets. In order to cover all ways of delivering service internationally, the GATS defines four types of cross-border service trade according to whether the service provider and/or the service consumer are in their home country and/or abroad:

- (Mode 1): *Cross-border supply*; a religious service crosses the border without the service consumer moving to another country; for example, online religious services;
- (Mode 2): *Consumption Abroad*; service consumers travel to the site of foreign service providers; for instance, Algerian Muslims traveling to Mecca for the *hadj* pilgrimage.
- (Mode 3): *Commercial Presence* where the service provider establishes operations in a foreign market; The Scientology Church has used Mode 3 consistently over time.

---

[1] Except in States which have an official religion supported by public authorities such as the Protestant religion in Canton de Vaud or Islam in Saudi Arabia. However, this is not the GATS perspective.

[2] The detailed structure and the explanatory notes on the CPC can be found on: http://unstats.un.org/unsd/cr/registry/regcst.asp?Cl=16&Top=2&Lg=2 (accessed March 4, 2011). The detailed structure of the WTO Service Sectoral Classification List can be found on: http://www.wto.org/english/tratop_e/serv_e/serv_e.htm (accessed March 4, 2011).

- (Mode 4): *Presence of Natural Persons* where the service provider, a natural person, temporarily crosses the border to meet foreign consumers, such as a minister or a missionary going to preach and possibly convert people abroad.

Religious services are a very small part of the GATS agreement. They are mentioned in category 12 of the WTO Service Classification, "other services not included elsewhere" which includes CPC 95 of which religious services are a subdivision (9591). Part II in the GATS defines general obligations and disciplines that apply across the board to all services (horizontal commitments). Countries may ask for an exemption of obligations according to article II of the GATS treaty. No country has asked for an exemption of obligations concerning Religious Services. The obligations and disciplines in part II of the GATS treaty apply for all WTO Member States as concerns Religious Services.

Part III of the GATS treaty deals with sectoral commitments made by each Member State on an individual basis according to the four cross-border service modalities cited above, the three main commitment categories (MFN, market access, and national treatment) and the type of service sectors covered (147 services). Combining these possibilities, one arrives at 150 countries × 4 modalities × 3 commitment categories × 147 services (CPC), that is, 264,600 specific commitments. Fortunately, commitments are made at the level of the 12 broad service sectors, which potentially means 21,600, this figure being still considerable. Member states in GATS have generally avoided committing themselves too hastily. As concerns religious services, no country has made a specific commitment according to Part III of the GATS Treaty.

This is necessary, however not sufficient to make the MoR paradigm a self-fulfilling prophecy. Beyond this, there is a need to create a metaphoric legitimacy by applying a vocabulary, that of economics and marketing, by considering worshippers as consumers, and by building reality through words in order for the MoR to become real.

Commoditization of Religion

Commoditization defined

Commoditization[3] is based on an object-centered view of economic exchange whereby subjects exchange a wide range of tangible and intangible commodities (*latissimo sensu*, i.e. products, services, rights, institutions, and social behaviors)

---

[3] The term "Commodification" would be used in the UK. There are also other meanings of the word "commoditization," such as the launch of a new technology item on a mass-market. I use a definition close to that of Kopytoff (1986), however insisting more on commoditization through market exchange.

on markets. "9591" is a direct reflection of this object-centered view: religion because it produces "religious services" becomes a commodity. Commoditization occurs when a previously non-market object (e.g. religion, blood, adoption, etc.) enters the market. The commodity itself is at the very center of the market process in which price, volume, and competition between suppliers to capture consumers are viewed as the central elements of market dynamics guided by unlimited free and rational choice (Warner, 1993; Stark, Iannaccone, and Finke, 1996; Iannaccone, Finke, and Stark, 1997; Ekelund, Hébert, and Tollison, 2006). Commodities must be fully comparable or at least as comparable as possible. The ideal commodity is completely standardized, devoid of any singular attribute that would make comparison, and therefore choice, difficult. Commoditization is an all-encompassing, snowballing, and self-perpetuating economic process which tends to swallow tangible and intangible items such as rights and obligations, institutions, social behaviors, and belief systems to transform them into commodities and introduce them into "competitive" markets. The key event in commoditization is when a "product," which is both part of a subject and an object (e.g. blood, or subject-related "objects" such as religious beliefs, trust, or reciprocity), becomes a commodity or when, conversely, objects leave the merchant sphere (see Kopytoff, 1986).

Assumption 1

The first assumption is based on the equation (identity) *economy = market*. This is assumed despite the fact that a large part of economics deals with costs and recognizes firms as internalized (i.e. out-of-market) arrangements of resources by entrepreneurs (Coase, 1937). Firms or their assets (business units, services, talents, patents, trademarks, equipment, etc.) can be outsourced, licensed to other companies, or the company can be sold out in part or in whole. The assumption is that the market supersedes any provisional and unstable resource arrangement planned and organized by entrepreneurs. the market will always be there for companies to internalize or externalize resources. Markets, through volumes and prices, are the final judges and organizers of the economic process. Following the first assumption of commoditization, we start from the obvious fact that there is an economic life of churches (e.g. Simonnot, 2005). Their need for resources cannot be denied and it follows that there is a MoR because economy = market. However, religions as rather stable resource arrangements, planned and organized by spiritual entrepreneurs are not primarily market objects.

Assumption 2

Another underlying assumption is that people, being objective by nature, are only concerned about utility. There is certainly utility in several religious services. However, marketing makes a difference between religion and religious services.

While the latter may, to a certain extent, be commoditized, this does not imply that religion itself should be considered a commodity.

Assumption 3

Identity is considered a threat to commoditization   Identity is considered a catalyst of division between individuals, groups, and nations because not sharing it may lead to misunderstanding and conflict. The doux commerce thesis (Hirschman, 1986) underlies commoditization with an identity-negating version of universalism. Idiosyncrasies based on language, culture, religion, ethnicity, etc. are considered potential obstacles to trade. Rather than being viewed as composed of permanent and collective traits, identity is treated as a set of changeable, individual attributes that become objects of choice. If switching or competition between religions is not a matter of deep-seated identity, religious switching occurs as a consequence of open, extensive, but peaceful rivalry between "commercial" religious suppliers. If assumption 3 is verified in practice, we should see a lot of conversions.

Assumption 4

The coexistence of market and non-market solutions is assumed to lead to suboptimal outcomes   Although this has been the case for centuries for many products and services (water, education, healthcare, safety and police, etc.). The assumption is that market-only solutions are more "efficient." As a consequence, non-market solutions should be changed to market-based solutions. In the case of religions, market and non-market solutions coexist in many countries and the issue is whether the market will remain marginal in responding to spirituality needs or whether it will absorb religions (Haddorff, 2000). Official religions are non-market organizations with state recognition and subsidies, as is the case in a number of European countries (see Bruce, 2000 on Nordic and Baltic Churches). They coexist with new religions which develop more on a market base such as the Church of Scientology or the Jehovah's Witnesses. Were it not for CPC 9591 and the GATS market opening obligations, public support in favor of official religions could go on. However, assumption 4 of the commoditization process is literally built-in in the anti-subsidy Article XV of the GATS Treaty ("Members recognize that, in certain circumstances, subsidies may have distortive effects on trade in services. Members shall enter into negotiations with a view to developing the necessary multilateral disciplines to avoid such trade-distortive effects"). In the long run, GATS article XV will allow new, commercial religions to attack public subsidies to locally recognized religions because of their "distortive effects on trade in services."

Assumption 5

Commoditization is assumed to be non-ideological   It is assumed that there is no ideology in commoditization, since, being object-based, it is also objective, facts-based. The self-interested and individualistic view of human nature underlying commoditization is considered the most realistic assumption. Commoditization is a TINA process, following the acronym often used by Margaret Thatcher (There Is No Alternative to commoditization). Choice, which is a key advantage of market processes, is paradoxically absent when it comes to the choice between commoditized markets and non-commoditized solutions. There is no choice but to have the choice.

The commoditization process: Introducing previously non market items into the market through property rights

Beyond tangible products that lend themselves easily to being marketed, new "objects" must be commoditized. Exclusion rights, mostly in the form of industrial and intellectual property rights, serve to withdraw knowledge from the public domain and/or keep non-paying users at bay from a commodity that would be utmost useful to them (e.g. ART drugs for AIDS patients in low-income countries). Brands related to a religious organization competing on the MoR should therefore be registered and protected by trademarks.

Rather than commoditizing the obviously animate part of subjects (as is done in enslavement), the process transforms segments of individual lives, skills and talents, and behavior into commodities. Furthermore, because human beings are partly complementary, partly substitutes to machines, they have historically been in competition with tangible commodities (i.e. equipment goods). The border between objects and subjects is not clear-cut because commoditization relies on the indirect reification of subjects. The same holds true for the difference between religion and religious services. Any minister providing religious services to worshippers is potentially a service provider rather than a figure of spiritual authority. Being a service provider, s/he is supposed to meet consumers' spiritual expectations, to deliver religious service quality, to be evaluated, and to be obliged to adjust if below expectations.

Opening markets and legitimizing the market of religions

The commoditization process requires the opening of markets, that is, to extend the scope of geographical markets to globally, rather than locally, confront supply and demand. Markets may still have some sort of fuzzy boundaries related to national languages and cultures, and to local idiosyncrasies, despite the near elimination of obstacles to trade. This is seen by the devotees of global commoditization to be a major impediment to economic efficiency and a threat to the maximization of global spiritual welfare in the case of religion. These fuzzy boundaries are defining traits of multidomestic, rather than global markets (Porter, 1986). *Laissez passer* dominates *laissez faire* in this part of the commoditization process, where national legislation must be almost completely harmonized so as not to be an obstacle to the free movement of commodities.

Legitimizing commoditization is not an easy communication task. It is a long-term, unilateral, persuasive, and somewhat subliminal communication undertaking. The trick is the systematic use of vocabulary and discourse to acquaint people with a newly commoditized (or a to-be-commoditized-in-the-near-future) object. The underlying, implicit rationale is that, if market language is used for items which were previously meant as orthogonal to the market, there must be some sound reason. In the legitimization undertaking, every human institution, especially non-economic, is presented as a market-based process by using the basic market vocabulary (e.g. supply, demand, consumption, competition, etc.) combined with terms related to the non-economic institution. This is how people progressively accept such oxymorons as "religious markets" (Iannacone *et al.*, 1997), "political markets" (Buchanan, 1968, 1987), "healthcare suppliers," "supply of religion," "competition in the global religious market," "consumption of spirituality," "brand loyalty and brand switching" for religious conversion, etc. as meaningful expressions. Over time, people progressively become acquainted with MoR oxymorons and develop ownership of such expressions. Cognitive assimilation, based on repeat-style persuasion, has shown to be efficient in the long run. Unilateral communication works provided that it overpowers other discourses by massive presence. The hoax is in the following syllogism, applied to religion as a potential commodity. Major premiss: There is obviously an economic life of any church and religious congregation. In fact, they have to maintain buildings, pay ministers and organize for the management of religious activities. Minor Premiss (i.e. assumption 1 above): Economy = market. Conclusion: Because they have economic concerns, religions should be organized on a market base with non-subsidized suppliers who compete for consumers of religion (worshippers).

The built-in argument in favor of this conclusion is that the "demand for spirituality" will be better satisfied by "religious firms" competing on a "market for salvation goods." However, the statement that religion should be organized as a market because churches and religious congregations have an economic life is a conceptual leap made possible only by assumption 1 (economy = market). This is backed by powerful TINA communication from business, media and politics based on the argument that global competitiveness requires dedicated participation of individuals and nations to extensive commoditization. What makes commoditization ultimately legitimate is when it is legally recognized at the highest level, that of international treaties that dominate national laws (i.e. GATS and WTO agreements). Having legally inscribed religious services in the WTO-GATS framework is a necessary, however not sufficient condition for commoditizing religion and globally opening religious markets. It needs the additional legitimizing power of practices and words, by applying marketing techniques to religious services.

Application of Marketing Concepts to the Market of Religions: Does It Really Fit?

Some marketing tools certainly apply to religious services such as media and non-media communications. However, many aspects of marketing do not readily apply to religion and there is some debate over whether they really apply and whether this metaphoric extension does not lead to over-commoditization (Bruce, 2006, 2008; Carrette and King, 2005). When looking at the marketing of religion metaphor, it is necessary to go into details of key marketing concepts and whether or not (or to what extent) they apply to religions. Is the application of marketing knowledge to religious markets an artificial metaphor or does marketing comprise a set of practical tools to be used without much *états d'âme*? We investigate below whether typical marketing concepts apply.

Consumer research and market segmentation

Is the member of a church a "consumer" of its "religious services"? Is the minister, priest or Imam, a marketer of such "religious services," a "spirituality salesperson"? Although one could argue that pastors, contrary to marketers and salespeople, tend to prioritize converting non-believers, they are also concerned with taking proper care of their own stable flock. There certainly exists an ideal tendency to consider every person as a potential switcher and people in other faiths as possible converts. However, it may be more prudent to cultivate one's own herd and keep it on one's own meadows, that is, in marketing terms, care for the actual customer base, rather than desert the loyal customers for hunting for far-away potential religious switchers. This is akin to the classical problem of allocation of marketing efforts between spending resources on the maintenance of the loyal part of the customer base versus spending on finding new customers among the potential brand switchers *or* any combination of both. Marketing can apply to religion, as both share a similar distinction between actual and potential "consumers."

Consumer behavior is the complex set of individual—psychological and collective—sociological determinants of meanings invested by consumers when they search for, purchase, possess, use, and finally dispose of products and services. Consumer behavior applies to religion, because religious products and services are exceptionally embedded in social and human life and have often being considered items related to cultural consumption (Belk *et al.*, 1989; Moore, 1994). Consumer research shows that consumption is deeply intermingled with social life especially as concerns the fuzzy boundaries between the sacred and the profane (Shachar *et al.*, 2009), which Belk *et al.* (1989: 1) call "the secularization of religion and the sacralization of the secular." Brands, for instance, are more and more considered in the framework of brand communities (Muniz and O'Guinn, 2001), which are based on a sense of shared responsibility and on social relations among admirers of a brand. They share rituals and traditions in quasi-religious ways, especially when they are a small group of fans of a declining star brand (Muniz and Jensen Schau, 2005). Similarly, spirituality and spiritual messages are increasingly used in advertising (Marmor-Lavie *et al.*, 2009), in particular to promote entertainment, art, and science (Scott and Stout, 2006). While brands use religious meanings to support marketing messages for profane goods and services, faith and religion have become themselves increasingly branded (Einstein, 2008). Although the mix of branding and religious messages remains often unnoticed by viewers and consumers, this blend of brands and spirituality may be confusing at times. As remarked by Beaudoin (2007: iv), "Christmas elevates the sale of toys made under noxious conditions in China."

Market segmentation and the targeting of particular demand segments is relevant for religion. It is difficult for universalist religions to officially state their dedication to particular segments of the population since the message is supposed to be for everyone. However, most religions have an actual (unofficial) age segmentation with the younger and the older being favored in minister dedication. In some cases, a gender-based segmentation may be actually practiced with men being offered a slightly different marketing mix as compared to women. Scientology corresponds to a specific target in terms of socio-demographic and/ or psychographic profile. Segmentation and targeting of demand segments is not claimed to be an official activity but is common practice (Vokurka and McDaniel, 2004). For instance Kuzma *et al.* (2008) compare the target markets of mainstream versus Megachurches in the United States showing that the latter attempt to reach different cultural and generational segments. Some key marketing concepts such as market share, competition, perceived risk (e.g. the social risk associated with changing religion), and consumer involvement apply well to the religious market. Religious market share is relatively easy to measure and has been an object of research in the scientific study of religion in particular to check whether smaller market share congregations try harder with the conclusion that their increased efforts are not due to religious competition itself (Hill and Olson, 2009). Similarly, other marketing concepts such as brand loyalty (Djupe, 2000), new product development and the management of consumer expectations (services marketing) apply well.

Primary demand for religion and religious consumer switching (i.e. conversion)

Marketers need a strong and dynamic primary demand with a significant base of consumers potentially switching suppliers to capture market share from competitors,[4] in contrast to religion, which has most often a very loyal "customer base." Religious market share dynamics have a strong relationship to conversion,

---

[4]   This statement is true in a restricted view of religious competition where churches would compete only among themselves. However, it can be argued that churches are in fact involved in a broader competition with secular institutions through activities competing in the overall time budget of consumers (Stolz, 2010). See Hischle in this volume.

that is, attracting new religious customers. It is difficult to estimate conversion rates, that is, consumer switching in the MoR. In the United States, the conversion rate seems to be relatively high with variability in religious preferences over time (Loveland, 2003). Roof (1989) based on the GSS (General Society Survey) estimates that about 28.8 percent of his sample have changed religion at least once over their lifetime with 10.1 percent having switched twice or more. Marriage and the family were the predominant reasons with more than 40 percent while theological dissatisfaction, related to purely personal choice, accounted for slightly less than 20 percent. Barro, Hwang, and Rachel McCleary (2010) study religious conversion on a large cross-national sample of 40 countries, through a diachronic design that enables them to estimate religious switching (Table 3, page 35). Except the United States with .158 (i.e. 15.8 percent), Canada with .171, Chile with .130, and New Zealand, many other countries display low conversion rates with some nations in the range of some per thousand in the population over a lifetime (e.g. Finland or Italy at five per thousand, Spain at six per thousand, etc.). Significant cross-national/cross-cultural differences in religion switching suggest that the MoR is very much an American phenomenon (Gill (2003: 327) for example, uses the expression of the United States being "a religious supermarket"). However, this may not hold true for the global scene. Even if we assume a 4 percent conversion rate for the world population, and on the basis of an approximate forty year choice period (in short, between early adulthood and early old age), we have an annual conversion rate of one per thousand, that is, a global base of actual religious switchers of about 7,000,000 per year. It seems to be a small base of actual switchers, which could be one reason for not undertaking costly marketing investments. However, the argument is fraught with endogeneity and therefore reversible. Low conversion rates in many countries could be the result of the lack of dynamism in the MoR with many potential switchers being passive because they are not offered attractive alternatives and therefore not becoming actual switchers.

Religion and the 4Ps of the Marketing Mix

The Marketing Mix is a combination of four action policies designed to coherently influence consumers and the market to maximize market share and profits. McCarthy first defined the 4 Ps in an influential book (McCarthy, 1975) as Product, Price, Place, and Promotion policies. The place and promotion dimensions apply well to the MoR while it is more difficult to force marketing policies into religion for product and price.

Place: Distributing religion   The "Place" dimension of marketing strategy is related to delivering products to final consumers through distribution channels and therefore making them available to potential shoppers and buyers. Companies can use short versus long, independent versus integrated (company-owned) channels, traditional (brick-and-mortar) versus virtual (online, Internet-based) distribution. All this applies to religions far beyond the simple metaphor. Churches and congregations have their own religious premises (e.g. churches, mosques, temples, monasteries, abbeys, spiritual souvenirs shops, etc.) which may be considered as company-owned channels. Religions are actively distributed on the Internet through dedicated web sites and also use outdoor locations (Kuzma *et al.* 2008). Finally holy places such as Lourdes, Mecca, or Varanasi, can be considered as distribution outlets with a strong symbolic value, even for non-believers.

Promotion of religion   Promotion of religion through media and non-media communication is clearly where the 4Ps metaphor holds the best and is near to "truth," that is, it is no longer a metaphor. There are many accounts of the importance of media communication for religions (Deacy and Arweck, 2009). Einstein (2008: 27) explains that 144 million Americans use some religious media at least once a month. 25 years ago, there was still some debate about whether marketing communications should be used for religions. McDaniel (1986) noted that churches were hesitant to use advertising feeling that it looked more commercial than spiritual. However, the general public was more reluctant than the clergy as concerns both the type of media and the message. Almost 20 years later Vokurka and McDaniel (2004) show that non-traditional churches (program and worship oriented) use significantly more of most marketing communications methods than traditional churches resulting in increased growth rate and less decline of church membership.

Religious product policy   is complex in the sense that the vast range of religious products comprises both tangibles (e.g. books and religious objects) and intangible items, some of them being religious services as defined by CPC 9591, others being related to the promise of a reward in the future, that is, goods of pure belief. Religious product policy in this sense could amount to nurturing, raising, and entertaining consumer expectation about the delivery of key benefits such as eternal life and enjoyment of celestial happiness. More pragmatically, religious product policy could deal with a borderline mix of social and spiritual services for accompanying people in life from birth (baptizing), marriage, to death (last sacraments and burial ceremonies). Stolz proposes an integrated definition of religious products as "salvation goods":

> ... an end or means to an end which is offered by a religion, embedded in a specific world-view and a system of life practices, and which may be aspired to or used by an individual or a social group. Salvation goods may be confined to certain points in time or lasting; set in the future or the present; transcendent or immanent, individual or collective; ascetic or contemplative; aspired to actively or given to the individual by an external power (Stolz, 2008: 59–60).

For tangible religious items marketing techniques readily apply. They may apply also for religious services with the caveat that it is difficult to establish whether religious services are public or private goods (or some combination of both). Park

Table 2.1   Product-price relationships for religious products

Tangibles ——————————>——————————>——————————>——————————>——————————> Intangibles
In-group oriented ——————————>——————————>——————————>——————————>——————————> Out-group oriented
Belonging needs ——————————— Self-esteem needs ——————————— Self-actualization needs
(in terms of Maslow's (1954) hierarchy of needs)

Categories →	Religious goods	Religious services			Salvation goods		
Religious products	Religious materials goods (books, statues, spiritual paraphernalia, etc.)	Religious Entertainment Services (festival, lotteries, fairs, charity fêtes, …)	Open social events designed to attract new members, potential switchers, with social and spiritual content	Church Membership related group activities, social/spiritual gatherings, intended for community members only	Sacraments, religious services related to birth, marriage, death and important life-events	Expectation-based salvation goods: both *this-worldly* and *other-wordly* benefits are expected from religious investment	Non-Expectation based salvation goods: no benefit of any sort is expected for this life or an afterlife.
Pricing policy	Traditional Pricing (displayed, non-negotiable, same for all, un-bundled price). Free-riding (not paying the item) is theft. Price elasticity, "magic pricing," etc. apply.	Entry can be priced as well as a number of individual items. Free-riding is limited if non-existent.	Gratuity is the rule with the possibility of free-riding for newcomers with the caveat that this could also appear as a pro-motional tool.	Bundled prices related to membership fees covering such services with different patterns (tithe, voluntary contribution, etc.). Free-riding very limited.	Unbundled prices with more or less explicit price list and a combination of gift (collection, donations) and *money-against-service* pricing. Free-riding possible.	Gift economy pricing dominates with financial generosity being granted in a latent, implicit exchange process. Free-riding is possible given benefits non-verifiability.	No pricing applies. *Sunk cost type of investment.* There is no monetary sacrifice and contributions are unscaled. Free-riding is non-existent.

Private goods ——————————— Mixed public and private goods ——————————— Goods of pure beliefs
Consumption goods ——————————>——————————>——————————>——————————> Investment goods

and Baker (2007) show that the consumption of religious and spiritual material goods (i.e. religious books, jewelry, art, clothes, etc.) is at the intersection between cultural consumption and religious practice. Table 2.1 shows that tangible religious goods are followed in terms of their degree of tangibility, in-group orientation, and consumption versus investment nature, by various kinds of religious services (which correspond to CPC 9591), and finally "salvation goods," corresponding to supernatural compensators, however with a narrower definition as compared to Stolz (2008). Within the category of salvation goods, a distinction between two subcategories can be made according to their being expectations-based or not. One cannot exclude purely disinterested religious participation, when a belief in predestination obscures afterlife expectations.

Pricing religious services   Pricing policy directly applies for tangible religious items because they are material goods. However, tangible religious items are a small part of the overall religious product offering. Many religious services have a public good dimension, which is evident in a human being in need of prayer, entering a religious edifice to pray, possibly receiving counsel from the minister, and leaving without paying. This can be considered free-riding in a commoditization perspective for which no benefit or service should be acquired without paying (see Brewer *et al.*, 2006). One may wonder whether religious pricing is really about pricing as there is most often no displayed price (a legal obligation in many countries), especially for sacraments. A list of prices leads to a clear allusion to money and this may lead to real embarrassment for the religious supplier. Bruce (2008) makes the additional argument that pricing of religious services is not enough for religious consumers to maximize their utility. Because of the complex combination of monetary and non-monetary sacrifices/benefits, the computation of utility against price is difficult.

> To talk about the price of religious involvement is stretching a metaphor too far. The metaphor is not salvaged from shipwreck by substituting the shadow price of time for money. How "costly" time spent on some activity is to us depends on the extent to which we find that passage of time rewarding ... In brief, the economicist model of human behavior requires that we are able to assess costs and returns from some neutral standpoint before we make a commitment to one religion rather than another. But the nature of religion does not allow such comparisons and measurements (Bruce, 2008: 93).

If religion is a set of consumption goods, religious goods should be priced on the basis of an unbundled pricing policy (Stremersch and Tellis, 2002), whereby each individual item is priced individually even if it is part of a set of complementary products/services. If religion is considered an investment good, related to long-term commitment, membership, and strong social/spiritual expectations as to the benefits derived from such commitment, bundled membership pricing should be the rule. In this case, only membership is priced and consumption comes in the form of a bundle of services accessible for those who have paid for membership in the religious organization. An alternative solution is religious pricing on the basis of a mix of gift economics *à la* Marcel Mauss (Mauss, 1924; see also Pace, 2008) and some pricing of unbundled services (Stremersch and Tellis, 2002).

It seems at first sight that pricing policy does not apply well to religion. However, it fits better if one takes into account three complementary avenues: The first, in which salvation goods are seen as an investment and membership is priced (especially in religions which have a clearly codified and almost compulsory tithe), the second, in which unbundled religious services are priced individually (which is the case of highly MoR religions such as the Church of Scientology for which profit maximization is the goal), and the third, in which gift economy provides for collection-based pricing. Beyond the evident heterogeneity of religious pricing, a constraint is manifest: To survive, Churches need resources for matching expenses with income, and therefore a minimal, partly covert, sales and pricing orientation.

It appears from the review and arguments above that 2 Ps (place and promotion) readily apply to the marketing of religions (as quasi-firms) and religious products and services. However it is more problematic for both product and price policy (often treated in the marketing literature as a product-price couple).

Religious Branding: Symbolic Competition in a Commoditized World

Few papers have investigated the issue of religious branding with the exception of Abreu (2006) on the Fatima sanctuary in Portugal, and Haley, White, and Cunningham (2001) on the case of branding Christian products. Branding is the most sophisticated part of marketing. On the mere basis of words and figures (i.e. brand names are most often alphanumeric), designs and logos (i.e. brands combine textual and visual content), branding can create economic value. This value (which we call brand equity) is purely based on meaning developed in the minds of consumers over years by advertising and marketing communications in the form of 1) brand awareness (consumers recall or recognize a brand) and 2) brand image (built on the types, favorability, strength, and uniqueness of associations; see Keller, 1993).

Religions like branding are meaning-based activities. This section first discusses whether branding can be applied to religion and concludes positively. Then it shows that the blurring of the boundaries between markets and religion leads to an unconfessed rivalry between commoditization/marketing and religion/ spirituality.

Religious brands

The first level is the corporate brand, that of the "religious firm," which is based on the name of the religion itself (e.g. Islam, Buddhism). The level of product branding logically follows and includes the title of holy texts (e.g. The Quran, the

Ramayana and Mahabharata), of key beliefs systems (e.g. Scientology's "Eight Dynamics"), main ceremonies (e.g. the Holy Mass, Roch Hachana), sacraments (e.g. Kalima), rituals (e.g. Eucharisty, Bar-Mitzvah), and religious practices (e.g. Ramadan, Lent). Religious branding also includes destination branding to holy places such as Lourdes, Fatima, Varanasi or Velankanni in India, Mecca, Jerusalem, etc., the field of destination or place branding being a target of interest for researchers in marketing (Dinnie, 2004).

There are strong elements of intentionality in branding. A certain meaning is intended based in particular on appropriate textual and visual contents (Usunier and Shaner, 2002) to augment brand equity. Protection of brand ownership from copies is also intended through industrial property, that is, registration of trademarks. If religious brands followed legal branding practices, they would be registered and names such as "Catholic Church," "Catholicism," "Roman Catholic," "Vatican," "Mecca," "Islam" would be registered as trademarks with the sign ™ or ® affixed to the brand name.

For most world religions, these names are considered generic names that cannot be registered as trademarks giving an exclusion right to the right owner.[5] For new religions such as Scientology the situation is quite different. Registered trademarks of the Scientology religion are numerous and can be defended in courts as brands names for which the right holders have a right of exclusion towards those who use the brand without permission. Neither Jesus nor Saint-Paul went to the patent office to register Christian trademarks. If existent, Christian and Muslim brand names and the associated brand equity were built through usage. Religious names were not primarily intended as a branding strategy. The intentionality dimension is lacking for most religions and religious brand building is generally unintentional. However the use of a name, even without it being formally registered as a trademark, gives rights against abusive use. In this sense, the portfolio of brand names of world religions described above is protected against opportunistic behavior. The practice of branding, in a marketing rather than legal perspective, applies fairly well to religious firms.

Unconfessed (too shameful to mention?) symbolic rivalry

Branding is the ultimate tool of Marketing because it is intended to destroy unwished symbolic associations, to alter value judgments, to neutralize negative sides of the brand's image, to render meaningless and therefore inefficient, rival associative meanings and to replace them by new, more manipulative meanings. Marketing communications, advertising, sponsoring, and public relations convey the desired meanings about the brand. As emphasized by Keller (1993: 14): "Marketers should define the knowledge structures that they would like to

---

[5] Historically, there were many conflicts between religions about which one had the "good product." However, these conflicts were solved through religious wars rather than through property rights.

create in the minds of consumers." Commercial meaning created by branding is intentional, at times superficial, often mutable and changing, so as to adapt to various publics and unstable environments and circumstances. While it is probable that churches and congregations have an implicit, or sometimes almost explicit marketing strategy, their beliefs, dogmas, and faith propositions are fairly stable over time. It is difficult to change beliefs and rituals to make them consistent with the messages to be conveyed by branding and marketing communications. If marketing is actually applied to religion, branding and brand management should be consistent with the 4Ps. As a consequence, product policy should be adapted to communication and branding, and place policy for a holy site could target a tourist rather than a religious market.

In the game of symbolic rivalry for meaning, commoditization has some key advantages (for a detailed account of this symbolic rivalry, see Beaudoin, 2007). It has the ability to undermine its competitors by blurring their symbolic base. Commoditization itself is a symbolic institution because it is based on fundamental assumptions that cannot be questioned as objects of faith in the market and its invisible hand. For commoditization, as the religion of the market, there is no choice but to choose. This choice is necessarily rational, based on utility maximization by a self-interested individual. Any vertical sociality that contradicts the peer-oriented view of commoditized socialization is considered an impediment for free choice. Commoditization is competing with other symbolic institutions on the market for meaning. Religions, in general, tend to take people out of the material world. Religion—because it generally promotes simplicity and soberness—may take objects out of the market, reducing the sphere of merchant exchange, and thereby threatening sales figures and profits. Promises of an afterlife increase involvement in *other-worldly* expectations and decrease *this-worldly* materialistic tendencies (Belk *et al.*, 1989). Commoditization on the other hand deals with products and services, including those in CPC code "9591." Religion promotes moral altruism and other-regarding orientation rather than self-interest and egoistic motivation as does commoditization. Because religion often implies non-choice (i.e. converting is considered evil and becoming an infidel), it violates the fundamental belief of commoditization in free choice and rationality. Rather, membership in most world religions is often driven by assumed identity and deep reluctance to change. In particular symbolic institutions that favor past orientation and/or fatalism are arch-rivals for commoditization (e.g. the Muslim religion, more generally the world religions, except Protestantism and its sects).

Conclusive Remarks

The MoR metaphor is rather well supported by the applicability of marketing concepts and practices. Low consumer switching and primary demand being reduced by autarkic production of spirituality would suggest that there is not much interest in spending on religious marketing. However, as emphasized above, these arguments are reversible due to endogeneity. Causality may run both ways. Low religious consumer switching could be the effect rather than the cause of a relative lack of investment in Church marketing strategies. The lack of marketing investments may have caused low switching and high out-of-market consumption of spirituality. There are no clear arguments against the application of marketing practices to religious services if not to religion itself.

There is a double effect of commoditization and deregulation of religion on Church attendance and more generally consumer interest for religious services. On the one hand, there is a positive effect of marketing techniques which result in increased interest, more comparison between alternative faiths and churches, and therefore increased commitment in Church attendance and religious activities. On the other hand, the religious message is partly blurred by the use of manipulative, short term, commercial messages based on advertising and branding. As shown in the last part of this chapter, there is a latent, unconfessed, however shameful side, of mixing marketing, branding, and religion. Marketing and branding are not separable from commoditization because they are the practical, everyday servants of commoditized markets. Consequently, there is symbolic rivalry between the systematic promotion of economic/market meanings and non-economic/non-market religious meanings. The resulting confusion may cause some "religious consumers" to switch to a disinterest for religions or to autarkic consumption of spirituality.

PART II
Marketing and Branding
Religion and Spirituality

Chapter 3

The International Christian Fellowship (ICF): A Sociological Analysis of Religious Event Management

Olivier Favre

Introduction[1]

The ICF (International Christian Fellowship) currently positions itself as one of the most militant and enterprising religious groups in Switzerland. Born out of interfaith services in 1990, this evangelical movement established as a Church in 1996 has now over 2,500 regular members in Zurich, as well as 16 new locations in Switzerland and about twenty others in Europe, mainly in Germany. Unlike other evangelical Churches, the movement did not start as a form of religious revival within an older Church, but rather as a missionary enterprise. From the start, the organization has aimed to attract young adults according to the "sociological profile" of a 27-year-old (!) inhabitant of Zurich. To reach this objective, the ICF has developed marketing tools completely new to Swiss Churches, which has prompted the religion researcher Friess to argue that "From the start, (the leaders of the ICF) have pursued a radical growth strategy, which allows us to place the ICF within the 'church growth movement' coming from America and the Third World" (2004: 23).

This type of religious marketing is overtly assumed and consciously publicized. Indeed, the ICF selects its target audience for each of its activities in the same way that a company seeks to place a product within a specific segment of the market. This is true to such an extent that a newcomer will soon feel out of place if he or she does not fit into the participants' average age group and their characteristic style of celebration.[2]

The successful development of the ICF seems to us a significant example of religious marketing adapted to the modern urban environment. This first impression

---

[1] I would like to thank Suzana Zink for her help with the English version and Jörg Stolz for his helpful comments on the text. The translations from German are ours.

[2] There are, of course, some participants (or even leaders) who are over 40, but I often noticed that they make sure to adopt a youthful, casual style of dress in order to fit into the group as much as possible. Even their language has to sound young, for example, in addressing newcomers with the familiar "du" form.

has provided the impetus for a more detailed analysis of the phenomenon from a sociological perspective. Thus, this study has two main objectives.

First, it aims to uncover the strategies and actions underlying the goals of the organization by means of qualitative data, notably in-depth interviews and participant observation, as well as by examining the movement within the broader category of evangelicalism.

Secondly, from a theoretical point of view, this study considers whether a description using terms inspired by the field of economics ("salvation goods" (Weber, 1995), "religious product," "religious market" (Stolz, 2008), etc.) takes on a much more direct and less symbolic significance with the ICF than with other religious institutions. The question is whether the ICF's competitiveness should be considered uniquely within the religious sphere or whether here, one gradually leaves behind the narrow field of systems of meaning to find oneself in the presence of a quasi-commercial—albeit originally religious—organization, whose product is, above all, in competition with the entertainment and socialization opportunities that a modern Western city has to offer.

Indeed, this study undertakes to show that the ICF uses modern means of communication and entertainment not only to make itself known or to communicate its message, but also as a constitutive component of its identity. Indeed, using the theoretical notions of *Erlebnis* and *Entgrenzung* derived from the sociology of entertainment, we argue that the ICF does not merely adopt certain strategies or wrap its message up in modern packaging; rather, its event-based strategy, borrowed from the world of entertainment, becomes constitutive of the organization's own identity and discourse.

Methodology

Firstly, this analysis aims to continue a wide-scale sociological study which examined all of the 1500 evangelical Churches in Switzerland (Stolz and Favre 2005, Favre 2006). The latter is a quantitative survey of 1100 individuals from a random selection of 60 Churches and religious communities. Different dimensions such as recruitment/conversion, religious practice, values, and beliefs were analyzed in depth with a view to answering an essential question: what are the main identities of present-day evangelicalism? The Zurich ICF features in this survey with 19 questionnaires returned. Moreover, as part of a follow-up study, 97 sixty to ninety-minute semi-directive interviews were conducted with members and official representatives of these Churches, the main aim being to understand how evangelical identities are being communicated and how the Churches manage to attract and recruit new members.[3] The interviewees were selected according to the identity sub-categories delineated in the aforementioned study (namely

[3]   Ongoing study funded by the SNSF (Swiss National Science Foundation) entitled *Evangelical Identity project* (no 100011-120483).

traditional, charismatic, and conservative). They also included former evangelicals who had left the milieu and others who claimed membership to Reformed parishes. Within this framework, four interviews were carried out with members and official representatives of the ICF, among whom its founder, Leo Bigger. Finally, participant observation, namely participation in the ICF celebrations (in Zurich and Bern), as well as the analysis of the ICF literature, sermons, and CDs have allowed us to thoroughly familiarize ourselves with the movement.

The ICF as a "Marketing Church" and the Recruitment of New Members

In Stolz's aforementioned forthcoming study, he investigates the methods and strategies used by evangelicals commonly understood as "evangelization" (cf. note 3). He notes that this preoccupation is so central as to account for a multiplication of relevant expressions in the interviewees' discourse. "Sharing one's faith," "talking about one's faith," "witnessing," "being a witness," "spreading the gospel," "speaking of God" are the most commonly used phrases. When evangelization is organized, evangelicals speak of "campaign," "action," "evangelization effort," etc., terms which are far less typical of the so-called traditional, Reformed or Catholic Churches. Moreover, if some interviewees claim to fulfill a specific missionary vocation and to have a special gift for it, the interviews clearly show that all evangelicals see evangelization as their mission. Indeed, evangelization seems to work; 50.8 percent of the evangelicals interviewed were not so during childhood and were therefore exogenous "converts." As Stolz points out, "Evangelization is considered as part of 'being Christian' itself. Converted Christians have a divine mandate to evangelize" (cf. note 3).

The ICF's uniqueness

As we will show, when it comes to this missionary fervor, the ICF does its share of work. Figure 3.1 shows the frequency with which the interviewees claimed to "witness," that is speak about God, to their circle in one way or another. The data show that traditional evangelicals are the least assiduous whereas two-thirds of Charismatics do so at least once a month. However, what is remarkable is the even higher incidence of this practice among the ICF members: none of these admitted to "witnessing" less often than monthly. This particular point is relevant for the analysis below. It indicates that all the ICF's initiatives, especially those regarding marketing, rely on a particularly fervent individual practice of "witnessing."

As we will show, the ICF distinguishes itself by the organization and promotion of resolutely modern celebrations unique in Switzerland. But this promotional force could not be understood without the evangelizing fervor of all its members.

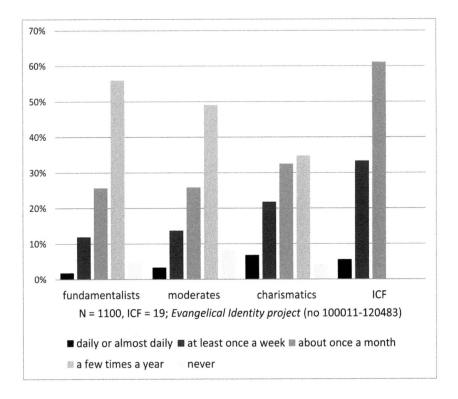

Figure 3.1 Frequency of personal witnessing (N = 1059, ICF = 18)

For Stolz (cf. note 3), the evangelizing fervor of the ICF can be explained by two main reasons. First, like The Salvation Army, for instance, the ICF has been from the start a mission-driven organization. Secondly, the movement has escaped, at least for now, the phenomenon of "routinization of charisma," given its recent origin and its founders' direct role in its management. Roman, the leader of the Basel ICF, is clearly aware of this:

> People are accustomed to things changing … . Of course, the ICF doesn't have a long history behind it so that one can say "we've always done things that way." We have only been around for nine years … Although we are no longer at the pioneering stage, we still have a pioneer spirit; we can change things and do them differently, we are experimenting with new forms of worship.

Regarding the entire evangelical movement, Stolz notes that "on a collective level, we can see that younger communities, i.e. those founded later, evangelize on average more frequently than older ones … . This can be explained by the theory of the 'routinization of charisma." Therefore, this young organization benefits from a strong emotional force and a revivalist atmosphere linked to the charismatic figure of its leaders. In other words, the charismatic authority has not yet made way for a form of authority defined through reference to the legacy of its forefathers. This evangelizing fervor is also what won over Sam, a young person in charge of the Lausanne ICF. Having grown up in an exclusive brethren community, he felt unbounded enthusiasm on discovering the ICF:

> I discovered ICF in Basel. There I joined a cell group and it was simply incredible, the way they talked about everything they experienced, it was very concrete, they were discovering new things about God, they were really happy to bring new people into their Church. ... For me, in my former Church, there was literally never anyone new, literally never (laughter) ... it was horrible.

In fact, it was not only people's inner experience which convinced him, but also the fact of being able to externalize it and attract new people.

Then, if the use of the media by evangelical groups or Churches is not new, what makes the ICF's initiative unique is its gradual, orchestrated incursion into public space. Whilst most religious groups nowadays publicize their convictions on the Internet, the ICF takes this a step further by occupying certain strategic places and spaces, literally as well as symbolically. For instance, its celebrations are broadcast by two private non-religious TV channels; its tenth anniversary was celebrated under the tent of the most famous circus in Switzerland, its fifteenth, at the Hallenstadion (which boasts a capacity of 13,000). Moreover, several Swiss public figures (Miss and Mr Switzerland, TV presenters, etc.[4]) have endorsed and promoted the movement.

If such a public investment has been made possible, it is thanks to a "flagship product," the main weekend celebrations. On this point, both external observers and the movement's founder agree: it is these weekly celebrations which have proved the greatest success. Each of them is, in fact, a carefully thought out event akin to a television show which aims to win over new participants. The lighting, rock music, performances, testimonials, etc. constitute an explosive multipack.

Principles inspired from the world of economy and event management

Based on our own participant observation as well as descriptions made by other researchers (Kunz 2004, Lienhard 2009), we have been able to identify five main characteristics which, in our view, contribute equally to the success of the ICF.

The first of these is its targeted offer. For Bigler, "to find a church where people, whether young or old, are all happy together is almost impossible." This observation has led Bigger and his team to offer "different recipients for different

---

[4]   Several Swiss public figures feel close to, or associate themselves with the ICF: Stéphanie Berger (former Miss Switzerland, actress), Carmen Fenk (winner of the MusicStar show), Claudio Minder (former Mr Switzerland), Jeanette Macchi (former singer, TV presenter).

ages." This manner of extending the offer over a whole weekend has the advantage of fulfilling specific expectations as well as mobilizing the maximum number of people willing to assist in the organization of the different services. The concept is coherent in that each celebration targets a specific age group or sub-culture (English or Spanish speaking) and has its own budget, pre-allocated at the beginning of each year. This implies not only great autonomy for each sub-sector, whose services are customized for its target audience, but also an expectation of success on the part of its leaders. This success can be measured quantitatively by means of a weekly count of the numbers participating,[5] the receipts and the number of new members in each small group.[6] The result is almost like a series of "Churches within the Church," as Bigger himself points out: "Like with a shopping mall there are lots of different shops inside." Here, the inspiration comes directly from shopping malls and their various shops.

Secondly, the celebration distinguishes itself from other Christian Church services thanks to its particularly appealing form. As Bigger notes, "we've found a form that will develop even further, which attracts many, many people, which is relevant." Bigger adds: "I know of many people who would never invite their friends to their church, because it's too boring. For them, it might be interesting, but they would never invite their friends." Thus, everything is done to preclude any feeling of boredom, the underlying idea being that a "boring" service may be enough for believers but not enough for them to take along a non-practicing Christian. In this respect, the ICF leader shows extreme self-confidence. In the television program *Zischtigsclub* (SF1, 24.2.2004) he affirmed peremptorily: "We are in no way behind Music Star." And indeed, as it was easily noticeable, the seven hundred strong audience were all captivated by the enthusiasm on stage, communicated by a young, nice looking lady (a TV presenter, as we later discovered) who introduced the meeting briefly, as well as by the modern rock band leading the "worship," with the lyrics projected on the main screen and the subsequent sermon in plain language accompanied by video-clips or sometimes sketches. Sam, for instance, describes the beginning of a celebration with a certain degree of candor:

> They open at 6. Around 6:25, the count down starts on the screens. ... Then the lights are dimmed in the corridors so that people go take a seat ... Then, on the count of zero, bang, the m.c., that is the master of ceremonies, goes on the stage, welcomes everybody, and warms up the audience by saying "greet your neighbor on the right, on the left." Other times, we try to see if the benches hold so we jump on them, ... really cool stuff!

---

[5]   It is only after many visits to the ICF meetings that I noticed an unobtrusive young man standing at the entrance, almost hidden behind the welcome staff, using a counting clicker.

[6]   *Small groups* allow participants to be integrated within small units of about ten people. These groups are reminiscent of the "cell groups" common in most present-day evangelical Churches.

To ensure the show-like quality of the celebration, the Basel ICF, for example, hired a professional singer from the start as the second full-time employee alongside the main leader. And ten years on, the Church has three professional musicians, which proves the importance of music in all their celebrations.

In fact, the ICF celebration is the main means of evangelization used. Other recruitment methods have been tested then discarded. As an example, Bigger cites a cold calling campaign he set up on the model of banks and insurance companies. On that occasion, 20,000 people selected from the directory were contacted. Among them, 2,000 non-practicing Christians expressed their interest in a different Church; 200 did attend the ICF events as a result, but only about ten remained committed to it. For the ICF leader, the result did not justify the effort: "I'll say it this way, if you compare income and expenses, that definitely doesn't pay off." Consequently, in Bigger's view, it is above all the "multipack" including sustained celebration, practical sermons, the participants' enthusiasm, etc., which constitutes the main source of success for the ICF: "people are excited and invite their friends or neighbors who are also in search of God. That's what we've been doing for years now." Sam confirms this: "what I find cool is that people are proud of their Church and so they like inviting their friends, they like taking part themselves." Still according to Bigger, 90 percent of the newcomers are there thanks to a word-of-mouth invitation, through a friend, etc. The remaining 10 percent attend a celebration after visiting the ICF website. This estimate is quite plausible. It actually supports the data on conversions and adherence which we have gathered about all evangelical Churches (Favre, ongoing study, cf. 3). The great majority of newcomers join an evangelical group following a personal contact, one which generally results in an insistent invitation.

Thirdly, the ICF follows a unique ideological line which is reflected in the movement's cardinal values[7] as well as in their attractive and practical sermons. Friess notes that "on stage there is acting and joking so that one can't help liking the performers" but above all, "the sermon is short and catchy" (2004: 26). After having reviewed dozens of the ICF sermons, we can affirm that one of their main forces is the constant use of visual or entertaining elements supporting and conveying the message. For example, to illustrate a series of sermons on the First Letter to the Corinthians, Bigger didn't hesitate to travel to the site of ancient Corinth to offer some filmed comments from the original setting. For Sam, this expressiveness on the celebrant's part is not always natural but nevertheless necessary: "we really try to remain passionate. My own job is to be in good shape

---

[7] "1. At the heartbeat of time: we constantly ask ourselves how church needs to be to attract people today. 2. Excited about life: we are excited about life with God and have a positive attitude towards life. 3. Experiencing fellowship: we treat one another with love and enjoy life in fellowship. 4. Developing potential: we support people and help them to flourish and develop their full potential. 5. Giving the very best: we give our very best for God. For we value quality. 6. Nothing is impossible: we believe for God nothing is impossible." (www.www.icf-movement.org/about/corporate-identity.html.)

on Sundays ..., I must be in good shape so I can inspire the others." He then goes on to explain how he prepares for it by doing less in the run-up to the celebration, for instance by enjoying various free time activities with his ICF leader friends.

As to the audience, we have noted that it includes neither extremely rich nor destitute people; rather, it is mainly middle to upper-middle class. Consequently, the sermons, which address themes stretching over several weeks, must always contain practical advice which is easy to follow on a daily basis. If the main leader is also the main preacher, generally a whole team contributes to producing the sermon, including, for instance, the event manager and the video people.

A fourth characteristic is that people must "live" something, "experience God": "And that's really our whole strategy, we say we offer a service where people experience God." Roman, a theologian and the person in charge of the Basel ICF, echoes this idea when he mentions his discovery of the ICF, for which he has chosen to work as a leader: "I have found a type of Christian being and Christian faith that excited and fascinated me, and also somehow delivered me." Thus, Friess notes that "The focus of the show is the experience of God, which has to confirm the authenticity of the message. They are encouraged by the presentation of emotional states such as ecstasy and awe. It sometimes happens that Leo Bigger falls to his knees and starts prophesying to the accompaniment of mystical keyboard sounds" (2004: 26).

Figure 3.2 confirms this: in this respect, the ICF is totally in tune with its charismatic orientation. However, it should be noted that, according to our participant observation, the charismatic dimension remains very restrained, nothing comparable to an ethnic Pentecostal Church, for instance. Indeed, according to Roman, the ICF avoids being incomprehensible to a visitor from outside: "If what is going on becomes totally incomprehensible, if people begin to speak in tongues or prophesy ..., then the new people will come to wonder: 'on which planet have I landed?'" Thus, the Pentecostal type of "experience with God" is never favored as a corporate experience, but can, on the contrary, be lived individually. Whilst otherwise deeming itself "charismatic," Roman's approach clearly shows the concessions that the ICF is willing to make so as not to shock the visitor. Thus, the event-based strategy used—which we consider from a theoretical perspective below—is not primarily charismatic in the way Pentecostal celebrations are; rather, it mainly aims to communicate the ICF's message.

Finally, the ICF owes its success to its great flexibility and extreme adaptability. This is what makes Bigger say that a conventional democratic structure would not be possible. How could a vote be organized on decisions which have to be made quickly, at any time of the year? "I'll say this again, a Church that is as big as our Church and is still growing, is so dynamic that you would actually need to have a vote every week."[8] The lack of a democratic structure goes hand in hand with the lack of membership status. However, the power of the five main leaders of the

---

[8] A member of the top staff of the ICF explained to me that it is sometimes necessary to temper the main leader's insatiable desire for change.

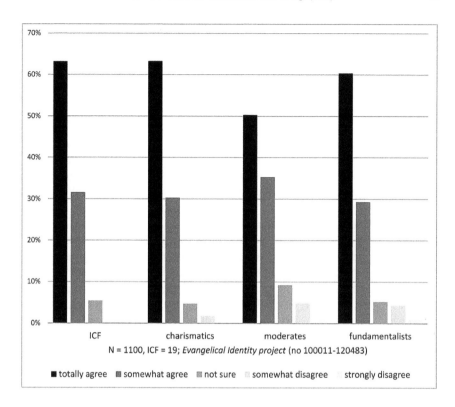

Figure 3.2   Perception of the presence of God (declaration: "I often feel the presence of God"; N = 1096, ICF = 19)

movement is counterbalanced by the great freedom enjoyed by the sub-groups and the section leaders. Thus, an individual participant with no elective power can, through his or her commitment to a sub-group, paradoxically have a greater decision-making power than that of a conventional parishioner.

Based on the above considerations, we can now proceed to situate the ICF phenomenon within the context of modern urban life. This is the aim of the next section, which puts forth several theoretical points.

Theoretical Considerations

Having highlighted the main strategies which ensure the movement's success, we now turn to the underlying reasons which, in our view, explain the phenomenon. The two explanations formulated below must be viewed as complementary and interrelated.

First, we argue that the ICF does not limit itself to competing on the religious plane, but trespasses on the field of entertainment, notably of event-based entertainment. To observe the strategy used, it is necessary to look at the phenomenon of event management within a much wider context. Indeed, this is not a marginal epiphenomenon of modern society, but a phenomenon which fulfills a significant social function.

The culture of event entertainment

Entertainment and recreational events generate strong emotions in the participants. It is the very purpose of event organizers to trigger positive and enjoyable feelings. According to Friess, this, in fact, meets a fundamental need of modern individuals as a reaction to stress and the technicization of modern existence: "In their search for the ultimate experience, people look for ... a product which conveys a promise of unparalleled authentic experience" (2004: 25).

Through *Erlebnis*,[9] individuals seek to feel their individuality, albeit temporarily, by means of intense experiences and relationships, in order to escape a sense of meaninglessness and up rootedness, and reconnect with their own history.

Thus, the event culture provides an emotional counterbalance, and as such, it is not necessarily an enemy of depth or serenity; rather, it bridges the gap between two worlds, the business world of the city dweller on the one hand, and on the other, the need to exist as an individual outside the sole logic of economics. The emotion generated by entertainment events, especially when coupled with an ideology, a religious one in particular, gives individuals a feeling of wellbeing and functions as a form of resistance to the trivialization of life. As Hell notes, "event culture is not just to 'make bad'. It shows that people hunger for a spiritual dimension" (2004: 33).

In a macro-sociological analysis entitled "Silent Battle" (2009: 253), Stolz convincingly explains that, in this respect, churches are faced with intense competition imposed by the secular event culture: "... many problems affecting Christian churches in western Europe such as the loss of members, the decline in religious participation, and waning interest in church activities are due to fierce and hitherto almost unnoticed *secular competition*." As far as religious services are concerned, for example, churches find themselves in competition with all the leisure activities currently on offer. Now, as many churches just suffer, the ICF aims to counter-attack on the same level.

In this sense, as far as the religious phenomenon analyzed here is concerned, the emotions induced by such events do not necessarily constitute a superficial reduction of religious feeling or worse, a perversion of the sacred, but much more the attempt to establish a link between the two realities, the world of commercial performance and that of individual spiritual needs. Roman's comments hint at this link: "We want to be a Church in the middle of this world, in the midst of society,

---

[9] By *Erlebnis*, we mean: "everything one has lived (experienced, perceived, thought, wanted, done, or influenced). ... *Erlebnis* is often translated as 'significant event'" (Mayzaud, 2005: 15).

with a passion and enthusiasm for Jesus …; we are not just event organizers for modern people; we speak about Jesus, we sing about Jesus, we live Jesus …."

The event, then, is supposed to function as a mediator between timeless values. This is a paradox: using ephemeral forms or fashions to communicate a message and ideology deemed existential and a temporal, the challenge of conveying an enduring message in perishable packaging.

The concept of Entgrenzung *or the dissolution of boundaries*

A second explanation seems particularly fertile. We owe it to scholars such as Belket et al. (1989), Muniz et al. (2001; 2005), Knoblauch (2009), and Gugutzer (2010) who are interested in the link between the sacred and the profane (and *vice versa*), religion and the outside world. If evangelicalism has often been characterized by a clear-cut relationship with the world (Favre 2006, 2009), the emergence of the ICF clouds the issue. The ideological content certainly remains evangelical, conservative as far as individual ethics is concerned, but their way of imagining spiritual life undermines the cliché. Gugutzer qualifies the narrowing gap between the religious and secular worlds as *Entgrenzung*: "Dissolution of boundaries for religion means 'crossing the boundary between the sacred and the profane.' The consequence of this is that even in secular societies, religion has not become irrelevant" (2010: 1). Muniz and Jensen go in the same direction: "Virtually everything is branded in this society, including water and dirt. Even religious organizations and sects have openly begun to brand. … Modernity may force the religious and magical to emerge in different contexts, displacing rather than destroying them" (2005: 737). For Gugutzer, just as sport has become a popular event, religion, too, can stage itself as a mass performance, for instance. Moreover, just as new sports appear and seek to justify their existence,[10] religion, too, is evolving and its new forms of expression can prove equally disconcerting. Like sport, modern religion capitalizes on the individual's need for experimentation and thrills. As a result, however, the external observer, used to more traditional religious forms of expression, is often disorientated as Belk, Wallendorf, and Sherry explain: "… mixing the sacred with the profane threatens to destroy the sacred, … having the potential to trivialize the sacred … ." (1989: 24) Anyway, the ICF meets the challenge to reconcile spiritual and entertainment needs by merging the two kinds of expectations into a single project. Now, such an enterprise may affect the content itself. Without going as far as McLuhan for whom *the medium is the message* (1967), it is apparent that for the ICF, the evangelical message transforms the Christian message to a certain extent, as Sam puts it, for instance: "being Christian is fun." Indeed, the many conversations between the ICF members witnessed were full of enthusiastic expressions. To put it differently, the usual evangelical insistence on repentance, personal devotion to God, etc.,

---

[10] This is the case of so-called extreme sports when the original framework reserved for the spirit of competition is widened to accommodate a desire for thrills.

has practically disappeared from the ICF vocabulary, whether it be in sermons or in everyday conversations. To understand Christian faith as thoroughly exciting seems sufficient to mobilize people.

Conclusion

To conclude, we argue that, from a sociological perspective, the ICF is neither a sect nor a Church (in the Weberian sense), but a religious movement which can be qualified as entrepreneurial in that it offers the possibility to live one's Christian faith in harmony with the world of modern entertainment. By organizing events, the ICF brings about an experience, an *Erlebnis* and, in doing so, it narrows the gap between the sacred and the profane. As we have shown, although the ICF conceives its "religious product" as having to adapt to its environment constantly, the "marketing" dimension does not explain everything. Indeed, if the use of specific strategies and of an attractive form plays an essential role in the concept, it does so as a catalyst of experience, blending strong emotions with religious aspirations which cannot simply be reduced to a question of form.

To put this differently, the ICF *meets non-commercial needs by means of marketing and events inspired by the world of commerce*. To attract, convince, and succeed, the ICF uses the resources made available by the *Erlebniswelt*, the world of entertainment. However, as we have shown, it is not only the form which is attractive; the content itself is transformed through festive celebration. The ICF thus satisfies latent needs through the immersion of spiritual aspirations into entertaining events. In this light, the ICF appears to be what Höhn (1998), a philosopher and Catholic theologian, would qualify as a "city religion" in the context of the new religious markets when structure and range match the typical characteristics of the City.

Finally, our analysis may shed a different light on the sometimes fierce criticism incurred by the movement. Indeed, if we expect Churches, and religion in general, to return to timeless values by means of alternative sites and forms of expression, evocative of serenity and meditation, then the ICF does not meet these expectations. On the contrary, if we accept the possibility of a return to essential values through sensory and instantaneous means, we may, then, refine our definition of authentic religious experience.

Chapter 4

Branding, Music, and Religion: Standardization and Adaptation in the Experience of the "Hillsong Sound"

Thomas Wagner

Introduction

Global brands, popular music, and evangelical Christianity are products of cultural flows (Appadurai, 1990) that facilitate interaction between the "global" and the "local," in what Roland Robertson (1995) has referred to as *glocalization*. Originally a marketing term, glocalization describes the processes by which "global" (usually western) ideas and products are adapted to local consumption contexts (ibid: 28–9). It expands the understanding of "locality" by eschewing "top down" or "bottom up" models of culture in favor of dialectical interactions (ibid: 30). For example, while McDonald's has become shorthand for the "hegemonic rationalization of culture" (Ritzer, 2010), Maharaja Macs in India and McLaks in Norway demonstrate local adaptations of its products. Once accepted, though, a brand like McDonald's may become so ingrained in the "local" consciousness that its foreign origins are forgotten (Belk, 2000). The global adaptation and transformation of popular musics such as Hip-Hop into sonic symbols of local identity speaks to similar dynamics (Mitchell, 2001). By the same token, many forms of evangelical Christianity have shown a remarkable ability to glocalize, adapting to almost every socioeconomic and cultural milieu into which they are introduced (Robbins, 2004).

Marketing, music, and religion can all glocalize because they are experiential vehicles for meaning making. As Robin Sylvan argues in his cross-cultural study of the religious dimensions of popular music, meaning in both religion and music is created by the interaction of multiple levels of individual experience—physiological, psychological, socio-cultural, semiological, virtual, ritual, and spiritual (Sylvan, 2002: 19–44). This is also true of the meaning of brands, which has been studied by scholars from each of these perspectives. For example, Lindstrom (2005) emphasizes sensory branding (physiological), Fournier (1998) treats brands as relationship partners (psychological), Muniz and O'Guinn (2001) explore "brand communities" (sociocultural and ritual), Manning (2010) focuses on brand semiotics (semiological), Book (2005) analyzes virtual world branding (virtual), and Muniz and Schau (2005) delve into religiosity in the Apple Newton brand community (spiritual).

The importance of experience in creating meaning has not been lost on practitioners of marketing, music, or religion. Several recent brand management books advocate encouraging "an almost religious zeal" in customers (Hanlon, 2006: 4; see also Lindstrom, 2005) and branding "like a rock star" (Jones, 2012). The religious-like activities of music fans are well documented, perhaps no more so than those of Elvis devotees, some of whom create shrines to the King and make pilgrimages to Graceland (Harrison, 1992). The intrinsic role of music in shaping religious experience has been evident to practitioners of the "great" religions for thousands of years (Beck, 2006). More recently, the explosion of religious branding consultancies shows that marketing is increasingly being embraced by religious organizations (Einstein, 2008). Although the marketing of religious experience is most familiar as a feature of evangelical Christian organizations, groups like the Jewish Kabbalah movement and the Japan-based Buddhist organization Soka Gakkai International show that sophisticated marketing efforts are a cross-faith phenomenon.

It is surprising, then, that while there have been several studies of music and branding, branding and religion, and religion and music, there seems to have been no attempt to study all three as a single rubric, even more so given acknowledgement of the roles of both marketing and popular music in the megachurch movement (Sargeant, 2000; Twitchell, 2007). This chapter begins to redress this, positing the experience of brand, music, and religious discourse as a gestalt "Sound." It takes as its case study Hillsong Church, the Australian megachurch whose brand is inextricable from its self-produced, internationally influential pop/rock worship music.

Hillsong's music "product" is one (if not *the*) main driver of its growth (McIntyre, 2007)—a glocalized offering adopted by Christian churches all over the world. Like McDonald's, Hillsong focuses on the consistency of its product, and achieves it by standardizing production and delivery. However, while McDonald's adapts the content of its product for local tastes, Hillsong does not. Rather, it offers a global musical product mix that is positioned through extra-musical communication and adapted by its worshipers through the frame of the brand in the local contexts in which it is offered and received.

The ethnographic data presented herein was collected during three years of research at Hillsong's London branch as part of the author's PhD project (Wagner, forthcoming), which involved participant observation and interviews with Hillsong London's congregation members, musicians from Hillsong's London and Australian churches, and Hillsong Church's trans-national leadership. This chapter is organized as follows: First, I provide background on Hillsong Church and information on its business model, mission, and message. The next section discusses how Hillsong ensures consistency by centralizing the production of its music around its flagship Australian church and standardizing its delivery in live performance. I next develop the concept of a branded "Hillsong Sound" as a product of stakeholders' social imagining of places and people in the Hillsong network. This is followed by a description of an abandoned attempt to create a distinct "European Sound" at Hillsong's London location by changing its musical product. The final section will give an example of Hillsong's use of extra-musical communication in shaping worshipers' social imaginations through a description of a video shown as a lead in to a weekly worship service at Hillsong London. The video positions the church as a "home" of overlapping communities that is a significant actor in a global evangelical project, glocalizing the brand and the music in the experience of the "Hillsong Sound."

Background and Business Model

Head Pastors Brian and Bobbie Houston founded Hillsong Church as the Hills Christian Life Centre in 1983. It initially had a congregation of 45 that met in a rented school hall in the Baulkham Hills district, a suburb of Sydney. Today, around 23,000 worshipers a week attend services at its purpose-built 3,500 seat flagship church (which remains in Baulkham Hills), its three other Australian campuses and 12 extension services, as well at Hillsong-branded churches in major cities such as London, Kiev, Cape Town, Stockholm, Paris, Moscow, and New York City. Hillsong's annual conference draws in excess of 28,000 people, while its European counterpart, the Hillsong Europe conference, draws about 16,000 people annually. The church's beliefs and practices are rooted in Pentecostalism (Brian Houston is a former head of Assemblies of God in Australia), but its website does not align the church with a specific tradition (McIntyre, 2007: 176). This is standard practice for most "seeker" churches (Sargeant, 2000). In this respect, then, Hillsong Church is better classified under a broad "evangelical Christian" rubric.

Hillsong is perhaps the most striking example of the confluence of sophisticated marketing techniques and popular music that has characterized the megachurch movement (cf. Sargeant, 2000). To date, it has produced over forty albums, sold over 11 million copies worldwide, and amassed over thirty gold and platinum awards.[1] These albums are separated into product streams meant for specific target audiences. For example, *Hillsong Kids* features music produced for children and *Hillsong Chapel* offers acoustic arrangements of Hillsong's songs for those who seek a "quieter" worship experience than that afforded by the electric guitar, keyboard, and drums-driven originals. Hillsong's global popularity, though, stems primarily from its two main product streams, *Hillsong United* and *Hillsong LIVE*. *Hillsong United* is the name of the band that grew out of the Australian church's youth program. Fronted by Brian and Bobbie Houston's son Joel, *Hillsong United* regularly tours the world, and is arguably the "Australian" face of the church. In contrast, *Hillsong LIVE* albums are meant to be the expression of Hillsong's "global" network: while relying heavily upon the Australian church's creative

---

[1]   http://distribution.hillsong.com/help/about. Accessed June 08, 2012.

team, *Hillsong LIVE* albums incorporate singers and songwriters from different Hillsong churches around the world. Despite separate marketing programs, there is a good deal of crossover of artists and songs between them (Riches, 2010; Riches and Wagner, 2012), which helps promote an overall Hillsong musical identity. While Hillsong's 23,000-person membership is relatively small, compared to megachurches that claim six-digit attendance, its worship songs have had an outsized influence on both the Australian and global Christian sonic (and theological) landscapes (Evans, 2006: 87–109). Every Sunday, songs written by its internationally known singer/songwriters such as Reuben Morgan, Joel Houston, and Darlene Zschech are heard and sung in thousands of evangelical and non-evangelical churches around the world.[2]

Like most modern megachurches, Hillsong is structured and operates like a secular business. According to its website, its governance policies are "based on the Australian Stock Exchange (ASX) Principles of Good Corporate Governance and Best Practice Recommendations, together with adherence to foundational Biblical values."[3] Senior Pastor Brian Houston is the head of its board of directors, which includes members with considerable business acumen, such as General Manager George Aghajanian, formerly of IBM, and Nabi Saleh, CEO of Gloria Jean's Coffees. Unlike secular for-profit companies, though, Hillsong Church is a registered non-profit organization, so it is income tax-exempt. Additionally, it lowers its cost structure by relying on a high proportion of volunteer labor in almost all aspects of its functioning.

Full access to Hillsong's financial dealings is restricted. However, a general picture of the church's finances can be constructed from its annual report. Income is generated from donations (its members are encouraged to tithe), ticketed events such as conferences, and numerous products, including CDs, DVDs, Mp3s, and books. Its 2010 Annual Report listed earnings of $64 million, with total assets of $28.7m and income from conferences of $6.7m (McMillan, 2011).

Hillsong's music is produced by its own publishing arm, Hillsong Music Australia (HMA), and distributed by EMI CMG in North and South America, and Kingsway Music in Europe and the UK. It can be purchased at church events like weekly services and conferences, through the Hillsong Music website, or via music download sites such as Amazon.com or iTunes. Aside from income generated from album sales, the church receives royalties paid by other churches who use its songs in services or other events. These undisclosed licensing fees, collected in part through the Christian Copyright Licencing International (CCLI) organization,[4] accounted for between 35 and 45 percent of all its total musical royalties in 2011 (McKenny, 2011).

Hillsong's mission and message is one of global transformation, seeking to "reach and influence the world by building a large Christ-centered, Bible-based

---

[2]   http://www.ccli.com/licenseholder/Top25Lists.aspx. Accessed June 08, 2012.
[3]   http://www.myhillsong.com/corporate-goverance. Accessed June 08, 2012.
[4]   http://www.ccli.com/Global.aspx. Accessed June 08, 2012.

church, changing mindsets and empowering people to lead and impact in every sphere of life."[5] It does this by building a globally networked community of local churches, and by promoting its brand tagline, "Welcome Home," which neatly sums up its glocalization strategy. Because Hillsong strategically locates churches in major international cities around the world, its trans-national congregation is culturally and linguistically diverse. This diversity is apparent at some of its larger venues, such as Hillsong London, which serves around 8,000 worshipers weekly, translating its services into seven languages.

The "Hillsong Sound"—A Global Language?

Musical style plays a critical role in creating and maintaining a sense of community and conveying social ideals (e.g. Blacking, 1973; Rommen, 2007). As such, Hillsong's music is key to the construction and maintenance of its global brand community and its brand identity. Its services provide an immersive experience for the congregation (Pine II and Gilmore, 2011: 45–6), emphasizing participation through singing and clapping, which also plays a key role in the socialization and emotional engagement that its members seek in a worship experience (Albrecht, 1999).

Hillsong is, of course, not the first church to appreciate the role of music in forging bonds and communicating with its followers. Indeed, music has occupied a central place in the spiritual experience offered by almost every religion throughout human history (Beck, 2006). This is especially true of experiential faiths, such as Hillsong Church, that seek an "ecstatic" or "transcendent" worship experience (Becker, 2004; Rouget, 1985). In these traditions, music and musicians are critical resources that facilitate a meaningful worship experience of the faithful. The HMA website highlights Hillsong's music as one of the church's "Christian Resources," which it offers to help achieve the following goals:

- To enable people to enter into a new dimension and atmosphere of praise and worship to the Lord.
- To empower people, ministries and churches through relevant, bible-based teaching, leadership and praise and worship.
- To share some of what God is doing here at Hillsong with other Christians around the world, as well as people outside of the Church. (http://distribution.hillsong.com/help/about. Accessed June 08, 2012.)

By positioning its musical offerings as Christian resources that can be used for worship and also as tools for church building and evangelical purposes, Hillsong differentiates its brand from the rest of the multibillion-dollar Christian music industry. This positioning is crucial to the branded experience of the "Hillsong Sound."

---

[5] http://www.hillsong.com/vision. Accessed August 19, 2012.

Branding is imperative for any organization that aspires to a global reach (Targos, 1998). In a globalized world, brands, music, and religion are all forms of cross-cultural communication. For a religious organization like Hillsong, clarity of communication is paramount, because its brand is bound to a claim of biblical Truth—the understanding of which is inevitably culturally-inflected. As a trans-national church, then, Hillsong faces a challenge of "global" proportions: it must deliver a clear, consistent, and coherent message across a range of offerings, through many people, in a variety of cultural contexts. Complicating the matter is the fact that this message is often delivered musically: While music is often easily absorbed into a variety of cultural settings, it is also subjective, so its ability to reliably communicate meaning through either sound or lyrics is debatable (Negus, 1996: 25–35). The culturally-specific medium of music thus presents Hillsong with unique opportunities for, as well as challenges to, communicating its brand to a trans-national audience.

Hillsong responds to these challenges by standardizing its music. Like food, music and religion are subject to the cultural norms and tastes of the localities in which they are consumed. For example, as noted earlier, McDonald's "glocalizes" in that it has a global strategy, in which it offers a standardized menu of products all over the world. However, it also practices a localization strategy by modifying some of these products or introducing new ones to appeal to the unique tastes of customers in different countries. Hillsong practices glocalization starting with the "Hillsong Sound," its global music offering. The "Hillsong Sound" begins as a standardized mix of products intended to communicate the fundamental message of transformation. These products are glocalized through extra-musical communication that adapts the Hillsong brand to its local context in each church in the Hillsong network. In the local worship context, individual members of Hillsong's congregations realize the meaning of the brand as they engage with and experience its music. Ultimately, the "Hillsong Sound" is inseparable from its worshipers' experiences of the Hillsong brand.

Although it is experienced in local contexts around the world, Hillsong's music largely originates from one place: its Australian church, the flagship location of the brand. The following section details the production process that seeks to ensure the level of cohesion and consistency that is necessary for the "Hillsong Sound."

Hillsong Australia: The Center of Production

A strong global brand communicates a consistent message across all of its offerings. One way to achieve this is through consistency of product. To ensure the consistency of its musical offerings, Hillsong has a codified production process by which songs travel from inspiration to recording. First, a creative team member submits a song for consideration. Hillsong's core song writing team is comprised of salaried pastors like Joel Houston and Reuben Morgan who are both internationally known and also intimately familiar with the church's mission and message. From a branding perspective, it behooves Hillsong to maintain a core of songwriters who are both recognizable and able to articulate its message consistently and accurately. Thus, while it is Hillsong's official policy that any team member may submit a song for consideration, according to an Australian worship leader I interviewed, the identity of the songwriter may influence the decision-making process:

> [Hillsong] has an idea as to whose songs they'd like to see on the next album. So they want to see a couple from [well known singer/songwriters like] Joel [Houston], a couple from Rueben [Morgan] … There may be two from random people in the congregation or the team … but it's pretty set (Jordan, interview with author. June 01, 2011).

When a song is submitted, Robert Fergusson—a Baulkham Hills campus senior pastor—reviews the song's lyrics to ensure that they are consistent with the church's teachings. If the song's message is deemed consistent with that of the church, it is then "field tested." This usually involves playing it in worship services at Hillsong's Australian churches, and observing the congregation's reaction. Since the primary goal of worship music at Hillsong is to afford a meaningful worship experience it is vital that worshipers engage with it. Therefore, if a song is received well, it will be retained. If not, it will either be discarded or re-written. Because songs are field-tested primarily in Australian locations, those congregation members become the *de facto* arbiters of taste for the entire Hillsong network. From a "top down" perspective, Hillsong Australia is the center of production of the branded music that carries the "Hillsong Sound," as it is written, tested, and approved in an Australian context.

It is tempting to label Hillsong's music "Australian." However, once it is released, the music is performed by Hillsong's worship teams and experienced by individuals in myriad "local" contexts around the world, (perhaps arguably) most intensely in live group settings such as weekly worship services. Hillsong thus seeks a further level of consistency by standardizing how the music is delivered in live performances across its network of churches, where it is experienced in the social imaginations of worshipers.

Musical Standardization and Social Imagination

Hillsong's members primarily learn new songs by listening to them outside of church and singing them in worship services.[6] Because worshipers are familiar with the recorded versions of songs, Hillsong's worship leaders work to maintain fidelity to those recordings in live performances in the belief that too much deviation will distract the worshipers' attentions from God. Because the music is

---

[6] Most of the songs sung in a service during a given period are from the most recent *Hillsong United* or *Hillsong LIVE* releases. For Hillsong's annual product cycle, see Riches, 2010: 144–7.

performed in a variety of acoustic environments by a large number of musicians in a variety of languages, variation is inevitable. To mitigate this, Hillsong institutes a variety of "quality control" measures. For example, the instrumental and vocal make up of worship teams is nearly identical across all of Hillsong's churches. Musicians learn to replicate parts as they are presented on album recordings. Additionally, click tracks are used to ensure that each performance is the same tempo regardless of who is playing the song or where it is being played. However, these attempts at standardization are moderated by an interdependence of place and identity that is equally, if not more crucial to the construction of the "Hillsong Sound" in the social imaginations[7] of those who engage with it. For example, when I asked Hillsong London congregation members if they believed Hillsong London's worship team to have its own "sound" or "style," several responded in a manner similar to this 28-year-old woman who hails from London:

> Our church plays everything faster and louder [than the Australian church], which *I guess is what you would expect from such a vibrant place* (Kimberly, email communication with author. May 03, 2011. Emphasis added).

As noted earlier, this is not the case: Hillsong worship teams use standardized instrumentation and metronomes to ensure that worship songs in performance are consistent with the recorded versions. The music in Hillsong London's worship services is meant to be, in an objective sense, the same as the music in Hillsong Australia's services. Nevertheless, it is experienced by worshipers as faster and louder by virtue of its being played in London.

The Hillsong London congregation members to whom I spoke also perceived Hillsong Australia and its music as more "laid back" than their own. One current member, who has spent considerable time in both the London and Australian churches, interpreted this in terms of culture:

> There is a lot of overlap. I mean, you get into church and it's Hillsong church, bigger and all of that. But it's slightly different because it's adapted to the culture, the Australian culture, so everything will be a bit slower (laughs), from the songs to—well, everything will be slightly slower (Emily, interview with author. December 07, 2010).

Both Kimberly and Emily's responses reveal that their perceptions—their social imaginations—of the location and the culture in which the music was produced influenced the ways they experienced it. Although there may be a "lot of overlap" between the cultures of the London and Australian churches, the relative

---

7   Here I am using "social imagination" in reference to Benedict Anderson's concept of an "imagined community," a community comprised of people who will never meet face-to-face but who nevertheless feel connected through mass media and the mediated images used to represent them (Anderson, 1983).

difference in the tempos of life was perceived in the tempo of the music, despite the latter objectively being the same. The role of the social imagination, then, has implications for any glocalization strategy's use of standardization and/or adaptation, as Hillsong's experiment with a "Euro Sound" shows.

Hillsong London: The "Euro Sound" Experiment

Because of its strategic location, Hillsong London is Hillsong's main base for evangelistic activities in Europe. Its worship team regularly tours the continent, performing music from *Hillsong United* and *Hillsong Live* albums at events in a variety of countries and cultural settings. One worship team member spoke to me about the evangelical success Hillsong London enjoyed in Italy:

> Well, actually (Hillsong London Senior Pastor) Gary (Clarke) said something about [touring] yesterday. He said they call it tours, but it's actually [evangelical] crusades. Because London goes to Italy, they go to Europe, and like a thousand people get saved in one night (Susan, interview with author. February 06, 2011).

When I asked what accounted for this success, another suggested that Hillsong London's music has a distinct "Euro Sound":

> The London stuff goes off really well in Italy ... It's "Euro," it's got its own flavor (Jordan, interview with author. June 01, 2011).

This worship leader believed Europeans are more receptive to this distinct "Euro Sound" than they would be to Hillsong's Australian sound, which they might hear as "foreign." It should be remembered, though, that Hillsong London plays music that is primarily written and recorded by the Australian creative team members and strives to reproduce those recordings in concerts. The objective elements of the music are not being adapted by the church musicians to local tastes. Rather, European "fans" appear to be experiencing Hillsong's music as local through their social imaginations.

The challenge to Hillsong's branding strategy, then, lies in managing how its music is "localized." The difficulty of this can be seen in a previous attempt by Hillsong London to cater to European tastes by offering an extension to its sonic brand, an experiment that was eventually discontinued in favor of a branding model that standardizes the product and allows local churches to adapt the context in which it is offered.

From 2004 to 2008, Hillsong London released a brand extension in the form of four self-titled albums. Although the London church's creative team wrote most of the songs on these albums, the music largely conformed to the overall rock-based style then coalescing between Hillsong's *United* and *LIVE* product streams (Riches 2010). There was, therefore, little in the way of sonic differentiation between the

London and Australian products. However, in 2007, London broke from Hillsong's musical convention with the release of *Jesus Is: Remix*. In an innovative offering, this album remixed the rock-based songs of its 2006 release, *Jesus Is*, as dance tracks. Synthesizers and drum machines largely replaced the electric guitars and acoustic drums of the originals, significantly changing the musical aesthetic. Much of the Christian music media applauded this new "Euro Sound." One reviewer wrote:

> Passionate Euro-styled worship has been a core driving force for the explosive growth at the new Hillsong London church. A group of talented and creative members of the church have taken 12 songs from the original *Jesus Is* worship project released in 2006 and remixed them from a pop and rock sound to electronic and ambient versions while maintaining the same lyrics and Biblical messages. Mixing a sound from their Hillsong Australia heritage with the current European/London music scene, this Euro-Worship has a fresh and exciting, yet familiar sound (http://www.christianscampus.com/2010/04/hillsong-london-jesus-is-remix2010.html. Accessed August 21, 2011).

In this review, the importance of place in the construction of a branded "Sound" is apparent; the reviewer posits Australia as the "heritage" of the music (cf. Gilmore and Pine, II 2007) while connecting the *Jesus Is: Remix* "sound" to an "European" music "scene" in London.

In (post)subcultural theory, a "scene" is defined in terms of the vitality and diversity of its musical life (Stahl, 2004: 55; see also Straw, 1991).[8] A "happening" scene is one that supports a diverse array of musics and a large number of stakeholders involved and invested in musical activities. In contrast, a "dead" scene is one with few opportunities to hear or perform music, and little diversity in musical style. Interviews conducted during my fieldwork indicate that, to Hillsong's musicians and congregation members, Hillsong London's "Sound" reflects London's status as a "happening" scene. The London "Sound" has a cosmopolitan "Euro-ness" that reflects the diversity of London's scene. This diversity is held in opposition to the homogenous musical scene of Sydney,[9] as this Australian worship leader indicated:

> Question: I've been asking if there is a "Hillsong Sound" and a "London Sound," and you seem to think there is.

---

[8]   As Stahl suggests, scenes "are dense array(s) of social, industrial and institutional infrastructures, all of which operate at a local and trans-local level" (2004: 55). Because of technological mediation, a scene can simultaneously be "virtual" and "global" as well as "local."

[9]   Interviewees from both London and Australia often used Sydney as shorthand when referring to Hillsong's Australian members and churches. Although Hillsong holds services in downtown Sydney, its flagship location is its Baulkham Hills campus. This is an example of the gravitational pull that "branded" cities exert on people's perceptions and expressions.

J: Yeah, I do. I think that I was hearing ... some Green Day influences, almost some Ska [On Hillsong London's first album]. And to me that's kind of indicative of England, where the Punk movement originated. I feel like that was something that was really appropriate. I also think that the Euro sound is so much more open to Electronica. I think they have a sense of that Soul influence in London. There are a lot of different influences that are just not present in Sydney (Jordan, interview with author. June 01, 2011).

If the "happening" Euro-London and comparatively "dead" Austral-Sydney scenes produce different "taste publics" (Russell, 1997), one might expect the congregation members of Hillsong London to prefer songs written by the London church's local songwriters. However, when I asked London congregants which they preferred, everyone I interviewed admitted a preference for the Australian songs. This preference was expressed by two of Hillsong London's congregants:

There's a lot of crossover between Hillsong London and Hillsong Australia, but most of the songs that I think are the better ones tend to be the Australian ones (Jason, interview with author. May 18, 2010).

It's weird, because at London, a lot of the good ones we sing are actually the Australian ones. Most of the ones London has written recently haven't been, I don't think, as good (Luke, interview with author. November 23, 2010).

In 2011, the Hillsong London recording line was officially discontinued. The original intent behind the Hillsong London albums was, as many of my interviewees suggested, to create a distinct "Euro Sound" that would appeal to a European audience. However, this didn't work in the context of Hillsong's global branding strategy, as recounted by Hillsong's general manager, George Aghajanian:

Question: Could you tell me a little bit about why Hillsong London no longer records its own albums?

GA: I think we got to a point where we felt ... we really wanted to make sure that Hillsong, when it was represented worldwide, didn't have a variety of different sounds. We wanted to make sure that everything we did was ultimately distilled onto one or two really good albums and not three, four, five, six different albums ... with all different types of sounds. Because London has a very specific sound; Sydney's got a different sound; Paris would have a different sound, and Kiev and so on.[10] So what we wanted to make sure of was that the Hillsong name

---

[10] Hillsong Kiev produces its own albums as a Hillsong brand extension. This highlights the role that language plays in brand translation. According to Aghajanian: "Remembering that the basis behind this is reaching people with the Gospel in song as well as in teaching, we take our worship experience, translate it, and release it into the Eastern

and the Hillsong reputation for worship was preserved while at the same time
being inclusive with what was happening with songwriters around different
parts of the world ... because if you have five albums, that's sixty songs you've
got to come up with versus two or three really powerful worship albums that
would then be the best experience for the greater Church (interview with author.
September 28, 2011).

As Hillsong expanded, it identified a need to maintain consistency and quality
across its product lines. To achieve this, it abandoned the attempt to create a
distinct "Euro Sound" for Hillsong London in favor of a more coherent "Hillsong
Sound" that could be recognized across product streams. This move towards
standardization involved centralizing the production of its music around its
Australian church and standardizing the live presentation of that music in services
across its network. However, despite the music being objectively similar across
venues, the music is still experienced differently, depending on where and by
whom it is being played, as it is adapted in the social imaginations of worshipers
in their local contexts.

To manage the "Hillsong Sound," then, Hillsong must go beyond musical
standardization to try to shape how it is "heard" by its local congregation members.
One way Hillsong does this is to position, by way of extra-musical communication,
each local Hillsong city and church within the global Hillsong Church community,
which is itself positioned as part of a global evangelical Christian project of Church
building. An example of this is provided in the following description of the three-
minute video that begins weekly services in every church in the Hillsong network.
This video, which is produced specifically for each church (e.g., Hillsong London
will present a different video than Hillsong New York) prepares congregants to
"hear" the "Hillsong Sound" by using image and narrative to orient them toward
certain ways of thinking about their city, their local church, and Hillsong Church
as "home."

The Hillsong Sound: "Welcome Home"

*Sunday, July 19, 2009. Hillsong London's 6 pm service at the Dominion Theatre,
London.*

*I have found a seat in row H of the Dominion Theatre, Hillsong London's
Sunday home in London's West End, front and center for the 6 pm service.*

European culture. That's why [in Kiev] they've probably had a little more autonomy to do
some of these albums, and London really hasn't. Because London, being in the English
speaking world, can contribute to our global expression of our worship. Kiev can't really
because of the language issues" (interview with author. September 28, 2011). Another way
Hillsong standardizes its product is by offering, free of charge, official translations of its
songs (http://distribution.hillsong.com/publishing/faq. Accessed June 08, 2012).

Since there are no tickets, you have to get there early. Around me, young, happy Christians talk excitedly to each other or rush to reserve the last seats for late-coming friends, silhouetted against a stage screen that reads "Welcome Home."

Right on time, the lights dim. A menacing industrial groove replaces what had formerly been unassuming, ambient background music. The word "London" flashes across the otherwise dark screen. The iconic Tower Bridge appears for a moment, followed by a succession of momentary, herky-jerky shots of anonymous Londoners rushing about their daily lives. Gradually, the pace grows faster. The camera begins to zoom out, revealing glimpses of London signifiers: here, a glimpse of a man handing out free newspapers at a tube entrance; there, a red telephone box. As the visual stimuli increase, so does the music's insistence. Just as silhouettes of the London Eye and Big Ben appear, the screen goes dark again.

An instant later, a bird's-eye view of the Thames at sunrise appears as the music suddenly becomes upbeat. The sun shines directly into the camera, becoming a glint off of the giant golden statue of Freddie Mercury that sits atop the Dominion Theatre's entrance. Inside, the busy lobby is filled with people that many in the congregation will recognize as friends (they might even catch a glimpse of themselves). These shots appear in rapid succession as the music continues to grow livelier.

The screen goes dark for a third time as the music morphs into a crunching, metallic guitar riff. A spinning globe appears, overlaid with the Apostle Paul's words: "The church is not peripheral to the world, the world is peripheral to the church." Ephesians 3:8–10 immediately follows, reminding the congregation that: "Through followers of Jesus like yourselves gathered in churches, the extraordinary plan of God is being known." This scripture shares the screen with images of people from around the world who, while nameless, are instantly recognizable by virtue of the ethnically marked clothing they wear. These shots are juxtaposed with sweeping visions of masses of raised hands, signifying a large, exciting evangelical event such as a conference, concert, or the service that has just begun. Thus, the second half of the video situates London and the church in the larger evangelical project of Church building. "Church" is understood here as not only the local church, but also the church with a capital "C," the global, borderless Body of Christ that is formed by believers. The video, which began with the single word, London, ends with a single name, Jesus. The band bounds on stage, seamlessly transitioning from the video's soundtrack to the live worship music experience. The service has begun. (Author's field notes, July 19, 2009.)

While an entire discussion could be devoted to the semiotics of the video described above, here I wish to focus on how Hillsong uses it to suggest ways of thinking about (and thus experiencing) the city of London, Hillsong London, Hillsong Church and the Hillsong brand in connection to evangelical Christian tropes of transformation and Church building. In order to do so, I borrow a metaphor from Timothy Rommen's study of Full Gospel Christians in Trinidad: the Hillsong brand exists in "ever widening concentric circles" that move outward from the individual congregation, through the Hillsong network, to global Christianity (and beyond) (Rommen, 2007: 41).

The first part of the video described above posits London as a place of promise and energy, but also one of loneliness and struggle. The second part of the video has a feeling of release from that struggle, a soaring journey above the Thames that lands at the door of the Dominion Theatre, the Sunday home of Hillsong London. Inside, friends await. Hillsong London is depicted as a "home"—an answer to the struggles of city life. This "home" is part of another "home"—Hillsong Church, which the third part of the video casts in a transformational role, this time as a globally significant builder of the global Church. The video takes the viewer on a journey from the unnamed (but easily recognizable) "third world," through an evangelical event that could easily be one of Hillsong's annual conferences, to the "Body of Christ"—the name commonly used by evangelicals to describe the "global" Church.

Much of the efficacy of the branded experience of Hillsong's music results from the connectedness that worshipers feel to the trans-national Hillsong network and the global Church. The "Hillsong Sound" is heard within a globally-oriented discourse that emphasizes Hillsong's ability to transcend boundaries. However, this is moderated by a simultaneous discourse that posits each of Hillsong's churches as the "local church" of the individual worshiper. Thus, the "Welcome Home" message that greets worshipers in Hillsong churches around the world simultaneously references Hillsong's individual churches, the Hillsong network, and the global Church; the "Hillsong Sound" may be promoted globally and *heard* in a local church, but it is *experienced* by its worshipers as a "glocal" phenomenon.

This chapter has explored some of the ways music, branding, and religious discourse coalesce as a branded "Sound" for Hillsong Church and its congregation members. It provides background on the church's business model, including its "glocal" marketing strategy, and presents a case based on ethnographic fieldwork carried out at its London site and through interviews with members of its trans-national leadership. The experiences that its congregation members encounter when worshiping through the church's music, which is presented in standardized forms, are derived from the gestalt of associations that is the Hillsong brand. The music is adapted in its members' social imaginations, which are themselves shaped through extra-musical communication that positions Hillsong as a "home" that exists simultaneously at multiple levels of (g)locality—a "home" that is a transformative agent in an evangelical project of Church building. The "Hillsong Sound" unites Hillsong's brand, its music, and evangelical beliefs in a single glocalized sonic experience. While this analysis is based on a single, context-specific case study, at the core of what has been discussed are basic forms of human communication and meaning making. Investigations along these lines in other religious, linguistic, socio-economic, and cultural contexts will contribute to our understanding of the processes of communication and meaning making that take place in an increasingly glocal—and branded—world.

Chapter 5

The Marketing of Spiritual Services and the Role of the Religious Entrepreneur

Markus Hero

Introduction

In Western European countries, since the 1980s a market for services has become established which offers a variety of suppliers the opportunity of promulgating spiritual support and therapies to help people cope with their lives.[1] The design of the relevant offerings in terms of their content exhibits a dual focus. On the one hand they focus on ideas which address questions of identity and identity management (cf. Barth, 2012): From "self-discovery," "self-awareness," "self-observation," "self-assurance" to "self-development," these offerings aim to achieve personal well-being, increased satisfaction with life and improved life skills. These offerings have been given a further overtone in terms of their content, as religious ideas are being turned into a fertile source of health-related services (cf. Andritzky, 1997; Deutscher Bundestag, 1998; Koch, 2005; Murken, 2009). The developments referred to are sustained above all by the variety of religious entrepreneurs (Hero, 2011) on the so-called "esoteric market," where new forms of "treatments for body and soul" (Bourdieu, 1992: 233) are propagated. The dimension which creates identity and offers healing can be regarded as a constitutive element of the respective offerings: "Shamanism," "Reiki," "tarot," "Bach flowers," "channeling," "rebirthing," "aura cleansing," "astrology," "geoaesthesia," "Qi Gong," "yoga," "meditation," and "hypnosis" and their psychotherapeutic and medicinal claims are accepted by a wide social public.

The present article deals with the contribution made by religious entrepreneurs' marketing and self-representation to the development and perpetuation of the spiritual services market. The following considerations are primarily of

---

[1]   There is a detailed description of what is on offer in the spiritual marketplace in Mayer (2007: 266 et seq.). As the classical article by Campbell (1972) states in respect of the origins of this milieu, the economic and intellectual motivations go back to the alternative culture of the late 1960s. An in-depth analysis of the reasons why the alternative milieu gave birth to new occupational areas is offered by Pierre Bourdieu (1982). Bourdieu places both the supply side and the demand side arrangements in the socio-structural context of the "new petty bourgeoisie." Chevalier (1981), Featherstone (1987) *inter alia* join this line of argument.

a conceptual nature. Drawing on micro and institutional economics, specific marketing activities in the environment of the contemporary spiritual market will be deduced. In particular this involves the question of which measures promote willingness to cooperate and trust between suppliers and consumers.

Spiritual Services as a Market Offering—Structural Considerations

To understand marketing measures in the area of contemporary spirituality we need to start from the assumption "that the characteristics of goods determine the way in which they are provided and the characteristics of a transaction [determine] how it is embedded institutionally" (Brinitzer, 2003: 159). Thus, first we need to look at the particular *problems of information and cooperation* associated with spiritual services. We shall then investigate how such services have been able to achieve increasing or lasting popularity despite the uncertainty associated with them. Particular significance will be attached here to the issue of how the suppliers and consumers involved generate *trust* amongst each other, and how the plausibility of the therapeutic ideas that are propagated is manufactured.

When goods and services are being purchased, they "divulge information about their characteristics to a differing extent" (Brinitzer, 2003: 160). Information economics distinguishes between goods and services whose quality the consumer can check before buying them ("inspection goods"), whose quality is only revealed to the consumer during consumption ("experience goods"), and finally goods whose quality largely remains in the dark even after consumption ("credence goods") (cf. Ekelund, 1995). Because in the area of spiritual services there are as good as no legal guarantees or equivalent securities as to the "quality" or the "benefit," potential interested parties find themselves in a situation of uncertainty.[2] Even after the actual act of purchase, namely during "consumption," the characteristics of spiritual services are revealed to the consumer only to a limited extent: There is a lack of specific criteria to judge the quality of either the process or the results of the service activity.[3] For this reason, in the microeconomic literature spiritual and health-related services have already been mentioned by various authors under the aspect of "credence goods" (cf. *inter alia* Ekelund, 1995; Dulleck, 2006; Richardson, 1999). This idea will be adopted below. However, this will not involve the modeling of prices and quantities of goods on the markets for

---

[2] Since it can be assumed that the actors are aware of this "uncertainty," the term "risk" can also be more accurately used. The term "risk" relates at the same time to both the awareness of the alternatives for action and the knowledge of the dependence of one's own outcome on the behavior of other players (cf. Brinitzer, 2003: 180).

[3] In a general sense one can assume that "religion involves a great deal of risk. Those who engage in religious acts cannot know that their efforts will have the desired effects" (Iannaccone, 1995: 285).

"credence goods," but rather the institutional and conceptual consequences that are associated with the assumed problems of information.

In what way are we justified in regarding spiritual services as "credence goods"? There are no simple verification methods available to the consumer for him to get a picture of the quality of the services to be expected from a service provider in advance. Especially in the case of the "exotic" techniques and processes offered on the alternative health market, there are scarcely any indications to help potential interested parties assess their value: Where, for example, does the benefit of a "magnetic field treatment" or "Reiki therapy" lie? An evaluation can at best take place at the expense of high "search costs," which will continue to exist as long as there are no networks of acquaintances or institutions to provide information about the respective offerings.

Defining the benefit of spiritual health services remains tricky even after the service has been consumed. The customer or client does indeed gradually gain more information about the change in his state of health if he follows its development over time. However, when it comes to evaluating a concrete service the consumer must be able to compare his situation with the state of health in which he would have found himself if he had not made use of the service. In addition, as the individual consumer possibly only gains information at a late stage, this can only help the scene further if institutional opportunities are created to communicate existing experiences and help other interested parties in their decision making.

The uncertainties mentioned are of particular significance for the dynamics of the market. Goods and services markets risk collapsing if the interested parties find no clear benefits to be reaped from the offerings, or have difficulty assessing their quality within an appropriate period. This is the case when skeptical consumers either fully withdraw from the market or exhibit only a low level of willingness to pay in view of the risk that exists. In the latter case, only low quality suppliers will remain in the market. To avoid triggering such "adverse selection" (Akerlof, 1970), support mechanisms are required to strengthen the consumers' *trust* and thus maintain their willingness to invest. On the other hand, market relationships always break down if there is no willingness to trust those who are involved.

In the context of market relationships, trust can be defined as an expectation by the buyer not to be deceived:

> Trust can be described as the social functional mechanism which expresses the suspension of the latent uncertainty of the provider of trust [the buyer]: trust operates as a calmative in social relationships which enables the provider of trust to remain calm despite the uncontrollable freedom to act of the recipient of trust [the seller] (Beckert, 2002: 36).

The problem of trust appears in its most pronounced form where the "value," "quality," and "benefit" of goods are very difficult, or even impossible, for the consumer to assess in advance. In such situations, appropriate institutional and communication measures, amongst other things, can provide assistance in creating "stable values" (Fligstein, 1996: 658). The corresponding supply-side measures are summarized in the information economics literature under the term "signaling" (Spence, 2002). As will be shown in the religious entrepreneurs example, a not insubstantial use of resources is required for the supplier to create the basic conditions for their service activities. Reliable expectation structures have to be created to strengthen the trust between suppliers and consumers.

As will be shown below using the example of the spiritual services market, this involves symbolic and institutional strategies which are intended to increase the suppliers' reputation and at the same time generate the potential for sanctions to be imposed (Section "Symbolic and institutional strategies for generating willingness to trust"). A further option consists in generating trust by means of performative action by the suppliers, namely religious entrepreneurs (Section "Generating trust by performative actions"). In contrast to institutional strategies for generating willingness to cooperate, "performative" means willingness to trust is produced "through acts of self-portrayal" (Beckert, 2002: 27), by which suppliers try to "convince [consumers] of the sincerity" of their "cooperative intentions to act" (ibid.) by discursive means. Particular attention will be given here to biographical self-portrayal on the supply side.

Symbolic and Institutional Strategies for Generating Willingness to Trust

If we assume that spiritual services can be classed as "credence goods," we now need to ask about the associated after-effects. If the constitutive uncertainty on the part of consumers were to continue to exist, the market would face the prospect of only modest growth opportunities. A broader public who are more willing to pay can only be addressed if they are enabled to gain information about the quality of the services offered, communicate the therapeutic experiences they have undergone and boycott any poor quality suppliers. In practice, different marketing mechanisms can be distinguished in the spiritual market in this respect: strategies of a symbolic, institutional, and performative kind.

The symbolic capital of naming

The following considerations are dedicated to those effects which emanate from the labeling strategies of spiritual suppliers, the aim of which is to bring off a positive reaction from the customer with respect to what is on offer. The manner in which potential customers perceive a brand name and keep it in mind is decisive for their attitude to a certain product or supplier (Keller, 1993: 2). The fundamental requirement for a particular service to be able to form the subject of communication amongst potential consumers (irrespective of whether it is a benevolent or derogatory assessment) is that the service concerned be identifiable. The continuity of the supplier's name and the service offered ensures recognition value, allowing it to be linked to past experiences and future expectations. Brand names, some of them patented, such as SENSITIVER LEBENSENERGIE BERATER®, PULSOR®ENERGIE THERAPEUT, ALEXAS-LIVETAROT®, CHANNELMEDIUM ASKARA®, OMEGATEAM® nowadays form part of the current manifestations of the spiritual services market. Through these names, the therapeutic ideas offered acquire a physically identifiable medium to which certain features can be ascribed, either to the person of the therapy provider (his name, his title) or to a symbol referring to the institution that is providing healing or to the healing service itself.

From the potential customer's perspective, the continuity of the brand name opens up the potential for sanctions. Both negative and positive experiences of a certain service offering can be permanently attributed, communicated and discussed with other people. From the supplier's perspective, the brand name thus goes hand in hand with an obligation: for the sake of his reputation he is obliged to maintain the symbols, labels, and names associated with his undertaking in a positive light. If the consumer can anticipate the direction a supplier's reputation will take, under certain circumstances he has a type of "hostage" or "security" at his disposal (Richter, 2010). As soon as the supplier delivers "poor quality," the consumer can retain the "hostage" or "security": in other words he can react by defection and negative assessment.

However, the economics of the brand name are not just restricted to opening up potential for sanctions. A spiritual supplier wishing to acquire a distinct identity so as to stand out from the mass of competing suppliers needs a name which will attract consumers' attention. Since the effect of these naming strategies on the visibility of the therapy supplier is hard to overestimate, the chosen names and symbols have to be "catchy" and meaningfully express the "special nature" of the respective therapy company.[4] This also includes the fact that the name must have a high recall value and be easy to commit to memory (Keller, 1993: 9).

As well as its functions of cognitive identification and differentiation, a company name is also of decisive importance from an evaluative point of view. For the supplier, a company name is above all about creating *positive associations*.[5] The "name and concept cult" (Goldner, 2000: 40) on the spiritual supply scene also assumes a function that supports the costumers self concept or identity. Brand names "serve as powerful repositories of meaning ... employed in the substantiation, creation und (re)production of self" (Fournier, 1998: 365). Names and titles in the spiritual scene must therefore adapt to the alternative self-definition of its public, which is expressed in typical attributes such as "holistic," "spiritual," "harmonious," or "creative." To gain approval from the public brings out an additional feature of the designations as well: Religious entrepreneurs largely resort to concepts which hint at their proximity to the social institutions that are recognized as legitimate. It is primarily the established educational institutions

---

4   For the varied effects of brand names see Welling (2006).

5   Pierre Bourdieu (1982: 748) talks of an "evocative capacity of linguistic expression, (...) which by modifying schemas of perception and evaluation allows us to see other things."

which serve as a point of reference, and above all state scientific and school education institutions ("academy," "school," "university," "center"). As well as suggesting professionalism, naming in the form described is also associated with another not unwelcome effect. A supplier's credibility or integrity is reinforced to the extent that he is able to keep the "economic truth" (Bourdieu, 1992: 188) of his company concealed. The connotations associated with "science," "research," and "teaching" essentially do not suggest any interest in private financial gain.

Institutional arrangements

While in the previous section the symbolic strategies of naming were at the fore, the next section will look at demonstrating institutional arrangements which structure the relationships between religious entrepreneurs and their clients. It is not just on the market for spiritual services that institutions are amongst the major requirements for cooperation between suppliers and consumers. Institutional arrangements are usually associated with normative role expectations and open up potential to impose sanctions. In this way institutional processes can "transform conditions of insufficient trust into ones of sufficient trust (for cooperation)" (Schmidtchen, 1993: 147).

Associations, special interest organizations and government regulations   The first opportunity to produce institutionally generated trust consists in the suppliers' membership in superordinate institutions. By pronouncing sanctions, an association can achieve a situation where suppliers display their "skills" and intentions properly and are also motivated to use these to the benefit of the consumer. The practices on the alternative health market above illustrate that suppliers become members of a plurality of associations.[6] As each association has a fundamental interest in maintaining its reputation, it will take care to sanction any members who damage this interest, for example by "unprofessional behavior" or "untrue promises." The relevant associations on the scene also take care of their members' reputations by preparing guidelines on training and continuing education[7] for the suppliers who have joined the association, as well as joint standards on ethics and procedures. In addition, the associations represent their members publicly, run advertising and try to represent the members' interests in terms of the creation of guiding political and legal conditions. Hence from the supplier's perspective, membership in a professional association represents an investment in the supplier's own reputation.

---

[6] Including "Berufsverband für Atemtherapie und Atempädagogik," "Verband Europäischer Ayurveda-Mediziner und Therapeuten," "Erste Deutsche Tarotverband," the "Deutscher Astrologen Verband," "Bundesverband für Feng Shui und Geomantie," "Reiki Verband Deutschland," or "Reiki Alliance Deutschland."

[7] The associations award titles and certificates, such as the certificate "Yogalehrer/in (BYV)" from the "Berufsverband der Yoga Vidya Lehrer/innen," or recognition as an "Anerkannte/r Heiler/in des Dachverbandes Geistiges Heilen."

In all markets for goods and services, the State can be considered as a third-party authority with the power to impose sanctions and establish reputations. In the case of the alternative health market, to date there have been relatively few government regulations. However, state-protected titles such as "alternative practitioner" or "psychotherapist," which permit their bearers to practice certain alternative forms of therapy, are relevant in this context. The responsible supervisory and authorizing bodies (e.g. the health authorities) can issue a "limited license for the professional practice of alternative medicine in the field of psychotherapy in accordance with the Heilpraktikergesetz (HeilprG) [*Non-Medical Practitioners Act*]." Government-awarded titles guarantee an effect on the reputations of the suppliers concerned, because acquiring them is associated with an established training course. Suppliers who use a title have made a credible commitment because they have to assume "that in the event of non-performance or poor performance they will be subject to state sanction" (Schmidtchen, 1993: 154). The national legal system also allows suppliers who have no explicit title as professional therapists to signal their trustworthiness to consumers. This can happen by their stating the general terms and conditions of their activity as service providers in an "advisory contract."

Intermediaries and brokers   The relationship with a third-party body which is capable of monitoring and sanctioning suppliers' behavior can also be set up on a more flexible basis. Obviously a large number of alternative therapy suppliers know the value of the infrastructure in adult education classes, seminar centers, further education institutions, communal events forums etc. Such intermediary institutions also include the operators of so-called "health fairs" and "esoteric fairs"[8]. For suppliers, the intermediaries' services are firstly associated with an opportunity to use suitable premises and address a broader public. The intermediary institutions or "brokers" (Rademacher, 2010: 123) take on an additional important function to generate trust on the alternative health services market. Since the institutions mentioned have a strong interest in expanding or maintaining their reputation, they will supervise the suppliers who organize "seminars," "workshops," or "educational courses" on their premises. From the consumer's viewpoint this offers relief, insofar as he can expect "brokers" to make every endeavor to identify "black sheep" and keep them away from their own business.

Various Internet platforms can also be considered intermediary institutions involved in alternative therapy events. Thousands of spiritual service providers use this medium. To emphasize the "professionalism" of this context, not just any supplier is allowed to set up operations on these internet platforms. Certain requirements must be met, such as previous activity as a professional life coach, qualifications in psychology, educational theory, or similar fields of study,

---

[8] These include events such as "Bioterra," "Esoterik und Naturheiltage," "Lebenskraft," "Esoterik-Tage" or "Energetika."

practical experience in the advisory professions and the intimate conviction of having received a calling.[9]

Longer-term relationships   Trust between suppliers and consumers can also be generated without the intervention of third parties, whether these take the form of associations or intermediary institutions. In the alternative health spectrum, as well as short-term customer relationships, longer-term *client relationships* also develop between suppliers and consumers. In this longer-term perspective, participants' willingness to cooperate is engendered from the benefit that suppliers and consumers derive from continuing the relationship. A supplier who offers unsatisfactory quality at a particular time can be punished by clients no longer considering him for future offerings. On the other hand, if the supplier offers services which keep the client permanently satisfied, then he thus acquires the prospect of a long-term business relationship. In this way the supplier's role entails an obligation towards the consumer which becomes an end in itself (cf. Brinitzer, 2003: 198).

The institutional arrangements mentioned above doubtless contribute to creating "reciprocal expectation structures" between suppliers, umbrella organizations, intermediaries, and consumers—yet the infrastructure of the alternative health market described here is insufficient on its own to eliminate all doubts in respect to the often "exotic" spiritual services which still appear strange to many people.[10] Thus the problem of trust can only be counteracted to a limited extent by institutional measures. Therefore the institutions mentioned so far cannot dispel all possible problems relative to communication and sanctions.

It is for this reason that, in practice, further strategies of generating trust are of significance in the alternative health market, which will be discussed in the following section. In contrast to the previously mentioned phenomena these strategies reside in the direct communication between suppliers and consumers. We have to consider the "performative acts" by the supplier "through which willingness to trust is generated in the activity situation itself" (Beckert: 34). Thus our consideration will now move from institutional arrangements to conceptual arrangements for generating trust.

Generating Trust by Performative Actions

Religious entrepreneurs will additionally try to add value to their services by means of a discursive argument. From an economic perspective, the phenomena we will now describe can also be classified as strategies for the production of willingness

---

[9]   See the portal www.questico.de.

[10]   This is also underlined by the fact that when choosing offerings, a large proportion of alternative health service users rely primarily on the recommendations of people they know, cf. *inter alia* Deutscher Bundestag (1998).

to cooperate. These involve creating a firm trust-generating foundation for the working relationship between customers and clients. However, to comprehend the social processes within these phenomena and the conditions in which such phenomena originate, we must supplement the purely economic perspective by a sociological one.

While the marketing strategies outlined in the previous section are also observable analogously in other, "non-religious," service economies, the phenomena to be discussed below involve a direct connection to religion. The "mobilization of willingness to cooperate" (Beckert, 2002: 41) here takes place through the communication of a religious narrative, which essentially relates to the biographical self-portrayal of the supplier. Credibility is signaled by the fact that suppliers present themselves as a guarantee of their product on the basis of their own "religious biography"; their personal career history.

It goes without saying that generating the impression of credibility is associated with certain requirements for the suppliers concerned. They have to make clear that their services and marketing strategies are not "free of charge" and easily accessible to any other supplier. A religious entrepreneur can provide proof of this by the fact that he "invests" in obtaining his status, his title, his professional career, and that he offers a "service" which can not be provided *ad hoc* by just any of his competitors. The strategies of advertising, giving titles, professional education, and the creation of outline contractual conditions mentioned in the previous section can be classed as signals of this kind. However, what the previously mentioned signals have in common is the fact that in their assumed effect they presuppose an abstract, calculative reasoning, but do not build on the direct interaction between supplier and customer. They remain reliant on an impersonal "trust in the system" (Giddens, 1996: 107 ff.). In the practice of spiritual services, on the other hand, above all it is those signals of trust which grow out of the personal meeting and communication between participants or at least reside at the interface between system and person (cf. Beckert, 2002: 37) which will have a motivating effect. The following section is devoted to the supplier-customer interaction and will show how the self-portrayal of religious entrepreneurs can generate trust and loyalty between participants.

The authenticity of the therapy provider

In view of the difficulties to validate the "therapeutic quality" of spiritual services, suppliers and consumers are very largely reliant on construing the healing or cure communicatively. It is therefore in the supplier's interest to develop shared categories of thought and attribution which the two parties can use to connect during communication. This requires that the supplier has a capacity for empathy, for which he is all the better equipped the more his own schemas of perception, thought and action overlap those of his customers, and the closer his own habitus comes to that of his customers. The spiritual service must be personal, and a "real" interest in the religious ideas proclaimed and in the concerns of the participants is expected.

What are the objective prerequisites which enable such "sympathy"[11] and which allow the impression of authenticity to be created in those involved? "In questions of credibility and trust, the partner's identity moves to the foreground" (Brinitzer, 2003: 185). The customer, as the provider of trust, is faced with the question of whether the supplier himself believes in what he claims to believe, and whether he has internalized the values he propagates (cf. ibid.). A religious entrepreneur's interest and attention appear convincing when he can make them appear credible and when he can empathize with the customer who is in need of advice and healing. This is especially the case when the supplier can show that he has experienced identical or similar problems, has been forced to confront them and has himself found support in the religious ideas he promulgates. A successful supplier should be capable of leading the way as a living example of his therapeutic idea. Customer trust is obtained from the supplier's identity, lifestyle, and past, which should be perceived as congruent with the therapeutic ideas on offer.

An examination of the marketing instruments specific to the scene, in particular the "short biographies" found on the suppliers' flyers, brochures and Internet sites provides us with unambiguous pointers. A universal pattern for the self-portrayal of religious entrepreneurs exists in the semantics of "personal development," of "moving forward," permanently "working on themselves," and the enduring willingness to "rediscover themselves." This is clearly signaled by the variety of training, continuing education and courses that most suppliers list as guarantees of their background. References to their own development also come to light (almost stereotypically) in the narrative biographical interviews of religious entrepreneurs. The metaphor of the "path" they have taken, frequently comes from a biographical crisis, as they aspire to a new identity with new thinking patterns. Höllinger and Tripold (2012) talk of a "holistic career" which the suppliers pass through and during the course of which the "identity of the players fundamentally changes" (ibid., 147). Their self-reliance as religious entrepreneurs not only stands for the step of freeing themselves from past working and living conditions which are now considered obsolete (cf. ibid., 148 ff.). It also offers suppliers the opportunity to envision and repeat their development and search for identity in their communication with customers, and thus implicitly confirm these aspects. The suppliers' biographical anecdotes in many cases reveal the theme of salvation, which consists in their emancipation from a past they experienced as crisis-laden.

The fact that a proportion of the suppliers on the spiritual market, which should not be underestimated, can communicate signals of this kind in respect to an "adequate" biographical history is proved by the membership study by the umbrella organization *Dachverband der Freien Gesundheitsberufe*: "Doubtless it

---

[11]   Early on, Adam Smith referred to the concept of "sympathy" in the context of his considerations of the way the "invisible hand of the market" operates (cf. on this Otteson, 2002: 16 ff.).

is the high intrinsic motivation of many suppliers which provides the incentive for their notable willingness to continuously educate themselves and develop further" (Freie Gesundheitsberufe o.J., 3). From this study it is apparent that a large proportion of the suppliers of alternative health services lead the way themselves as examples of spiritual "self-empowerment," thus anticipating a central motive on the part of consumers.[12]

The invisible hand of homology

Viewed sociologically, the ability to "sympathize" or "put ... yourself in somebody else's shoes" (Luhmann, 1973: 28) is anything but self-evident, but is instead associated with specific social enabling conditions. The following remarks will focus on the question of which socio-structural conditions are responsible for the convergence between the motives of suppliers and consumers—despite the relative autonomy of the respective interrelationships between their actions.

From a socio-structural perspective, religious entrepreneurs frequently belong to the human services professions in the social, educational, advisory, and care sectors, in which the step toward autonomy means a continuation of their previous service activity (cf. Hero, 2008b), albeit extended by a repertoire of religious ideas which are used for the purposes of advice, education, and healing. However, without being able to fall back upon established careers, the representatives of the new service professions expose themselves to substantial risks. The newly arising fields of activity do not offer the same income opportunities (cf. Freie Gesundheitsberufe, o.J.) and security of established professions. However, the lack of definition of the alternative job descriptions (there are no rigid and reglemented definitions) grants a much broader scope for an "alternative" lifestyle, for strategies of self-staging, bluffing and euphemization. The new religious entrepreneurship also allows such ambitions to be unequivocally recognized. The very semantics of religion offers players the opportunity to anticipate the desired upward valuation of their own identity (at least symbolically). This ambition reveals itself purely externally through the choice of "job titles," which are enhanced with transcendent references. The titles of the new healers are part of a "spiritual self-empowerment." They aim to transcend the present social existence by anticipating their professional emancipation. For the religious entrepreneur it is a question of lending higher recognition to their own existence and the services they offer: "Certified Shamanic Counselor," "Certified Astrologer," "Reincarnation Therapist," "Hildegard Physician," "Qualified Rebirther," "Holistic Aura Consultant," "Force Field Prophet."

The needs in respect of identity, self-portrayal, and stylization that are characteristic of the consumer thus find their complement in the symbolic

---

[12] As Gebhardt *et al.* (2005) state, the "self-empowerment of the spiritual subject" has to be regarded as a central predisposition which drives people to turn towards non-church, new religious offerings.

presentation and representation strategies of the new healers. For both groups, due to their relatively unsecured biographical position there is an increased need for identity-related techniques of self-discovery and self-representation (cf. Höllinger and Tripold, 2012). So it is possible for many religious entrepreneurs to sell themselves alongside their services as a model for their "product," which can be considered a form of self management. The religiousness they propagate with strong connections to self-referential, subjective patterns of interpretation is their very own.

The congruence of the value orientations or world views of patient and therapist (Kaptchuk/Eisenberg, 1998) is shown to be both one of the central enabling conditions and also an amenity of the alternative healing scene. The more similar the habitus of suppliers and consumers, the more likely it is that the discursive construction of salvation and healing will come about. Thus the supplier, as the "recipient of trust," can better succeed in addressing the expectations of the "provider of trust": similarity of status, similarities in their biographies and a similar appearance correlate with a higher trustworthiness (Plötner, 1994: 156).

Conclusion: The Role of the Religious Entrepreneur and the Spiritual Market

The purpose of this article consists in identifying supplier-side strategies and arrangements which bring about cooperation between suppliers and consumers in the market for spiritual services; a market which is burdened with uncertainty. Since the origins and expansion of this market are distinctly connected with the identity and "performance" of the suppliers, we shall attempt to systematize the features of the role of the religious entrepreneur that can be derived from the above considerations.

Undoubtedly the term "religious" entrepreneurs is not always in accord with the (professional) self-definitions of the suppliers in the field, who often reject a characterization as religious and prefer other attributes such as "spiritual" or "holistic." Nevertheless, observed from a scientific point of view the reference to religion is still obvious; attention here is directed towards those suppliers who take over or create religious interpretations and offer these to their buyers seeking services. Going beyond the suppliers' social origins and biographical progression (cf. here also Hero, 2011: 37 ff.) we can derive certain structural characteristics of their "professional" activity from the above remarks, which identify them as central agents in the development of contemporary spirituality.

Firstly we shall address the issue of distinguishing this new type of religious expert from traditional religious experts. Whether it is an "Ayurveda therapist," "aura cleaner," "Reiki therapist," "Shamanic adviser," or "holistic astrologer"— the decisive characteristics of the new religious entrepreneurs consist in the fact that they are not legitimized by any religious organization or religious group or community. In terms of numbers, the many centers run by *individual companies* dominate, where religious ideas and practices are propagated but scarcely any connections extending beyond individual episodes of service provision are created between those involved.[13] Such relationships are distinguished by their relative lack of commitment, flexibility in terms of their content and also by the permanent "exit option" of those involved. Because such relationships are unable to resort to any traditional potential for information and sanction that has developed, trustworthiness and willingness to cooperate have to be engendered by means of institutional and conceptual support mechanisms. Markets are reliant on communication mechanisms which the players keep up to date via past and prospective transactions.

As well as the aspects of contemporary spirituality relating to its content, which are frequently mentioned in the literature on the sociology of religion (cf. Heelas, 2008; Knoblauch, 2005), it is therefore essential to make reference to the general organizational conditions of the new manifestations of healing. It is precisely here that the figure of the religious entrepreneur takes on a decisive role. The marketing activities outlined in this article are constitutive for the proliferation of this new religious scene. For religious communication to take place, potential exchange partners must be made aware of their mutual concerns, and informed about past episodes of service provision and future cooperation opportunities. Thus the proliferation of contemporary spirituality would be inconceivable without the marketing activities which transmit information between suppliers and consumers. In other words, adequate conditions for the practice and fulfillment of contemporary spirituality only result from the symbolic, institutional and performative activities on the supply side.

As we have shown, the religious entrepreneur takes on a dual function in contemporary religious change. On the one hand he drives it forward by his organizational actions, not the least of which are the marketing activities outlined in this article—but on the other hand he is also an innovator in terms of its content, because he embodies the maxims of the "self-empowerment of the spiritual subject" (Gebhardt *et al.*, 2005) *in persona*. The figure of the religious entrepreneur brings together a multitude of present-day social technologies and technologies of the self, whose joint vanishing point forms the focus of a lifestyle on the behavioral model of self-discovery and responsibility for oneself.

---

[13]   There is in fact no reliable total overview of how many esoteric therapeutic health practices and centers offer their services in the German-speaking regions. However, to get an impression of the alternative healer scene we can draw on the data from a full survey of the scene in North Rhine-Westphalia, where in 2007 more than 1000 locally based suppliers were identified. This number does not include the state-recognized professions of "non-medical practitioner" and "psychotherapist"; cf. Hero, 2008a: 172.

Chapter 6

Non-fortuitous Limits to the Concept of Branding in the Popularizing of "Justly Balanced Islam" in France

Jason Dean[1]

In June, 2008, the recently founded French Muslim Rally (RMF[2]) won the presidency of the French Council on Muslim Worship (CFCM[3]) using the slogan "justly balanced Islam."[4] At first blush this victory might appear to be the result of the effective marketization of a religious brand. By "brand," I understand the exclusive designation of a good, product or service, in a market economy. For the sake of discussion, I will use the word "market" in the way in which it is employed by Gary S. Becker (1976), to designate a self-correcting mechanism for the allocation of resources and the distribution of goods and services. It follows from these definitions that the relevance of brands and branding is directly proportional to the number of competitors in a given religious market and to the distinctness of the goods they offer. This chapter will first demonstrate that the social structure of religions in France does not conform to Becker's model of a market. Second, it will show that in this highly regulated environment, the RMF did not so much seek product differentiation as identification with Muslim values. Third, it will argue that "justly balanced Islam" is better understood, not as a brand competing for shares in a religious market, but as symbolic capital which Muslim religious agents strive to accumulate in order to gain hegemony over their field.

---

[1]   Associate researcher at the Center for the Sociology of Religions and Social Ethics of the University of Strasbourg, France. The author would like to thank Christian Grappe and Jean-Pierre Bastian, directors, respectively, of the EA 4378 and the CSRES for providing support for this chapter. He is also indebted to Mark R. Johnson who read an early draft of this chapter, making many useful comments.
[2]   Rassemblement des musulmans de France.
[3]   Conseil français du culte musulman.
[4]   In French: "*Islam du juste milieu.*" The phrase is based on Q 2:143, in which God, in Yusuf Ali's translation, says that he made the Muslims an "Ummat [nation] justly balanced [*wasaṭ*]."

Regulation of Religion in a Secularist State

In "A Supply-Side Reinterpretation of the 'Secularization of Europe,'" Rodney
Stark and Laurence R. Iannaccone predicted that "increased pressure" from
"competing religious firms" would lead to the deregulation of Western European
religious economies (1994: 248). Yet as the institutionalization of Islam in France
over the last twenty years shows, the French state continues to pursue a policy of
religious regulation known as *laïcité*. This section first describes the steps that
lead to the inclusion of Islam in the system of restricted religious pluralism that
characterizes the social structure of religions in France through the creation of a
representative body governing Muslim worship and ritual practice, the CFCM.
Second, it places the CFCM in historical perspective by retracing the tradition
of national religions in France. Third, it analyzes current state efforts to exclude
undesirable religious groups.

The CFCM, an instrument for the control of Muslim religious practice

The CFCM is a state sponsored representative body which serves as an interface
between the government and the Muslim community on matters of religious
practice.[5] The concerns that led to the creation of the CFCM in 2003 can be traced
to significant social and demographic changes that affected the Muslim population
in France during the 1970s and 1980s. In April 1976, the conservative government
of Jacques Chirac authorized family reunification, allowing immigrant workers
to bring their wives and children to France. Hitherto, immigration for economic
motives had been almost exclusively masculine; under the family reunification
policy, women and children came for personal reasons. This created new needs
ranging from better housing and education to religious, cultural and linguistic
concerns. In October 1981 the newly elected socialist government of Pierre Mauroy
granted foreign nationals the right to found community organizations eligible for
public funding as a means of meeting some of these demands. This led to the
creation of cultural centers in industrial areas and ghettos where Arabic, regional
customs and religious principles were taught. The political scientist Gilles Kepel
subtitled a 1987 study of these groups, "The Birth of a Religion in France." A year
later, he published an op-ed piece in the French newspaper of record, *Le Monde*,
calling for the creation of a "representative body of Islam in France" charged with
the responsibility of promoting a "form of Islamic religion that harmonizes with
our secularist institutions" (Kepel, 1988). Beginning in 1990, successive French
governments strove to attain this goal. It is not necessary to describe these efforts
in detail here, but I would like to highlight some crucial points.

---

[5]   In the year 2000 the High Council for Integration estimated that four million people
then living in France were of Muslim ancestry. A 2011 study by the National Institute for
Statistics and Economic Studies evaluated at 2.1 million the number of "declared Muslims."

In 1990 socialist Interior Minister Pierre Joxe appointed 15 prominent leaders from different segments of the Muslim community to form the Council on the Future of Islam in France (CORIF[6]). In an interview published in *Le Monde* on March 17 of that year, he expressed his confidence that "Muslim ritual practice on our soil will take on a particular character as it integrates national traditions, specifically those concerning education and women's rights." Carrying a big stick he added, "In France, religious tolerance is enshrined in a legal principle: *laïcité.*"

During its three-year existence, the CORIF was beset with internal dissentions. In 1993 newly appointed Gaullist Interior Minister Charles Pasqua broke with his predecessor's broad-based consultative approach, naming the Rector of the Great Paris Mosque, Dalil Boubakeur, to chair the newly-created Representative Council of French Muslims.[7] The Council drafted a Charter of the Muslim Religion in France, intended as "a legal framework for resolving all points of tension that might arise within the Muslim community and between this community and the public administration" (Boubakeur, 1995: 35). The Charter proclaimed that the emergence of what it called "Islam of France" was predicated on the existence of representative institutions (52) and declared the Council to be "the representative body of the Muslim community at the national level" (53). Officially submitted to the Interior Minister on January 10, 1995 the Charter failed to gain support from those parts of the Muslim community who were not affiliated with Boubakeur's Great Paris Mosque and never took effect.

In January, 2000, after a hiatus of nearly five years during which the Socialist Party came back into power, Interior Minister Jean-Pierre Chevènement convened a "consultation" of leaders representing most, though not all, segments of the Muslim community. Not only were attendees given the opportunity to contribute their ideas toward the future "representative body of Islam in France," but the Minister unabashedly hinted that support could be found for the construction of new mosques (Chevènement, 2000). In return, participants were required to pledge allegiance to the laws of the French Republic, specifically Articles 10 and 11 of the Declaration of the Rights of Man and of the Citizen concerning freedom of thought and religion, Article 1 of the French Constitution stipulating that France is a secularist (*laïque*) Republic, and the Law of 1905 governing the separation of church and state (COMOR 2000).

In July, 2001, the third plenary session of the Consultation ratified a General Framework on the Future Organization of the Muslim Religion in France, which instituted a system of indirect suffrage to elect the members of the national body. Under this system, the number of representatives that each officially registered mosque or prayer room sends to the regional body is proportionate to the area of its prayer hall, expressed in square meters. The regional bodies then elect the members of the national body, now referred to as the CFCM.

---

[6] Conseil de réflexion sur l'avenir de l'islam en France.
[7] Conseil représentatif des musulmans de France.

The first CFCM elections were postponed a number of times as candidates jockeyed for position. Dalil Boubakeur accused mosques he did not control of fostering fundamentalism; his rivals responded by denouncing undemocratic procedures. During a high-level meeting in December 2002, Interior Minister Nicolas Sarkozy brokered a deal which enlarged the future executive board from 11 to 16 members in exchange for a promise that the presidency would go to Dalil Boubakeur whatever the actual outcome of the elections. When these finally took place on April 6 and 13, 2003, they showed that Boubakeur had reasons to seek a guarantee: his Great Paris Mosque alliance ran a poor third behind the National Federation of French Muslims (FNMF[8]) and the Union of Islamic Organizations of France (UOIF[9]).

With the inauguration of the CFCM Kepel's goal of a establishing a "representative body of Islam in France" was met. The promotion of a form of Islam compatible with the political institutions of the secularist French state could now begin. President of France from 2007 to 2012, Nicolas Sarkozy summarized the problem from his point of view in a pithy statement: "What we want is Islam of France, not Islam in France."

National religions in the French tradition

The will to place the activity of religious organizations under the control of the state is neither new nor specifically directed against Islam; rather it is a constant of the French political tradition.

The idea of a sovereign state exercising its authority over a delimited territory can be traced back to the legal advisors in the court of Philip the Fair (r. 1285–1314). In order to finance the war against England, the King in Council decided to tax the churches of the kingdom. Pope Boniface VIII responded by issuing the bull Clericis laicos (1296) prohibiting the catholic princes from collecting the tax. He was forced to retreat in 1297 when the bishops in Paris voted in favor of the tax.

In a position of political and military strength after his victory at Marignano in 1515, Francis I (r. 1515–1547) sought to increase his control over the Roman Catholic Church in France. Made public in 1516, the Concordat of Bologna granted the king the right to name church officers, including bishops. The autonomy of the Roman Catholic Church in France was further reduced by the Ordinance of Villers-Cotterêts (1539), which separated secular and ecclesiastical jurisdictions, discontinued the use of Latin in official acts, and created a register of births and baptisms.

The Edict of Nantes (1598) is a landmark of religious tolerance. It is also a testament to the pragmatism of the King in Council who understood that Catholic exclusivism no longer served the interests of the monarchy. By granting a general amnesty for crimes committed during the wars of religion that had ravaged France

---

[8] Fédération nationale des musulmans de France.

[9] Union des organisations islamiques de France.

for more than thirty years in exchange for a pledge of loyalty to the monarchy, Henry IV was able to consolidate his government and avail himself of the diplomatic and military skills of his Protestant subjects. He thereby set a precedent for the integration of demographically important religious minorities in a highly centralized political system through the recognition of state sovereignty.

The French Revolution represented a particularly radical experiment in the regulation of religion. Beginning in 1789, the Constituent Assembly voted a series of laws limiting or repealing the privileges of the Church. These measures were summarized in the Civil Constitution of the Clergy (1790): nationalization of church property, conjunction of religious and administrative circumscriptions, election of church officials by the citizens, obligation for the clergy to pledge allegiance to the new regime, prohibition of referring to the authority of foreign bishops. After the proclamation of the First French Republic in 1792, other measures were taken to reduce the influence of the Roman Catholic Church on society: eradication of remaining religious orders; nationalization of birth, death, and marriage registries; establishment of a republican calendar abolishing references to saints; abrogation of salaries paid to the constitutional clergy; prohibition of public religious ceremonies, such as processions, bell ringing, and the wearing of ecclesiastical garb. These anti-religious measures were seen by their proponents as an application of the principle of the sovereignty of the people contained in the Declaration of the Rights of Man and the Citizen (1789). In their view, any intermediary form of social organization, such as religious communities, between the individual and the state was a potential source of inequality. In order to achieve the republican ideals of Liberty, Equality, and Fraternity, it was incumbent on the state to control the public space, ridding it of religious symbols.

When the Republic went bankrupt, it sought its salvation in a providential hero. As much by pragmatism as by conviction, Napoleon Bonaparte broke with the revolutionaries' antireligious ideology and sought a compromise with the Roman Catholic Church. The Concordat of 1801 recognized Catholicism as the religion of the majority of French citizens and reestablished many of the prerogatives of the Roman Church. Bonaparte however did not wish to restore the Catholic monopoly on religion. The Organic Articles, which he unilaterally joined to the proclamation of the Concordat (1802), provided a legal framework for the practice not only of the Catholic religion but also for the Lutheran and Reformed faiths. Under these laws, church buildings remained the property of the nation, but the state agreed to pay the salaries of the ministers of the three officially recognized religions in exchange for their contribution to the moral upbringing of citizens.

A fourth religious community attracted Bonaparte's attention. Promising to "abolish all humiliating distinctions between the Jews and his other subjects," the emperor convened, in October, 1807, a "Great Sanhedrin" of 71 Jewish leaders in Paris in order to discuss ways of harmonizing Jewish law and the Civil Code. Five months later, a decree officially recognized the Jewish religion, now organized according to a system comprising a Central Consistory and seven departmental consistories. The creation of the Israelite Consistories, which were later integrated into the framework of the Concordat, demonstrates that, in its desire to develop national forms of religious worship, the state was not deterred by the absence of a clearly identifiable clerical hierarchy. Working with representative community leaders, it offered political and financial incentives in exchange for the emergence of an exclusive arbitrator on questions of worship. The final architecture was a two-tiered system of local and national bodies. These elements can be found *mutatis mutandis* in the institutionalization of Islam in France.

During the nineteenth century, the role of religion in society became a central political issue opposing clericalists who strove to maintain the influence of the Catholic Church and republican secularists seeking to exclude religious expression from the public space. After the victory of the Coalition of the Left in the 1902 parliamentary elections, the government of Emile Combes moved aggressively to close Catholic schools and ban teaching orders. Paradoxically, this highly polarized debate took place at a time of loosening restrictions in other areas of French life. In 1901, the government granted French citizens the right to associate without having to obtain legislative authorization. Could not these 1901 Law associations serve as a model for relations between the state and the churches, suggested the socialist deputy Francis de Pressensé. This proposition provided the basis for the 1905 Law on the Separation of the Churches and the State. Under this law, churches were no longer governed by public law, but religious groups were given the possibility to organize themselves as 1905 Law associations in order to organize worship services and benefit from tax exemptions.

The Law of 1905 was a uniquely liberal moment in French history: believers could continue to think of themselves privately as the Church of God or the Chosen People, but in public life they become associations, similar to trade unions, political parties, and sporting clubs. The French state however did not abdicate control over religions. Article 1 of the Law of 1905 stipulates that "the Republic insures freedom of conscience [and] guarantees the free practice of religion." These precepts are open to different interpretations; but it is worth noting that both Pierre Joxe (*Le Monde*, March 17, 1990) and Jean-Pierre Chevènement (2000) saw in them a justification for state intervention in the organization of Muslim worship.

Laïcité has historically been a rallying cry for parties on the left of the political spectrum. With the emergence of Islam, however, conservative political parties, whose constituencies include many Catholic voters, have taken up this cause as a way of defending traditional French values. In order to limit expressions of Muslim belief in the public space, they have sought to extend the obligation of religious neutrality to civil servants, children in the public school system, parents accompanying school excursions, and workers in private businesses that provide "public services," including day care centers.

Prohibition of undesirable religious groups

Until now, I have been concerned with showing how successive French governments have developed a system of limited religious pluralism by associating, explicitly under the Concordat and implicitly since the Law of 1905, accepted religious organizations in the construction of the social order. That Islam was admitted into this select club is a tribute to the demographic importance of the French Muslim community, but also an indirect acknowledgment of a perceived threat posed by Muslim extremists. Not all religious groups however are so fortunate. For there is another side to the regulation of religious pluralization in the secularist French state: the exclusion of undesirable religious groups, called "sects" or "sectarian movements" in government parlance.

In 1996, the Gaullist government of Alain Juppé responded to repeated parliamentary demands (Vivien, 1985; Gest and Guyard, 1996) for greater scrutiny of unconventional religious groups by creating an Interministerial Observatory on Sects. After a change of government, the Observatory was restyled, in 1998, as the Interministerial Mission for Combatting Sects. The Mission took its current appellation in 2002 when it became the Interministerial Mission for Monitoring and Combatting Sectarian Deviances (Milivudes[10]). Its responsibilities include "observing and analyzing the phenomenon of sectarian movements whose activities infringe on human rights and fundamental liberties, constitute a threat to public order, or transgress laws and regulations" and "facilitating the coordination of preventive and corrective measures by public authorities against these activities, while respecting civil liberties" (*Journal Officiel*, November 29, 2002, 1966).

In addition to the existing legal apparatus,[11] the predecessors of the Milivudes developed two original instruments in the "fight against sects," one judicial, the other intended to win the battle of opinion.

The 2001 About-Picard law "reinforcing the prevention and the correction of sectarian movements" introduced a new offense in the French criminal code, that of "fraudulent abuse of a state of ignorance or weakness" in minors and "particularly vulnerable" people, such as the elderly, the handicapped, pregnant women [sic], and those in "a state of physical or psychological servitude." Co-author Catherine Picard hailed the law as a "world premiere." However, the concept of "abuse of weakness" proved to be difficult to establish and the law has only been used once, when the leader of the esoteric group Néophare received a three-month suspended sentence in 2004.

As early as 1983 the Vivien Report (1985: 114–16) urged using the mass media, including the state-controlled television networks, to draw public attention to the danger of sects. In 1996, the Gest and Guyard Report grabbed headlines by publishing a list of 173 "sects," based on information provided by the intelligence service of the French police. Although human rights groups quickly accused the

---

[10]   Mission interministérielle de vigilance et de lutte contre les dérives sectaires.

[11]   The Vivien Report (1985: 73–90) enumerates the 1901 Law on associations; the 1905 Law on religious associations; criminal laws penalizing a variety of offenses including scams, "illegal practice of medicine," "failure to assist people in danger," "corruption of minors," as well as "affront to common decency;" regulations governing the use of the public space; tax laws; and more.

French government of violating religious freedom, the Miviludes only formally retreated in its 2004 annual report, stating that "France has no official definition of a 'sect,' neither does it maintain a data base or a list of these [sic] movements whose illegal activities come under the relevant provisions of the Criminal Code and are punished by the law enforcement agencies of the state" (Miviludes, 2004: 87). Despite this disclaimer, the 1996 list is still referred to by politicians advocating stronger anti-sect legislation.

The change in terminology from "sect" to "sectarian movements" is a semantic precaution that did not fundamentally alter the government's determination to establish a distinction between respectable "religions" and dangerous groups in order to, as Vivien (1985: 119) put it, "restore the moral backbone of the nation." The former receive official recognition, symbolized by the annual reception for religious leaders at the Elysée Palace or the presence of government officials at religious ceremonies; the latter are stigmatized or prosecuted.

The divide between implicitly recognized "religions" and explicitly ostracized "sects" leaves little neutral ground. The Church of Scientology and the Jehovah's Witnesses, two religious groups that appeared on the 1996 parliamentary list, have challenged the public authorities in court in order to obtain equal treatment with other religions.

In 1996, a court in Lyons convicted 15 members of the Church of Scientology of fraud, sentencing them to heavy fines for promising "artificial paradises" to their victims. In its 1997 review of this decision, an appeals court ruled that the Church could, on the objective criteria of having a congregation and a dogma, be considered a religion and that its members should be given the benefit of doubt concerning the sincerity of their beliefs, on which the court refused to make "value judgments." Reconsidering the case within the limits of the anti-fraud laws, the appellate court reduced the sentences of six high-ranking Church officers and acquitted nine other lower ranking ones. This decision made subsequent prosecution of Scientologists more difficult, and though some convictions have been obtained, the courts have consistently denied prosecutors' demands to dissolve the Church.

Over the last decade the Jehovah's Witnesses have won a series of legal battles on the right to refuse blood transfusions (2002), eligibility for tax exemptions on church property (2000) and tax deductions on donations (2011). Recently, they lost an appeal before the administrative court contesting the Justice Ministry's refusal to authorize Jehovah's Witnesses as prisons visitors. This and other court battles for equal treatment will likely go on.

The antagonistic approach to church-state relations adopted by the Church of Scientology and the Jehovah's Witnesses represents a challenge to the regime of restricted religious pluralism which characterizes the French Republic at the beginning of the twenty-first century. By deciding which religious groups are worthy of public recognition and which represent a danger for its citizens, the state asserts its right to determine what is good for its citizens. But neither the Scientologists nor the Jehovah's Witnesses are asking for state approval; what they seek is state neutrality. This might seem like a minimal demand, but it has the potential of undermining the centuries-old tradition of national religions. I therefore believe that the French state will continue to resist demands for the deregulation of religion. In this, it will receive support not only from republican secularists but also from those religious organizations which have historically fought pluralization, foremost among them the Catholic Church.

The social structure of religions in France contrasts with the Beckerian model of a market economy in four significant ways. First, state regulation limits the number of competitors by setting up barriers to entry for undesirable religions. Second, the state modifies the internal structure of implicitly recognized religions to meet the requirements of its own centralized organization. Third, the state grants unequal access to such limited resources as real estate, public funding, privileged tax status and the media. Fourth, it controls religious expression in the public space, which tends to conflate with the political space.

Salvation Goods in Highly Regulated Religious Environments

Laurence R. Iannaccone (1995: 77) has remarked that "in competitive environments, religions have little choice but to abandon inefficient modes of production and unpopular products in favor of more attractive and profitable alternatives." For competitors in such markets, branding can be an important tool as it increases product identification and fosters consumer loyalty, thereby creating brand value. But what strategies do religious agents in highly regulated environments adopt? This section attempts to answer this question by examining a salvation good, "justly balanced Islam," in the French system of restricted religious pluralism. It first establishes that the Qur'ānic-based phrase "justly balanced Islam" cannot serve as the exclusive designation of a particular religious product. Second, it considers the idea that "justly balanced Islam" should be seen, not as a brand, but as a public good. Third, it examines rivalry in "justly balanced Islam." Fourth, it discusses three theoretical models for the description of competition between religious groups.

The property of non-excludability

To speak of "justly balanced Islam" is to refer to the Qur'ān, the common heritage of the Muslims. Unlike such taglines as "The Real Thing" or "Just do it," "justly balanced Islam" is not the copyrightable invention of an advertising agency but a traditional concept elaborated by successive generations of Muslim scholars. In the last decade of the twentieth century, Muslim thinkers in France and North Africa translated the Qur'ānic term *wasaṭ* and its jurisprudential derivative *wasaṭiyya* into French, popularizing "justly balanced Islam" as a way of speaking about their religion. Indeed, when the RMF chose this expression as its slogan for the 2008 CFCM elections, it was already in wide use.

A search of the electronic archives of the French newspaper of record *Le Monde* shows that the concept of "justly balanced Islam" was first introduced into French public discourse following the January 1992 military putsch in Algeria. Two days after the High Security Council annulled the results of the first round of parliamentary balloting that promised to bring the Islamic Salvation Front to power, a former minister, Mustapha Cherif, explained, in an interview published January 14, that the state sought a "happy medium"[12] between fundamentalism and secularism. When Islamic terrorism became a domestic issue in France, *Le Monde* ran an article in which it cited Q 2:143 as evidence that Islam does not advocate blind violence (September 19, 1995). During the parliamentary debates on the About-Picard anti-sect bill, the Rector of the Great Paris Mosque, Dalil Boubakeur, was quoted in an article on October 21, 2000 as saying that Islam was a "justly balanced community" which abided French law. In an interview on May 4, 2002, Fouad Alaoui, the secretary-general of the UOIF, dismissed concerns that his federation held extremist views by saying that his interpretation of the Qur'ān was that of the "happy medium."

These references, among many others, show that "justly balanced Islam" had become part of French public discourse prior to the 2008 CFCM elections. As such, it could not be claimed as the exclusive designation of a particular brand of Islam; in economic terms, "justly balanced Islam" is a non-excludable good. The RMF was, of course, conscious of this and its choice of slogan indicates that it was not primarily concerned with creating a differentiated presence in a religious market. Two explanations can be advanced to account for the RMF's relative lack of interest in appealing to potential consumers. First, religious affiliation in the Muslim world is transmitted from father to son or daughter; Muslims do not have to convert non-believers in order to gain members, although conversions are welcome. Second, in a highly regulated religious environment, public acceptance is at least as important as proselytism. These factors point to two publics that the RMF could have been targeting when it adopted the slogan "justly balanced Islam": coreligionists and political authorities.

Public goods, knowledge goods and salvation goods

One of the consequences of state regulation of religions is that in order to gain recognition and acceptance religious organizations must offer products and services perceived as beneficial to society as a whole. As the survey of the incidences of "justly balanced Islam" in the newspaper *Le Monde* shows, this phrase became a byword for mainstream Islam; it was used to assuage fears of terrorism, attest the civic-mindedness of Muslims and associate Islam with positive social values such as family, education and personal integrity.

Jörg Stolz (2007: 72) has suggested that moral guidance, counseling and social services provided by religious groups to members and non-members alike

---

[12]   In French: "*juste milieu*." In Arabic: "*wasat*."

can be likened to public goods in that they are non-excludable. Since there is no market for non-excludable goods, they are typically supplied by the state and paid for through taxation. Governments may, however, feel it is more efficient to outsource the promotion of moral values and the administration of some social services to religious organizations. This is notably the case in Germany where churches receive public funding for their hospitals, daycare facilities, family planning clinics, and retirement homes. And even in secularist France, the state pays salaries to chaplains and subsidies private denominational schools that agree to teach the national curriculum.

However, a second property of public goods must also be considered here, that of non-rivalry. Goods are said to be non-rival when its consumption by one agent does not affect its use by another agent. This is typically thought to be the case of knowledge goods. A mathematical formula, a law of physics, or a software code can be used simultaneously by an unlimited number of individuals. Nevertheless, in a seminal study of the economic conditions of scientific innovation, Michel Callon (1994) has questioned the non-rival character of knowledge goods by identifying four types of investments that must be made before a particular knowledge good can be used to produce something new. He writes,

> the property of nonrivalry, which holds only for the very few who have borne [the cost of the four types of investments] (and which in the case of science or technology constitutes the community of specialists), is the result of a series of strategic (investment) decisions taken by those actors. It is in no way an intrinsic property of the statements themselves: it would be better to call it an extrinsic property and to consider variable degrees of (non)rivalry (406).

Four aspects of this conclusion should be underscored. First, the property of non-rivalry is not an essential attribute of knowledge goods, but is rather a result of the social structure of scientific labor which produces and applies them. Second, this structure is characterized by a division between "specialists" and the general public. Third, knowledge goods are non-rival only for those specialists who have made the necessary investments to master them. Fourth, these investments entail competition for funding, talent, and equipment.

Like knowledge goods, many salvation goods are formally non-rival. If Callon is correct that the property of non-rivalry only applies to the few specialists who have achieved dominance through competition, we should expect to see evidence of competition between specialized religious agents for the use of "justly balanced Islam."

Rivalry in "justly balanced Islam"

Incidences of "justly balanced Islam" and related expressions from a survey of French language Muslim Internet sites conducted from November 2010 to June 2011 can be divided into two major categories according to the types of social relationships they induce. Occurrences in one category identify the "happy medium" with a particular school of Islam. Valuing authenticity over popularity, these groups cultivate dense social networks of likeminded believers. Because they come very close to the Weberian ideal type of the sect, I qualify their method as the sectarian approach. A second category gathers incidences that witness to an understanding of *wasaṭ* as a "happy medium" between two extremes, an approach I describe as pragmatic.

The sectarian approach is exemplified by Sufī networks and Salafī associations. A French convert to Islam, Jean-Louis Girotto asserts that "the Sufī path can rightly be called the 'happy medium.'"[13] And Khaled Bentounès, the leader of the ᶜAlawiyya fraternity, declares that the "fulfilled Sufī inhabits the happy medium."[14] With equal assurance, the Salafī site Al-Ghourabaa defines its purpose as "defending the Authentic Tradition and the Way of the Happy Medium."[15] In a similar vein, the site Salafs explains to visitors that the "justly balanced nation" of Q 2:143 refers to those who "witness to the oneness of God," a periphrasis for the Salafīs.[16] That the sectarian approach is illustrated by two ideologically opposed schools of thought lends credence to the idea that it constitutes a sociological type independent of particular beliefs.

An oft-cited *fatwā* by the Saudi *muftī* Muḥammad ibn Ṣāliḥ al-ᶜUthaymīn (1929–2001) provides a convenient definition of the pragmatic approach: "the happy medium in religion means staying within the limits set by God, neither exaggerating nor neglecting one's duties."[17] Groups that adopt this method counsel their members to practice religion in a way that does not alienate other believers or provoke negative reactions from non-Muslims. This general framework can also be used to demonstrate the capacity of Islamic law (*sharīᶜa*) for finding practical solutions to problems as they arise in the lives of believers. In recent years, the "happy medium" principle has been used to answer such diverse questions as the proper length of the veil, the amount of money that should be spent on Ramaḍān festivities and the lawfulness of cosmetic surgery.

As this short survey shows, Muslim religious scholars and activists compete with each other for control of the phrase "justly balanced Islam." But how should this competition be conceptualized? Are these agents competing for shares in a market, for resources in an environment, or for something more fundamental?

---

[13] L'accès à l'intériorité, c'est toute la Voie. http://www.soufisme.org/site/spip. php?article203 (accessed March 7, 2011).

[14] http://oumma.com/Histoire-des-Prophetes-Adam-sur (accessed November 19, 2010).

[15] http://www.alghourabaa.com/index.php?option=com_content&view=article& id=27:qui-sommes-nous-&catid=10:messages&Itemid=26 (accessed March 16, 2011).

[16] http://www.salafs.com/modules/news/article.php?storyid=10199&keywords=juste +milieu (accessed December 31, 2010).

[17] This *fatwā* can be accessed on several Websites such as IslamQA, Fatawaislam or Ibnothaimeen.

Markets, niches, or fields?

The dichotomy I have just sketched between the sectarian and pragmatic approaches to "justly balanced Islam" might seem to mirror the "religious niches" described by Roger Finke and Christopher P. Scheitle (2009: 16): a "niche is where [an organization] looks to acquire resources … If niche size is stable and a religious group has exhausted the existing resources in the niche by converting all who are willing to join, a group can only grow through expanding its niche outwards." In this perspective, the pragmatic approach to "justly balanced Islam" might be seen as an attempt to enlarge the membership pool, a strategy the authors call "niche stretching." As Scheitle (2007) has shown, the niche and market models have much in common: both conceive of religious pluralization and morphogenesis as rational adaptation to external conditions.

In his sociological theory of "fields," Pierre Bourdieu develops a different view of competition between religious agents. He defines "fields" as "spaces structured by positions whose properties depend on their position in these spaces" (1984: 113). Fields come into existence when "specialists" acquire skills and knowledge that allows them to distinguish themselves from "laymen" (1971: 304); they are, therefore, multiple and relatively autonomous. Participation in a given field is predicated upon on belief in the value of the risks and rewards inherent in it (1984: 114). In order to enter a field, new entrants must acquire "symbolic capital," qualities and characteristics recognized by incumbent agents as consistent with positions in their field. Competition within each relatively autonomous field is therefore essentially rivalry for the symbolic capital that defines the structure of positions within the field. Within each field, agents compete with each other to achieve dominance (1971: 299); yet their rivalry must not undermine the values that define the field. Rivals are therefore united in an "objective alliance" that transcends their "underlying antagonism" (1984: 115) and insures the "reproduction" of the field (1970: 23). The state of a field at any given time is the sum of past struggles between specialists (1984: 114). Although the internal power structures of the different fields that compose society are often similar—Bourdieu speaks of "homology" (1971: 319)—specialists in one field do not directly compete with specialists in other fields. Rather, dominant agents in different fields exchange the goods they administer. Such inter-field exchanges, called "transactions" (1971: 313), are conceptually distinct from intra-field competition.

To summarize, Bourdieu's "fields" differ from "markets" and "niches" in four important ways. First, competition is seen not as a response to external circumstances, whether economic or ecological, but as an internal condition of the field itself. Second, the aim of intra-field competition is not a share, *i.e.* a limited portion, of the field, but true hegemony—Bourdieu speaks of "monopoly"—which alone confers the power to conduct inter-field transactions. Third, competition in Bourdieu's fields has an existential character; rather than developing rational strategies to achieve quantifiable goals, agents are driven by interiorized beliefs that engage their survival as social beings. Fourth, competition between agents is tempered by the imperative, common to all those who derive their social status from the field, to maintain and perpetuate it.

Bourdieu's theory of fields anticipates Callon's observation that competition originates in the distinction between specialists and non-specialists. Like Callon, Bourdieu identifies the ultimate goal of competition as control over the goods produced by the field. His view differs somewhat from Callon's in that he sees access to resources commanded by specialists in other fields, whether material (funding, for example) or symbolic (recognition), as a result of successful competition for dominance rather than as a part of the contest. In the next section, I will examine the capacity of Bourdieu's theory of fields to account for competition between Muslim religious agents who use the motto "justly balanced Islam."

"Justly Balanced Islam" in the Discursive Practice of Three National Muslim Federations

That the National Federation of the Great Paris Mosque (FNGMP[18]), the UOIF, and the RMF all refer to "justly balanced Islam" is clear evidence that they consider themselves as part of the same religious field. A closer look, however, reveals slight but significant differences in the way each federation uses this phrase. I identify three distinct discursive practices depending on whether "justly balanced Islam" is conceived of as 1) a national religion of the secularist French state (FNGMP), 2) an equilibrium between the demands of Islamic law and the requirements of French society (UOIF), or 3) the ecumenical religion of all Muslims (RMF).

FNGMP: "Justly balanced Islam," a national religion of the secularist French state

In its quest for recognition as the representative organization of Muslims in France, the Great Paris Mosque sought to identify itself with the French Republic in three major ways: appropriation of the memory of the Muslim soldiers who "died for France," willingness to lead the fight against Islamic extremism, and endorsement of the compatibility between Islam and *laïcité*.

The Great Paris Mosque proudly traces its origins to a 1920 decision of the French Parliament to grant a subsidy of 500,000 francs to the Algerian Society of the Habous of the Holy Sites of Islam for the construction of a "Muslim Institute" in recognition of Muslim servicemen *"morts pour la France"* during the First World War. On the 90th anniversary of the battle of Verdun in 2006, the President of the Republic, Jacques Chirac, and the Rector of the Great Paris Mosque, Dalil Boubakeur, stood side by side at the inauguration of the Douaumont memorial which commemorates those deaths. The website of the Great Paris Mosque

---

[18]   Fédération nationale de la Grande Mosquée de Paris, name taken by the Dalil Boubakeur's coalition.

continues to pay homage to those battles "consecrated by collective sacrifice in the defense of the ideals of Liberty, Equality, and Fraternity." By presenting itself as the guardian of Muslim patriotism, the Great Paris Mosque seeks to secure its place in French national history.

Until the creation of the UOIF in 1983 and the FNMF in 1985 the Great Paris Mosque held a *de facto* monopoly on the representation of Muslims. The GMP responded to the presence of these rival organizations by raising the specter of Islamic extremism. We have seen how Dalil Boubakeur obtained the promise to become the first CFCM president by convincing Interior Minister Sarkozy that he was a rampart against "fundamentalism." He used this same strategy in the 2005 election campaign, warning against "activists and demagogues" and publically labeling his rivals as "fundamentalists."

In its quest for official recognition, the FNGMP has consistently reaffirmed its respect for the laws of the Republic. We have seen that Dalil Boubakeur assured French public opinion during the debate on the About-Picard anti-sect law that Muslims were a law-abiding "justly balanced community." This legitimist position led him in 2003 to caution the controversial headscarf ban. Indeed, he consistently supported what he called "Islam of France," meaning a French national form of Islam compatible with the principle of *laïcité* (Boubakeur 1995: 55–6).

UOIF: "Justly balanced Islam," an equilibrium between sharia and society

The statutes of the UOIF define the purpose of the federation as "promoting Islam, its values of openness and tolerance, its ethics and morals, through an understanding of the happy medium, moderation and authentic religious practice."[19] UOIF president Ahmed Jaballah interprets this as a mandate for social action: "We call for an equilibrium between the intransigence of textual literalists and the laxity of modernists who sap Islam of its substance; we call on Muslims to be active citizens who take part in society."[20]

The UOIF has taken an activist stance on many social issues, sometimes appearing inconsistent as it sought to reconcile the conflicting demands of Islamic and Republican law. In 2003, the UOIF defended the rights of Muslim girls to wear headscarves in public schools. Then, after rejecting a conciliatory offer from the government, it called for legislation prohibiting the veil in order to avoid compromising itself (*Le Monde*, October 14, 2003). At the height of the 2005 riots in the Paris working-class suburb of Clichy-sous-Bois, the UOIF issued a religious opinion (*fatwā*) calling for respect of private property and an end to the violence.[21] Accused of introducing religion into public debate and attempting to infringe on the government monopoly on law enforcement, the UOIF issued a statement

---

[19] http://www.uoif-online.com/v2/spip.php?article787 (accessed December 14, 2010).
[20] Interview in *Le Monde*, April 7, 2012, p. 10.
[21] www.uoif-online.com/print.php?sid=414 (accessed March 7, 2006; the *fatwā* was subsequently removed from the UOIF website).

justifying its action.[22] Education is another domain where the position of the UOIF continues to evolve, as Rhône-Alpes regional leader Azzedine Gaci explains:

> Although I was opposed to creating denominational schools ... I now feel that such establishments are necessary; for young girls who want to wear the headscarf ... and also in order to teach Islam as a religion of peace, coexistence and tolerance. That is the true meaning of "justly balanced Islam."[23]

As tense as it can sometimes be, the UOIF's relationship with French society is peaceful compared with its dealings with the CFCM. In May 2005, the UOIF suspended its participation in the CFCM to protest "misgovernance." In 2008, Fouad Alaoui, General Secretary of the Union, criticized the CFCM for creating a "religion of colonized minds," which he contrasted to the "citizens religion" advocated by his organization (*Le Monde*, May 13, 2008). In 2011, Fouad Alaoui resigned his position as CFCM vice-president, explaining that "on the streets, no one trusts the CFCM" (*Le Monde*, June 4, 2011). These attacks point to the ambition of the UOIF to use the legitimacy it has gained in the defense of Muslim values to either take control of the CFCM or circumvent it.

RMF: "Justly balanced Islam," the ecumenical religion of all Muslims

Beginning in 1992, French Muslims of Moroccan descent gained control of the FNMF with the support of Morocco's Interior Ministry. However, the FNMF was deeply divided. The rift was so serious that in January, 2006, a new federation, the RMF, was created to represent the interests of the French-Moroccan Muslim community, effectively replacing the FNMF. In 2008, the RMF's candidate, Mohammed Moussaoui, was elected president of the CFCM.

The surprising success of the RMF can largely be attributed to its ability to convince the French Interior Ministry, final arbitrator of the seats on the Executive Board of the CFCM, that it was a responsible partner who could be entrusted with the presidency.[24] The RMF's mission statement defines its goal as "bringing about a moderate form of Islam, tolerant and respectful of French republican laws: a 'justly balanced Islam.'"[25] These words would have remained unconvincing however if the RMF had not been able to overcome the internal divisions of the French-Moroccan community, uniting its constituency around traditional Muslim

---

[22]   www.uoif-online.com/print..php?sid=420 (accessed April 20, 2006; this text too has disappeared from the UOIF website).

[23]   http://www.vousnousils.fr/2006/09/28/apprendre-lislam-du-juste-milieu-239672 (accessed February 2, 2011).

[24]   Despite winning both the 2003 and 2005 CFCM elections, the FNMF never obtained the presidency.

[25]   http://www.lermf.com/Objectifs/les-objectifs-du-rmf.html (accessed December 14, 2010).

values. To emphasize its ecumenical approach, the Charter of the RMF invokes great religious figures of the past: "The RMF is deeply committed to the shared doctrine of the Pious Predecessors of the Umma, the doctrine of the People of the Sunna and the Collectivity, such as the Imams Mālik, Abū Hanīfā [sic], Al-Shāfiʿī, Ibn Ḥanbal, Al-Bukhārī, Muslim, Abū l-Ḥasan al-Ashʿarī and the other great names in the History of the Muslim religion. They personify the justly balanced Umma: neither extremism nor neglectfulness in religious practice ... and no disputes about dogmas."[26]

One year after his election as president of the CFCM, Mohammed Moussaoui's ambition to steer a middle course between "extremism and neglectfulness" was put to a severe test. On June 18, 2009, the French National Assembly voted to create an Investigative Parliamentary Commission on the use of burkas and *niqāb*-s by Muslim women. Testifying before the Commission on October 14, Mohammad Moussaoui explained that "In accordance with the opinion of the great majority of Muslim theologians, the CFCM considers that the use of the full veil is not a religious duty, but rather a religious practice based on a minority opinion." He concluded by saying,

> It is not our purpose to approve or disapprove the use of the full veil. Our priority is to insure that the Muslims in France, in their entirety, are not stigmatized and that the peaceful coexistence between the communities that make up the nation is protected from all types of extremism.

Mohammed Moussaoui's reluctance to condemn use of the full veil came under attack from the Socialist Deputy Jean Glavany: "You said that the use of the full veil is not a religious duty but a minority religious practice. But this 'minority religious practice' is a fundamentalist practice! ... Why don't you help us fight this kind of fundamentalism?" Politely declining the invitation to participate in a government campaign against fundamentalism, Mohammed Moussaoui argued that the responsibility for discouraging use of the full veil should be entrusted to "the imams and Muslim religious authorities of France who promote moderate Islam and justly balanced Islam" (Mission d'information, 2009). This appeal reflects the RMF's understanding of "justly balanced Islam" as a religious, not a political, matter. In contrast to the UOIF, the RMF does not use social issues to gain leverage in the Muslim community; at the same time, it distinguishes itself from the legitimist position of the Great Paris Mosque by refusing to sacrifice Muslim unity on the altar of French ideological secularism.

A major difficulty for Muslim religious agents in the French system of limited religious pluralism is that they must address two distinct audiences: their coreligionists and political authorities. The distinction that Bourdieu draws between intra-field competition and inter-field transactions provides a fruitful framework for understanding the decline of Dalil Boubakeur's Great Paris

---

[26]   http://www.lermf.com/Objectifs/charte-du-rmf.html (accessed December 14, 2010).

Mosque alliance. Confident in its position as the historical representative the French Muslim community, the FNGMP attempted to exchange a salvation good alternately named "Islam of France" or "justly balanced community" for official recognition. The French government initially endorsed this arrangement, securing the election of Dalil Boubakeur to the presidency of the CFCM in 2003 and 2005. But when it became apparent that the FNGMP lacked the support of large parts of the French Muslim community, the government abandoned its traditional ally. This move did not reflect a change of opinion concerning the intrinsic value of specific Muslim salvation goods, but rather the recognition that the FNGMP was not a credible partner because it did not control the production of those goods. This observation is consistent with Bourdieu's postulate that only those specialists who have achieved hegemony through intra-field competition are able to negotiate transactions with dominant specialists in other fields.

While FNGMP courted approval from political authorities, the UOIF and the RMF concentrated their efforts on building legitimacy within the Muslim community. They, too, spoke of "justly balanced Islam." The choice of this Qur'ān-based motto shows that the UOIF and the RMF were primarily concerned with identifying themselves as authentic representatives of the Islamic tradition. Only after establishing their claim did they then compete with each other for dominance in the Muslim community by developing different understandings of the "happy medium." Far from being contradictory, the coexistence of ostensible agreement and internal rivalry is cogent with Bourdieu's description of agents in a field, united by an "objective alliance" that transcends their "underlying antagonism." In this perspective, "justly balanced Islam" can be understood as a symbolic capital that Muslim religious agents use to compete for dominance in their field, a necessary condition for conducting inter-field transactions with the state authorities who regulate religion in France.

Conclusion

The concept of branding posits that competing religious firms seek product differentiation in order to gain shares in a religious market. Contrary to this expectation, all three major Muslim federations in France chose to use the slogan "justly balanced Islam." Rather than targeting individual consumers, they addressed two distinct social groups or institutions: their coreligionists and the state. The internal organization of these two publics affects the forms that competition between religious agents take. In the Islamic tradition, religious scholars define the standards of belief and behavior that followers observe. To control the production of these standards is, therefore, to control the Muslim community. Competition between specialists is further intensified by state regulation of religious organizations which places high barriers to entry on new competitors and encourages incumbents to centralize their activities. In such an environment, salvation goods are produced, on the one hand, to assert and reinforce the position of religious agents within their field and, on the other, to gain acceptance and recognition from the state by endorsing widely-shared social values. Rather than being a competitive advantage, product differentiation has the potential to isolate an agent within the religious field, designating her/him/it for scrutiny from the state. Considering that all religious organizations are characterized to a degree by a division of labor between specialists and laypeople and that all political systems regulate religious activities to some extent, these historical constants constitute non-fortuitous limits to the concept of branding as applied to salvation goods.

Chapter 7

Healing by Islam:
Adoption of a Prophetic Rite—*roqya*—
by Salafists in France and Belgium

Hanifa Touag

Since the 1990s in Belgium and in France, Salafism, a large scale intellectual and social movement has been developing and contributing greatly to modifying the European Muslim landscape. With its influences rooted in the teachings of theologians like Ahmad Ibn Hanbal, Muhammad Ibn 'Abd Al-Wahhab, and Ibn Taymiyya, Salafism intends to purify religious practices of innovation—*bid'a*—thought to have compromised the original Islam. The Salafist creed[1] is seen as a return to the religion's primitive sources by imitating the "pious ancestors," *salaf al-salih*, and by affirming mistrust for the multiple interpretations and legal schools—*maddhab*—accused of having divided Muslims. In practice, the Salafist preacher extols a literal application of the Koran and the Sunna, constituted of *hadiths*.[2] This literal understanding is coupled with intransigence with regard to other Islamic tendencies—notably Sufism and Shiism, considered as deviations. In short, the Salafists see themselves as the depository of an Islamic orthodoxy which they consider to be mismanaged, not only by the West, but by Muslims themselves.

The new reality of Salafism in Europe owes much to the logistical and financial support of Saudi Arabia, but also to the decline of the ideology conveyed by the Muslim Brotherhood movement (Maréchal, 2009) and the Tabligh movement (Dassetto, 1988, 2011). The Salafist religious "offer" presents the "force of the word" (Haenni, 2008) as a comparative advantage, with conservative and strongly anti-Western accents, whereas, in institutionalizing itself, the Brothers increasingly courted politics (Geisser, 2006) and developed a decreasingly subversive rhetoric.

But the force of the word alone does not exhaust the salafist religious offer. An important aspect of their activity in the field relates to healing by the *roqya*, a

---

[1] The sociologist Samir Amghar (2011) notes that in the history of Muslim societies, returning to a primitive Islam is recommended whenever those societies are confronted with an economic, political or social crisis.

[2] A *hadith* designates the Prophet's words and, then, by extension, a collection including an ensemble of the traditions related to the Prophet's acts, words, or even silences.

method for extracting *djinns*[3] and evils linked to sorcery by the evil eye. The new therapeutists—the *raqis*—take their stance in opposing other Muslim practitioners-marabouts, *talebs*[4] and seers, whose practices they criticize, judging them to be approaching associationism, *shirk*.[5] For their part, they recommend returning to a purified exorcism, centered on Koranic psalmodies and treatment by Koranized water. Of course, not all *raqis* consider themselves *Salafists* or *Salafi*.[6] However, the non-Salafists and Salafists have the same thing at heart: the desire to transmit a reduced and strict practice of the *roqya*, copied on an idealized model of the Prophet and his companions. In both cases, the felt need to purify the therapeutic field is beyond doubt.

The renewal of interest engendered by these new Koranic healers in Europe raises a number of questions: first of all, how can the *raqi* compete with other actors in the market of Islamic healing to the point of setting out to correct them? What forms of self-legitimization does he implement? Are there substantial differences between the *roqya* and other practices associating therapy and religion (like maraboutism)? Lastly, does exposure to the *roqya* produce a *salafization* of the patients (with a return to the religion for sociological Muslims and a conversion for the others)?

Our brief research, spread over six months, involved eleven *raqis* and some twenty patients in three geographical zones in Europe: the Brussels-Capital region, the Lille region, and the Paris region. The *raqis* were quite accessible; they were rather prolix about their profession, which they wish to publicize to gain credit. As for the patients, they were rather reticent for, in their view, talking about the *djinn*, supposed to inhabit the afflicted, can lead to exciting and frustrating the demon whom they rather want to calm and rid themselves of.

The recovery is generally a long process for patients: it is thus difficult to determine the symbolic effectiveness of the *roqya* in a rather short investigation period. Hence what in our view deserves to be indicated in this study of Salafism in the *roqya*, is the transition from an elitist conception of membership in a

---

[3]   In pre-Islamic Arabia, the *djinns* were genies likely to appear in various human or animal forms, or remain invisible. Sabrina Mervin defines them as "intermediaries between the world of *ghayb*, mystery, of hidden things, and that of men; they inspired poets, in good or evil" (Mervin, 2010: 220).

[4]   The *taleb*, a seeker after wisdom, is the plural of *tolba* in Algerian dialect and literally means "student": it notably designates the student who has followed studies in Islamic sciences as well as other courses like Arabic grammar and calculation or who has received spiritual instruction and therapeutical gifts from a *sheik* within a Sufi brotherhood (*zawiyya*). The Salafists actively oppose Sufism, so it seems logical that *talebs* be the targets of the Salafist *raqis*.

[5]   Regarded as a serious sin in the Koran, associationism or *shirk* consists in associating God with something other than himself.

[6]   We also had the occasion to question *raqis* from the Muslim Brotherhood movement, the *Jama' at-Tabligh* movement, and other practitioners who said that they do not identify with any movement or religious tendency in particular.

Salafist group (Amghar, 2011: 93–137) to a suppler, more "popular" conception of Salafism. As opposed to sectarian logics, the Salafist *raqi* does not just "look after" brothers with Salafist convictions; he is capable of rethinking the codes of the *roqya* and his treatments in terms of the consultation and his patient's particular needs. This article is the occasion to deepen our awareness of a practice that social science research on Salafism has barely touched on.[7]

The *roqya*: An Historical Overview

Roqya and Islam do not go hand in hand historically: studies (Hamès, 2007) refer to the presence of professionals of exorcism, conjuration, and incantation well before the Revelation. Exorcism was a practice already firmly rooted in the society of the pre-Islamic period, or *jahilliya*,[8] among the Mecca polytheists, who drew on various materials (among which poetic material) to ward off whatever evils arose.

Since Islam could not eliminate belief in *djinns*, who belonged to the daily lives of the Arabs of the time, it integrated them into it. Thus, the *djinns* assumed their place in the Revelation; the idea of invocation was also integrated into certain Koranic verses[9] and *hadiths*, which were subsequently interpreted by commentators and scholars. Their procedure—namely, Al-Bukhâri, Al-Baydawi, Muslim, and Ibn Hanbal—consisted in *religifying* the *roqya*: the Koranic text was even promoted to the rank of a healing incantation. Two celebrated episodes of the Prophet being bewitched and Al-Baydawi and Al-Bukhâri's celebrated interpretations facilitated annexing the *roqya* to the prophet's experience.[10] Recourse to it came to be encouraged over the centuries.

Yet neither the Sources nor the Tradition provide a clear idea of the nature and status of *djinns*, those invisible intermediaries between the world of mystery and that of men. Are they liable to attack a human at any moment? Are they usually "bad"? Imprecision still reigns concerning the incantator's role and the need (or

---

[7]   Generally, literature on the *roqya* in Europe is sparse: Moussa Khedimallah's monographic study (2007) on the case of a *raqi* in Lorraine and Fatima Cherak's doctoral thesis (2007) exploring three different terrains by comparing them (Algeria, Egypt, and France) pay scant attention to the question of the bond between the *roqya* and the rise of fundamentalists in Europe. Conversely, in political science works relating to Salafism, the *roqya* is never deeply investigated.

[8]   In Arabic, *jahiliyya* means "ignorance." That ignorance is that of the Arabs before the Revelation of Islam.

[9]   The *roqya* is not clearly defined in the Koran, but the lexical field making allusion to it is (Hamès, 2007: 17–45).

[10]   Two Muslim exegetes, Al-Bukhâri (m. 870) and Al-Baydawi (m. 1286), interpret the origin of verses known as "talismanic" ("al-muawwidhatayn," suras 113 and 114) in establishing a correspondence between the number of knots untied in the history of the Prophet's bewitchment and the number of verses contained in the two suras (Hamès, 2007: 17–45).

lack of it) of mediation by a self-proclaimed professional. Finally, the *roqya*'s very contents are marked by a certain wavering: nobody can indubitably affirm that it should include such and such a treatment. However, and despite the blur characterizing the *roqya*'s sources, Islamic exorcism is to be found under the most varied of forms—maraboutism, clairvoyance by writing, etc.—in the Muslim world and in Europe, thus calling the traditional dichotomy of "religion against magic" into question.[11]

The remarkable phenomenon in the last few years has been the dissemination of a new understanding of the *roqya*: under the influence of a new generation of Muslim therapists who, for the most part, are calling for an Islam of fundaments and the *salafiyya*, the *roqya* is being narrowed to Koranic recitations and prescriptions of drinks or ablutions with "Koranized" water. Moreover, recourse to the *roqya* is not the privilege of the first generations of Muslims. As Felice Dassetto has underlined regarding Brussels, "these beliefs are not just characteristic of the first generations: they also continue in the following generations" (Dassetto, 2011: 158). It is thus important to understand how these new healers construct their legitimacy and the extent of their influence from a sociological point of view.

New "Healers with the Koran"

A discourse of disenchantment and the construction of re-enchantment

These new healers are positioning themselves in two distinct manners. On the one hand, new *roqya* practitioners entering the field of Islamic healing embody a revision in the concept of scientific therapeutic legitimacy. Indeed, *roqya* professionals are consulted when the solutions proposed by medicine are deemed insufficient. On the other hand, the *raqi* also fits into a market of Islamic healing whose "deviations" he hopes to correct *vis-à-vis* Islamic orthodoxy. In his view, they are generated by the marabouts, *talebs*, dervishes, *chawwafas* ("seers"), and sheikhs of the brotherhoods. In a highly competitive market, the *raqis* criticize both doctors, for exciting the *djinn* by administering doses of "chemicals"— medicines—and Muslim practitioners for not relying entirely on God. In Roubaix, *raqi* H. discredits these "*talebs* who claim to be, or who really are, married to *djinnias*"[12] who help them in their therapeutic treatments. Unlike marabouts, the *raqi* claims to reject any instrument establishing a distance between himself and his patient. The use of trace materials (*athar*), to detect the origin of evil is seen as distancing (whom?) from the divine power and its healing prerogatives.

---

[11]   Claude Rivière challenges this paradigmatic opposition between religion and magic and the debates it has occasioned in the anthropological approach to religions (Rivière, 1997).

[12]   The female version of the *djinn*, a demon, an invisible being.

The discourse of the Salafist *raqi* relies on a strategy of "disenchantment" of the practitioner figure. For salafistes, the *raqi* is not a Prophet[13] insofar as he interacts directly with the divine power; he manipulates no form of *sihr*—"magic"— naturally possessing no particular gift. Having no natural faculty to intercede between men and the world of the invisible he, paradoxically, can obtain things through intense religious training. Hence ways of learning the *roqya* oscillate between an individual do-it-yourselfism mixed with family acquisitions, recent literature on the *roqya* and knowledge obtained in mosques and other learning centers. Participation in rituals organized in mosques and private locations contributes to training future *raqis*. The Ettaouba Mosque in Evere (Brussels) organizes instructional sessions on the *roqya*, reserved for women, as well as round-tables to discuss the benefits of the *hijama*, a treatment related to the *roqya*.[14] Former patients participate and mention that they have been cured—djinns who were earlier persecuting them have been converted into Muslim *djinns*, assistants, and protectors of future *raqis*.[15] Two *raqis* explain that they were trained in *roqya* at the Belgian Islamic center, the former bastion of Bassam Ayachi.[16] Another *raqi* in Brussels claims to have been trained by Sheik Aznagui Abou Chayma, in the context of an initiation to *roqya* proposed at his "la Plume" association. Word of mouth between patients refers to the authority of these centers which, even if closed, continue to benefit from a good reputation.

At the end of his training, the future *raqi* states that he observes providential aid during his first consultation. Confronted with a patient complaining of uncontrollable suffocations and unexplained fevers, *raqi* M. of Anderlecht (Brussels) claims to observe God's help at work. His female patient changes her mood little by little and goes into a trance after having drunk Koranized water prepared for her by the *raqi*. For both him and the patient (whose subsequent narrative plays a role in recognition of the *raqi*'s powers) the uncontrolled agitations are indeed a sign of his divine gift, authorizing the neophyte *raqi* to

---

[13]   The *raqis*' insistence on recalling this aims at protecting them from any accusation of wanting to usurp divine or prophetic attributes (or *shirk*, associationism).

[14]   *The hijama* or "exiting the *djinn* by the blood" consists in applying suction cups to make the patient's blood circulate. This method resembles that employed in Chinese medicine. Consultants of the second generation often establish a parallel between the two to diminish the atypical character of their approach.

[15]   However, some *raqis* reject consulting *djinns*. This notion of "*isti' âna bil djinn*: asking for the *djinn*'s help" corresponds with the practice of orthodox *roqya* in their view.

[16]   Bassam Ayachi's arrest in Italy, in November 2008, returning from Syria with illegal immigrants suspended the Belgian Islamic Center's activities. But the difficulties of the center and its founders do not seem to concern the *raqis* who, once trained, distance themselves and, on the whole, practice remotely from the groups who trained them. The Islamic Center of Bassam Ayachi, known in Belgium and Europe for its former proximity with Abdessatar Dahmane (the killer of Colonel Massoud in 2001), is not representative of the ideology in other *roqya* training centers in Belgium. In fact none of the *roqya* training centers advocate revolutionary action but rather a quietist vision of Islam.

pursue his practice. The first therapeutic experience amounts to a "license to exorcise" that the *raqis* call the *hikma*, as opposed to the *baraka*[17] among the marabouts or sheikhs of the brotherhoods: obtained by an unfailing diligence in their religious training, the *hikma* is a reward in recognition of the new *raqi's* religious willingness.

But, *in fine*, the notion of the *hikma*[18] grants the *raqi* a quite particular role. It permits any Muslim so trained to exorcise and, hence, to enter into contact with the world of the invisible. Indeed, when it took over the *roqya*, practiced earlier in France and Belgium, the Salafism movement radically decompartmentalized itself by breaking with its elitist and hereditary character. In "disenchanting" the role of the therapeutist by insisting on the acquisition of a body of knowledge, Salafism, far from having limited the practice of the *roqya*, has undoubtedly contributed to extending it and, thus, contributed to "re-enchanting" the real.

The *raqis* come from a variety of social and intellectual groups. Some are engineers,[19] doctors,[20] imams,[21] or unemployed. The purpose of *roqya* is not necessary to improve the practitioner's quality of life—for that matter, he sometimes requests no financial compensation.[22] Specialization in the *roqya* is also aimed at transcending the stigmata of "sorcerer" inherited from a marabout father or grandfather, thus reconciling the past and present.

Supporting organizational networks and transmitting the roqya

A product of a religious globalization of Islam, Salafism entered France and Belgium via specific paths of dissemination: bookstores and telecommunications. Hence it is logical that the Salafist *roqya* should use the same channels.

The *roqya*'s major postulates—belief in *madakhils*, bodily openings suitable for the entrance of a *djinn*, plus the jinn's strictly demonic dimension—find widespread support in demonological literature. This literature shows a diversified range of procedures for diagnosing evils, employable techniques, and various interventions the author has tested on his patients.[23] Initially disseminated by Saudi and Egyptian publishers, and today by French and Belgian publishers, this

---

[17] The notion of "baraka" does not appear in the discourse of *raqis* to explain the obtaining of a power of knowledge or a power to heal. In the *raqis'* conception, *baraka* refers to an occult knowledge and to the marabouts' pretensions to be the intermediaries between God and Men.

[18] In Arabic *hikma* designates wisdom. The root h-k-m also refers to the idea of power.

[19] A.H., a French-Morrocan *raqi* and member of the Tabligh movement and the French "Al-Istissal" network of *raqis*, shows no hesitation in recalling that was trained as an engineer and was once an Olympic champion of mathematical games.

[20] A.M., a *raqi* for ten years; he receives in his doctor's office in Clichy.

[21] Two Imams from mosques took part in the survey.

[22] The patients can, of course, bring food or gifts when the raqi does not request pay. This is particularly the case for Imams.

[23] Quite often the author will leave his address in a book so readers can contact him.

"clairvoyant" literature banks on the *roqya*'s visible character (Cherak, 2007) through the covers, the titles, and the images. In making it be seen that he resolutely opts for transparency, the *raqi* wants to show that his practice, organized under the public eye, aims at strict conformity with Islamic orthodoxy. The practice's intense mediatization attests to this. Thus, several Arab satellite television channels like the Egyptian Dream, Orbit, and *Iqra* ("Read"), the Saudi *al-Majd* ("Glory"), *al-Nass* ("People"), and *al-Haqiqa* ("the Truth") propose programs on the Koranic *roqya*. Recently, the Belgian Internet chain "Median TV" broadcasted an interview with *raqi* Abderraouf Ben Halima and transmitted the colloquium "A paranormal world," held in April 2011.[24] The Web's immaterial waves stage *"jalssa*: meetings" leading to conversions of the sick.[25] Practicing *roqya* in this way has become part of the daily lives of Muslim households in France and Belgium.

This mediatization embodies an economic dynamics. It fosters the construction of a therapeutical capitalism based on a geographical "division of labor" for the *raqis*. Thus a certain number of *raqis* have decided to form themselves into "national" networks, which put the *raqi* in Internet connection with a patient according to criteria he/she formulates. Thus, A.M., member of the alliance *Al Maherr*[26] ("the Savant") and S, member of the group *Al Istissal*[27] ("the fact of tearing up, uprooting") agree in saying that forming networks "also meets the patients' needs": "most patients prefer consulting an exorcist near home, but others, on the contrary, feel that they would be embarrassed were one of their neighbors to find out… ."[28] In their view, the patient might be afraid of happening on his sorcerer. As for young girls, still unmarried, the stigmatization of their neighborhood would tend to orient them towards geographically distant *raqis*. In certain quarters a bad reputation might interfere with their marriage project. In other words, forming wider scale networks would seem to benefit both the new *raqis* and cautious patients.[29]

However, this professionalization does not escape the polemic over the commercializing of religion. Indeed, if the practitioners legitimize the *roqya* as

---

[24] A colloquium, held April 16 and 17, 2011 and organized by the Al-Hikma Center in Brussels, brought together preachers and *raqis* insisting on the need to prevent *djinnic* attacks.

[25] Cf. the staging of a conversion by a *raqi* of the Al Maherr network: http://www.youtube.com/watch?v=pMT4shtZb4A, accessed July 12, 2011.

[26] http://www.maherr.com/, accessed March 28, 2011.

[27] http://www.alistissal.com/, accessed March 28, 2011.

[28] Discussion with S. of the "Al-Istissal" alliance, September 15, 2011.

[29] The new *raqi*, lacking in experience and legitimacy, can thus benefit from a certain "job security": the network ensures him customers he doesn't have to look for; in exchange, he concedes part of his potential market to the network. Consequently, once the *raqi*'s clientele is ensured in his city and beyond, he more or less parts company with the network which he no longer needs. The turnover is thus rapid and sharing the same Salafist convictions is not the whole story.

aiding a Muslim brother,[30] that help loses its meaning if the practitioner requires a financial compensation. Thus, the *roqya*'s adversaries insist that one should not "sell" the word of God for vain wages or grow rich on the community's misfortunes.[31] They add that a *raqi* remaining at his patients' bequest all day can't help but neglect his five daily prayers. These controversies have slowed down neither the *roqya* nor the promotion of a "therapeutical capitalism": at this point, the exorcists defend themselves in pointing out that the alleviation of a suffering believer deserves spending time and legitimizes their request for payment.

The raqi *looks after the social more than the religious*

Finally—and this is one of the aspects legitimizing *raqis* that is often raised[32]— the *raqi* plays an undeniably social role. Indeed the *raqi*'s efforts are not strictly limited to administering a treatment and accompanying the patient in the social difficulties he encounters. Social regulation is thus an essential aspect of the *raqi*'s functions.

He initially plays a *soothing* role within the family: confronted with silence on the part of official medicine, the patient's family is often helpless and at pains to understand his/her pathological state. Some patients acknowledged to me that they themselves felt guilty towards their family, or even marginalized by them. They were taken for "fools" whereas they felt themselves to be in full possession of their intellectual faculties. In Brussels, Fatima-Zahra expressed a sense of guilt when her husband came to identify his crisis of dementia (the husband's view) with a crisis of possession (the *raqi*'s view). "I saw it as shameful; I really felt guilty. So I tried to hide it from my children and the family."[33] The diagnosis of possession by a *djinn* 'achiq ("in love") rehabilitated Fatima-Zahra, casting her in a victim role and not to be neglected by the family—for the risk of contagion is obvious.[34] The theory of the distribution of *djinns* into families, as the exorcist explained to the husband, quite often consolidates intra-familial ties. In this way,

---

[30] An Islamic hadith, famous in the *raqi* milieu, states: "he who can help his brother, let him do it" (*Sahih*, Mouslim, the Book al-Salâm, hadith 4076) thus applies to practicing the *roqya* (Cherak, 2007).

[31] The same ethical questions arise with regard to the Muslim funeral sector.

[32] Moussa Khedimellah (2007) insists quite keenly on the social role of the young *raqi* he interviewed in Lorraine.

[33] The case of Fatima-Zahra deserves some attention. A 52-year old, employed mother, having devoted her entire life exclusively to educating her children. the ages of her children range from 10 to 31. She thus insists on the fact that her maternal mission is far from finished. Linked to a certain perception of the disease, her guilt feelings were reinforced by the feeling of a maternal task not having been correctly accomplished.

[34] The idea that the possession or sorcery is contagious is admitted by some exorcists, thus explaining attacks striking several family members simultaneously. *Raqi* K. from Courneuve told me that one day he felt pins and needles in his hand after having exorcized a person: the jinns may also be transmitted by touch.

the *raqi* assumes a moderating role in regulating the social strains which animate relationships between patients and their entourage faced with the disease.

The *raqi*'s social role is not reduced to managing intrafamilial relationships (a man and wife, a mother and her daughter-in-law, etc.). He often sets out to remove a series of mental barriers and hindrances touching on all aspects of the patient's life: the separation of couples, the impossibility of giving birth, or prolonged unemployment are the cases frequently encountered. Often the *raqi* is in tune with his patient's pessimistic vision, considering himself to be the target of a generalized misfortune involving his/her health, material well-being and social relationships. All of their evils come together in an exclusion from all social and affective life. The *raqi* then invokes a destructive sorcery on the part of jealous parties, or stemming from an intense conflictual relationship.

The role of social regulator is not unique to *raqis* in the field of Islamic healing. Just like his therapeutical predecessors,[35] the *raqi* interacts with a reality marked by fragilization and risk to the individual, as well as by the multiplicity of rivalrous situations experienced daily—at work and in the family. He "unties the knots,"[36] symbolic of social barriers. After a fashion, he normalizes social relationships, in a context where, for young Muslim women under 30, the search for a partner in a matrimonial project is not as easy as it was in the past.[37]

The eminently social role the Salafist *raqi* plays leads us to reflect on the very nature of Salafism. In granting therapeutical aid to a public that is non-Salafist and sometimes not even Muslim,[38] the Salafist *raqi* breaks with the stereotypes that are traditionally attached to the salafiyya: insensitive to social and family questions, enshrouded in sectarian logics, the salafiyya was said to be satisfied with generating and feeding theological disputations and acting as the transmitter of religious theses from Saudi Arabia. With the *roqya*, the Salafists, on the contrary,

---

[35] Liliane Kuczynski's study on the marabouts of the Paris region thus revealed that jealousy and envy are the most frequent topics in consultations (Kuczynski, 2007).

[36] Fatima Cherak analyzed the Arabic lexical field used by patients and *raqis* to indicate their misfortunes: it refers to "*rbat*: knotting." It is said of a young girl who has not managed to find a husband that she is "*marbouta 'ala ezzwaj*: knotted for marriage," of a woman who is sterile, or considered to be, that she is "*merbota 'ala al-wlada*: knotted for childbirth" (Cherak, 2007).

[37] Fatima Cherak develops the following hypothesis: Muslim women today are stymied due to transformations in women's networks. Such networks left the choice of bride entirely in the hands of the future mother-in-law, whose son granted her *carte blanche*. The progressive individualization of social relationships is leaving an increasingly narrower space for manoeuver for the mother's intervention, because today men prefer to know and date young girls before asking their hand in marriage. This new mode of recruiting marriageable young girls condemns those who are mostly absent from the public space of men, particularly workplaces, schools and universities (Cherak, 2007).

[38] Among those questioned, two non-Muslim women at an impasse in finding solutions for their sufferings, presented themselves at a *raqi*'s, after having heard of the *roqya*'s benefits from a Muslim girlfriend or neighbor.

widen the Muslim public concerned by Salafist ideas of purification. But doesn't that unavoidably come at the price of a leveling of their dogmatic demands? In short, what red lines does the Salafist refuse to cross, and what does he agree to concede as long as it doesn't interfere with his therapeutical procedure?

The Unfolding of a Salafiyya *roqya*: Permanences and Adjustments

The patient's symptoms are studied on the basis of two principal etiologies: possession: "al mess" and sorcery "al 'ayn." This interpretational model, common to all *raqis* doesn't prevent their formulating certain requirements before the session, related to their conception of orthodoxy. But those demands are not rigid and may be continually renegotiated depending on the patient and situation.

The relationship with the patient: between dogmatic demands and therapeutical pragmatism

Salafist *raqis* formulate a series of requirements addressed to their patients, who are supposed to comply with them if the *roqya* session's procedure is to conform with "Islam." Yet, quite often the *raqi* changes his conditions to simplify the ritual procedure

The *raqis* demands involve various aspects of the ritual (the time, space, and human organization). Thus, *a priori*, it would seem that Salafist *raqis* refuse to work during Ramadan:[39] it's a sacred month, "for needed rest 'to bolster' one's spiritual forces and multiply acts of piety" (Cherak, 2007). Yet certain emergency cases were able to shake the *raqis* out of their Ramadanian lethargy: the *raqis a fortiori* justify their interventions by mentioning cases of the chronically ill, the surety of whose cure was at stake just before Ramadan. As for the space of the ritual, while, in principle, it corresponds to a private place arranged by the *raqi* for consultations,[40] it very often happens that the *raqi* moves around and penetrates a space of familial intimacy, often impure as regards Salafist demands.[41] The minimal demanded by a Salafist *raqi* concerning the space where he will proceed to the ritual is the absence of statues or dolls: they declare that they would prevent angels from entering the house and that the Koranic psalmody would thereby be deprived of providential grace. Similarly, the question of *mahrem*, a male relative who must accompany the patient at the exorcist's, represents an obstacle for certain

---

[39]   They refer to this *hadith*: "During Ramadan, the doors of paradise are opened, the doors of hell are shut and the demons chained up," hadith 1793, the book: *al-Siyam* (the Fast) of *Sahih* Mouslim (quoted in Cherak, 2007).
[40]   Including a chair, rugs and all aids to the ritual (suras pinned to the wall, prayer beads, etc.)
[41]   In certain Muslim families, no Islamic ritual object was present, neither prayer beads, nor a Koran, etc. when the Salafist *raqi* entered.

female patients who would feel embarrassed in complying with it as a condition of the practice's legitimacy.[42] The idea, of Hanbali origin, and taken up by the Salafists, that women presenting themselves at the exorcist's would automatically "sow" *fitna* ("division") unless they be accompanied by a man, is admitted by all Salafist *raqis* since, in their view of things, outside of a relationship "legalized" by marriage, isolating a man with a woman would expose the individuals to the sin of "*zina*: fornication." But this condition, which *de facto* protects the exorcist against all charges of fondling or rape—which could destroy his reputation[43]—is nevertheless circumvented for the simple reason that women represent at least 80 percent of their patients. Consequently, the Salafist *raqi* chooses to officiate in a group: some twenty women come together to hear the *raqi*'s psalmody. If it turns out to be an expensive transaction, the group visit is often poorly perceived: the relationship with the patient is depersonalized, she seeing herself as a cash cow and not really taken into the *raqi*'s care. Lastly, the most skillful solution for the *raqi* is to initiate his wife into the *roqya*, with the therapeutist guiding his wife in the gestures to be enacted, particularly if they involve touching the patient.

The *roqya*'s professionalization and the increasing competition of Salafist *raqis* among one another have led them to seek pragmatic solutions so as not to lose their clientele, accommodating them while still affirming the licit character of their practice. Besides economics, other types of determinisms weigh on the Salafist *raqis*, compromising their achieving their project of "religious purity" (Roy, 2008).[44] In practice, Salafist *raqis* do not wipe the slate clean in their milieu and draw upon a universe of varied references.

A raqi *inserted into a universe of cultural references*

Religion is not the sole resource of the *roqya*, even among the Salafists. One need only observe the moving reality of these curative techniques *in situ* to be convinced of that: if most Salafist *raqis* say they succeed in excorporating the evil with Koranic psalmodies alone, they resort to methods they do not justify religiously when the evil persists, like "emptying" the stomach and treatments by bleeding. Moreover, not all the practices of traditional exorcism are condemned by practitioners of the salafiyya *roqya*; certain techniques and representations find favor and even recognition in their eyes. Using a stick, traditionally associated

---

[42] Three patients—all active women—entrusted to me that *vis-à-vis* the intransigence of *raqis* who refused to receive them without *mahrem*, they had to give up *roqya*.

[43] Another role of the *mahrem* is to assist the exorcist should there be a question of physically handling the patient to control her when in trance, should she manifest aggressiveness *vis-à-vis* the therapeutist.

[44] The concept of "religious purity" refers to the inclination of religions to abandon their territorial and cultural anchoring (Roy, 2008).

with marabouts and *talebs*, has thus been rehabilitated by some raqis.[45] For example the fact of inserting a fingernail under the patient's to force the *djinn* to talk or leave his victim is a commonly used *taleb* technique (Cherak, 2007). Along the same lines, is the technique of burning a piece of cloth with God's name or attributes written on it and making the possessed smell it or, further, burying his body, or its afflicted part, in cemetery ground are recommended to patients by the exorcist. These *raqis* find themselves in the continuity of a family heritage; their having observed many of the marabout or *taleb* father or grandfather's meetings is incapable of being entirely erased.

Hence, when it invests in the *roqya*, a popularization of Salafism indeed exists, with the inevitability of taking certain principle (economic, therapeutical, and familial) realities into consideration, thus constraining Salafism to position itself otherwise than via theological jousts.

Measuring the *roqya*'s Symbolic Effectiveness

Evaluating the effectiveness of a treatment like the *roqya* is complex in more ways than one. First of all on a methodological level, during a short investigation (six months), it is hard to draw definitive conclusions on the patient's fate. He may feel he is cured from the first and manifest a consequent religious enthusiasm, only to soon sink into the depths of the disease.

After a certain number of meetings, the *raqi* places responsibility for the healing on the patient's shoulders, healed or not: non-observance of the religious principles of Islam being regarded as a principal factor in possession, any sin ("*ma'siya*") or even any religious indifference opens the path to a *djinnic* attack. For the *raqi*, whose role gradually diminishes, only a strict and rigorous observance of Islam and its practices can alleviate the patient's woes.

But this conversion-healing (or intensification of practice-healing) relationship is, in our view, a factor explaining the lack of *salafization* observed after consultation. Causality has brought out the limits of the *raqi*'s symbolic efficacy, for things appear profoundly paradoxical in the eyes of the patient, who is completely mixed up: the *djinn* supposed to inspire immorality and the abandonment of religion makes the sufferer the victim of a possesser *djinn*; yet the patient who commits a sin exposes himself to possession (Cherak, 2007). The patient's supposed part in complicity with the evil, making him a "culprit," is of course not accepted by the patients, whose ill-being or disease is lasting and unbearable. Sonia, sick for over five months, summarized this confusion as follows: "at the beginning, I was sick, I was attacked by a *djinn* ... and now *al-haj* tells me that I am the cause of the attack. My *wesswess* ("distress") has increased since I found that out." Others, disappointed, call for the *raqi*'s "resignation": Zaher explains that his *raqi* failed to

---

[45]   M. (Roubaix), K. (Courneuve), and L. (Molenbeek) use a traditional stick so as not to touch the patient directly. Marabouts use this means of excorporating *djinns* too.

try everything to extract the *djinn* (notably, imprisoning, hitting, burning, cutting its throat or killing it); he rather set out to convert the *djinn* and the patient by reciting the five pillars.[46]

For the patients, a return to health or a normalized social life being an imperative prevailing over the rest, constructions of a causal religious meaning making the patient feel guilty do not help in establishing loyalty in a volatile and pragmatic clientele.

Indeed, among the vast majority of patients observed, pragmatism is key. The term "effectiveness" comes up very often in the patients' talk. The therapeutist's strict observance of an Islamic orthodoxy is not a decisive criterion in the search for healing. Thus, out of 24 patients questioned, 23 had already consulted other practitioners (*talebs*, marabouts, clairvoyants), 20 continued to consult the others and practice the *roqya* simultaneously, and 14 had returned to or rediscovered "official" medical pathways (often psychiatry) after a few *roqya* sessions.

The *raqi* attributes the difficulties in establishing a loyal clientele to the confusion reigning in the spirit of many patients. *Raqi* A. of Schaerbeek underlines it as follows:

> Women dare to come and see me to ask what they ask their marabouts. They come to bewitch their husbands, to make them fall in love, or to break the ties between him and his mother. But I can't do that, myself, I don't play with *djinns*. I don't bewitch Muslims. I don't take myself for God or the Prophet.[47]

Despite the media arsenal set up by the Salafist *raqis* to distinguish themselves from marabouts, the *roqya* always seems to be the object of regular confusions on behalf of the patients. Undoubtedly because the borderline between exorcisms is thin and is located primarily in the order of speech of the practitioners.

---

[46] As the *raqis* explain it, converting the *djinn* is a sign of preventing a future *djinnic* onslaught.

[47] Discussion with *raqi* A. of Schaerbeek (Brussels), September 16, 2011.

PART III
Religious and Spiritual Consuming

Chapter 8

Adding Imaginative Value: Religion, Marketing, and the Commodification of Social Action

Jochen Hirschle

Introduction

The aim of this study is to theoretically account and empirically test for the impact of economic growth on religious change. While a variety of studies have analyzed this relation and have shown that for many countries a negative correlation exists, most of them have employed secularization theory to theoretically account for this result. From this perspective, economic modernization leads to a decline in religious values, which is followed by diminishing rates of religious service attendance (Weber, 2000; Berger, 1967; Bruce, 2002; Norris and Inglehart, 2004).

In contrast, this chapter aims to explain the relationship between economic growth and religious change from a supply-side perspective. I argue that under affluent conditions, individuals cease attending religious services not because they become unreligious, but rather because economic growth (firstly and very practically) leads to an increase in the purchasing power of households. This ultimately leads to an expansion of the consumer market, and to waxing marketing activities of companies. Secondly, and consequently, individuals incrementally engage in consumption-related activities to meet needs that were previously fulfilled by traditional religious activities and products (Stolz, 2010; Gruber and Hungerman, 2008; Belk *et al.*, 1989).

Even if this hypothesis does not match the mainstays of secularization theory, it is theoretically rooted in Emile Durkheim's religious sociology. In his classical treatise on *The Elementary Forms of Religious Life* (1912), Durkheim argued that religion is an eminently social issue. It facilitates engagement in collective action by providing tangible, symbolic material, and rites that enable individuals to meet, communicate, and commune.

Under affluent conditions, however, the market incrementally intervenes in this field of delivering intermediaries to reproduce and organize social practices. First, there are products that are indicative of social status or affiliation with certain subcultural groups, and thus mainly serve socio-cultural functions (Bourdieu, 1979; Holt, 2006). Moreover, there are social infrastructures of consumption—clubs, theme parks, hotel resorts, restaurants, shopping districts, and fitness gyms—that operate as explicit opportunity structures for individuals to meet and interact. These new social infrastructures are not just cold facilities where individuals can be in contact with others. Rather they are, like the branded products, culturally up-valued by means of marketing measures and elaborate designs. They are culturally significant settings for individuals to commune.

The central hypothesis to test in this chapter is that under conditions of affluence, individuals incrementally enact social relations in these new infrastructures of consumption instead of relying on traditional church-related practices. As a consequence, churches are losing their monopolistic position of delivering the "tangible intermediaries" (Durkheim, 2008: 175) that allow individuals to commune.

In what follows, I theoretically delineate the above sketched arguments in more detail, and locate them in the context of the classical treatises on the development of the capitalist economy and religious sociology. In the second part, I operationalize and empirically test the consumption hypothesis using longitudinal data from the German Socio-Economic Panel (SOEP, 1984–2009) on a sample of German Catholics. I conduct bivariate and panel regression analyses to determine whether the increasing engagement in consumption-related leisure activities (attending clubs, cinemas, concerts, theaters, and museums, and engaging in sports) diminishes individuals' propensity toward attend religious services.

Capitalist Dynamics, Marketing, and Religious Change: A Consumption-Oriented Interpretation

The origins of capitalism

In his studies on *The Economic Ethics of the World Religions*, Max Weber argued that the rise of capitalism was primarily a result of two religious developments: first, the Jewish-Christian tradition had in general (and more than the other world religions) fostered the development of rational ways of thinking (systematization of ideas) and conducts of life (asceticism) (Merz-Bens, 2008: 24; Tenbruck, 1975: 683). Second, and as a consequence of these processes, Christianity gave rise to the Protestants sects, who finalized the process of rationalization by releasing "Christian asceticism" from the religious sphere "into the market-place of life" (Weber, 1971 (1920): 154). They achieved this by giving "every-day worldly activity a religious significance" (Weber, 1971: 80). Specifically, the Calvinists religiously up-valued profane occupational life by determining that material success was a sign of a *state of grace*. As a consequence, individuals who were adherents of these religious sects were increasingly motivated and forced to engage in economic transactions in order to reassure themselves about their grace.

The combination of these two facets paved the way for the victory of capitalism. By up-valuing secular activities, the Protestant sects provided a bridge for rationality to flow from the religious sphere—where it was encapsulated in the Catholic tradition—to the economic world (Weber, 1971: 181). From now on, individuals were not only highly motivated to earn a profit, but they were also equipped with the tools and conduits of life that enabled them to pursue this goal in the most efficient way.

While these religious phenomena were the mainspring for the economic revolution, the emerging capitalist system was soon able to survive without its religious root. Through institutionalization, the modern economy established its own moral order and socialization mechanisms within the firm and the market. Although these occurrences on their own may not be able to produce the values that are required to keep the system running by imaginatively charging working life in the same way the Protestant sects were able to do, they do effectively produce conformity to the system's normative requirements by sanctioning deviant economic behavior: "The manufacturer who in the long run acts counter to these norms, will just as inevitably be eliminated from the economic scene as the worker who cannot or will not adapt himself to them will be thrown into the streets without a job" (Weber, 1971: 54f).

The process of rationalization and the disenchantment of the world which started in the religious sphere was continued and finalized with the establishment of capitalism. Therefore, the rise of capitalism, which from Weber's perspective goes along with the death of its religious roots, was also long interpreted as the central cause for the secularization of society (Berger, 1967; Bruce, 2002; Dobbelaere, 2004). Peter L. Berger concluded that "the original 'carrier' of secularization is the modern economic process, that is, the dynamic of industrial capitalism" (Berger, 1967: 109); and Schumpeter argued that "[t]he capitalist process rationalizes behavior and ideas and by so doing chases from our minds, along with metaphysical belief, mystic and romantic ideas of all sorts" (Schumpeter, 2009 (1942): 127).

The rise of marketing

While this concept of economic modernization has dominated different disciplines for a long time (economic sociology as well as the study of religion), in the last decades it has been criticized from different sides. In economic sociology, John. K. Galbraith argued that from a certain stage of development (that is, when original needs of most inhabitants of a society are already fulfilled), the central problem of capitalism is no longer that of rationalizing and increasing production, but rather that of selling the huge amount of commodities it produces (Galbraith, 1975: 149).

Galbraith therefore concluded that in the modern context, the natural order of production and consumption has been reversed. Production no longer satisfies the original wants of individuals; rather, to keep economic growth stable under conditions where these wants are already fulfilled, "production creates the wants it seeks to satisfy" by itself (Galbraith, 1975: 149). The central aim of the economy has changed from developing the units, technologies, and organizational principles of production to developing the means that allow companies to increase consumer demand.

While Galbraith clearly understood that the "institution of marketing" (Sheehan, 2010: 32) plays a crucial role in these attempts to control demand (Galbraith, 1975: 150), he barked up the wrong tree when it came to explaining how these measures actually operate (Baudrillard, 2009: 74). Galbraith argued that marketing measures artificially create the wants that are necessary to sell a product under conditions of affluence (Galbraith, 1975: 151). Conversely, contemporary sociologists and marketing experts agree that marketing is hardly able to seduce consumers by means of designing and implementing new wants; rather, they try to attach positive connoted cultural value to a profane "use-value product" in the hopes that a fusion of the two enhances a product's desirability (O'Shaugnessy and O'Shaugnessy, 2002: 533; Twitchell, 1996; Baudrillard, 2009: 74; McCracken, 1990: 77).

Marketing lends desirable values from the cultural sphere when providing products with additional values (McCracken, 1990: 71ff). Hence, consumers in the modern context decreasingly buy products or services because their use-value relates to pre-existing or artificially synthesized wants. In the act of buying, individuals rather try to relate to the cultural values that have been attached to products via marketing. This perspective implies that the economy has carried over and systematized a process that had its origins in the religious sphere. Not only is the process of fetish consecration similar to branding in that both provide a bridge for the sacred to flow into the sphere of profane activities; in addition, the rise of capitalism itself goes back to a process of adding imaginative value to a profane activity, as described by Max Weber. Because the Protestant sects defined material success as a sign of a state of grace, individuals started to seriously engage in the process of production and consequently established the capitalist economic order (Weber, 1971: 181).

The recent marketing activities of companies acting on the consumer market are a reflection of these original religious principles (Belk and Tumbat, 2005: 208). When companies add cultural values to commodities by means of advertising, sponsoring, and product or package design, they virtually try to lift these products out of the secular world of use-values in order to relocate them in the world of positively connoted imaginative values:

> For whatever else advertising does, one thing is certain: by adding value to material, by adding meaning to objects, by branding things, advertising performs a role historically associated with religion. The Great Chain of Being, which for centuries located value above the horizon, in the World Beyond, has been reforged to settle value on the objects of the here and now (Twichtell, 1996: 12).

Consumption—a social matrix?

The success of marketing in boosting consumer demand is not due solely to the effect of adding imaginative values to commodities. Furthermore, marketing does not only seduce consumers to buy products by addressing hedonistic wants of isolated egos (Baudrillard, 2009: 74). Rather, the up-valuing of commodities has paved the way for new consumer products and services to become part of the basic social and cultural practices of individuals (Cova, 1997: 310; Baudrillard, 2009: 78; Hirschle, 2011: 268).

This commodification of social action first occurs because the imaginative values that advertising attaches to products are borrowed from the cultural sphere of the society in which these values are embedded (McCracken, 1990: 79). Products are an object code. "They help to give the ideas of culture, which are by their very nature intangible, a certain concreteness" (McCracken, 1990: 133). Consequently, commodities are used by individuals to express and manipulate cultural meaning (McCracken, 1990: 131); this becomes apparent in Bourdieu's treatise on the relevance of lifestyles and consumer products to communicate class status (Bourdieu, 1979).

Secondly, the market increasingly provides imaginatively enhanced products that not only operate as inactive vehicles or languages in the social process, but are at the core of the social process itself. Clubs, bars, theme parks, hotel resorts, cruise ships, fitness studios, restaurants, and climbing gyms are "foci of activity" (Feld, 1981) in that they operate as opportunity structures in which individuals meet and communicate. They offer activity schemes that facilitate people's engagement in social relations. The market provides, extends, and permanently changes and upgrades the facilities that allow individuals to enact existing social relations and to generate new relations.

The process of up-valuing products by means of marketing measures plays a crucial role in this process: the attractiveness of the range of infrastructures is a function of the imaginaries that individuals associate with them. Music clubs are not only mundane places where individuals have the opportunity to meet; their imaginary value is loaded with the music of a certain subculture, with light shows, and elaborated interior designs. Equally, the attractiveness of theme parks is a function of their ability to stimulate the imaginations of customers; that is, their ability to take them to a journey away from the routines of daily life. Holiday resorts create these imaginations by associating the stay with a certain natural setting: the landscape, the sea, the beach, and the taste of an exotic culture (Day *et al.*, 2002). This imaginative value added to or associated with the infrastructure is not consumed by separated individuals. Rather, the images that are created by these facilities form the background for individuals to engage in social relations (Illouz, 1997: 262).

By providing tangible infrastructures, the market has expanded its scope of influence into the core matrix of the social process. The economic act of selling products and services has been emancipated from the explicit purchasing situation. Beyond reorganizing the economic life of individuals, capitalism has made society an "appendage of the market" (Polanyi, 1968: 77) by implementing new means and intermediaries that initiate and structure social action. In this way, products have become an important factor in catalyzing the social bottom-up.

On the competition between religion and consumption

From a Durkheimian perspective, this process of recreating society through consumption-related intermediaries necessarily initiates "a silent battle" between religious and secular products (Stolz, 2010: 253). Emile Durkheim conceived of religion as "something eminently social" (Durkheim, 2008: 11). Whatever else religion does, it is at any rate "the means by which society is made and remade: religion is instrumental in creating society" (Pickering, 1984: 309). Durkheim, as an adherent of a positivist position, was mainly interested in the empirically assignable mechanisms that fulfill this purpose (Marica, 1932: 141). Therefore, he viewed *rituals* and *collective representations* as the core of every religious system (Durkheim, 2008, 323). Rituals, on the one hand, "set the collectivity in motion— groups gather to celebrate them. Their primary effect is to bring individuals together, to increase contacts between them, and to make those contacts more intimate" (Durkheim, 2008: 258).

Collective representations, on the other hand, are the basic elements of the religious system at the cognitive level, but they are dependent on their enactment within concrete practices, which require tangible intermediaries: "Collective representations ... presuppose that consciousnesses act on and react to one another; they are the result of these actions and reactions, which are possible only through tangible intermediaries" (Durkheim, 2008: 175).

Moreover, the production and reproduction of social practices and collective representations are not only secondary by-products of religion. By instructing individuals to act collectively, the religious material helps to evoke a transcending mental state that is the source of religious sentiments: "The very fact of assembling is an exceptionally powerful stimulant. Once the individuals are assembled, their proximity generates a kind of electricity that quickly transports them to an extraordinary degree of exaltation" (Durkheim, 2008: 162). In fact, Durkheim conceives of religious ideas and the sacred itself as products of the energies that are released within these social practices: "it is in these effervescent social settings, and from this very effervescence, that the religious idea seems to be born" (Durkheim, 2008: 164).

While focusing on the symbolic means that he conceived of as instrumental in catalyzing the social process, Durkheim came to the conclusion that the semantic properties of these means can vary considerably between different religions: "The circle of sacred objects ... cannot be fixed once and for all; its scope varies endlessly from one religion to another. Buddhism is a religion because, in the absence of gods, it accepts the existence of sacred things" (Durkheim, 2008: 37).

This concept invites scholars to not only compare between different religions, but also to compare religions with secular institutions that might be able to produce equal (social) outcomes (Featherstone, 2010: 119; Stolz, 2010).

If one of the central functions of religion is to "set the collectivity in motion," and if tangible intermediaries are central in doing so, because "[s]ocial life ... in every aspect and throughout its history, is possible only thanks to a vast body of symbolism" (Durkheim, 2008: 177), it seems reasonable to argue that marketing capitalism has spawned a mighty opponent for traditional religions. By providing products and infrastructures that serve as imaginatively up-valued intermediaries for social action and as attractive opportunity structures in which to realize social relations, the consumer market might be able to replace traditional religions as the main providers of the symbolic material necessary to reproduce social life.

From this it follows that if both consumption and religion fulfill social purposes, and if an increase in purchasing power means that individuals incrementally increase their engagement in consumption-related leisure activities, they should, correspondingly, incrementally decrease their attendance at traditional religious services.

Analyses: The Development of Income, Consumption-Related Leisure Activities, and Church Attendance Among German Catholics

In what follows, I test the above delineated hypothesis by means of empirical analyses using longitudinal panel data from the German Socio-Economic Panel (SOEP, 1984–2009). The analyses focus on the question of how the development of purchasing power relates with changes in consumption-related leisure activities and church attendance behavior.

In order to empirically treat this question, I use a subsample from the unbalanced SOEP data consisting of individuals from Western Germany aged 18–35 years who are members of the Catholic Church. I employ these sample criteria for two reasons: first, many products, services, and infrastructures in the leisure economy aim at young, socially active groups. Moreover, the young are generally less fixed in their choice of activities (Ryder, 1985: 31); that is, individuals in the adolescent or post-adolescent life stage tend to be more willing to adopt new cultural practices. Second, in comparison with Protestant churches, the Catholic Church provides a variety of rituals, symbols, and objects explicitly aimed at integrating the individual into the community (Durkheim (1897) 1986; Weber, 1971: 104). Therefore, the competition between consumption and religion should be particularly evident in this group. When these individuals adopt consumption-related intermediaries, they should—if the hypothesis applies—cease attending religious services.

Operationalization

To test the above delineated hypothesis I use the relevant indicators to operationalize the concepts involved. These are: income, consumption-related leisure activities, and religious practice.

• To study income development, I use the net income variable available from the SOEP (1984–2009) and adjust it in terms of household members in accordance with the OECD scale (OECD, 1982). I adjust for inflation using the Consumer Price Index (OECD, 2011; Reference year: 2005).

• To examine the engagement of the sample in consumption-related leisure activities, I rely on three spare-time activities surveyed in the SOEP by means of a four-point scale (never [0], less than once per month [1], once per month [2], once per week [3]). These are a) "go to the cinema, pop or jazz concerts, dancing or disco clubs;" b) "go to the opera, classical concerts, theater, exhibitions;" and c) "do sports." Since I am not interested in differentiating between social milieus, I use an aggregated consumption-related leisure activities index (CrLA index) in the main analyses. The index bases on all three items. Its value ranges between 0 (performing none of the described activities) and 9 (attending all of them at least once per week). Due to the fact that the SOEP does not survey these leisure activities every year, I can rely on information gathered across 17 points in time between 1984 and 2009.[1]

• To operationalize for religious practice, I use the standard indicator of church attendance. The SOEP file includes this variable measured on a 4-item scale. I use the original indicator as a dependent variable in an (ordinal) regression analysis. I dichotomize the variable by aggregating the categories "every week" and "every month" to better display its development for the descriptive analyses. Since the SOEP survey only began collecting information on church attendance since 1990, I additionally draw on data from the European Value Study (EVS 1981). By applying the same sample criteria and variable specifications (monthly church attendance), I obtain additional information on church attendance for the year 1981.[2]

Analytical procedure and hypotheses

In the first step, the analyses aim to describe the development of income, consumption-related leisure activities, and church attendance across the specified timeline. If the hypothesis on the competition between consumption and religion applies, the analyses should reveal a positive correlation between income growth and respondents' engagement in consumption-oriented leisure activities, and a negative association between leisure activities and church attendance.

While the descriptive analyses are conducted on the basis of the aggregated means of the sample in terms of church attendance, income, and leisure activities, in the second analytical step, I aim to test the delineated consumption hypothesis

---

[1] Information on leisure activities is available for the following years: 1985, 1986, 1988, 1990, 1992, 1994, 1995, 1996, 1997, 1998, 1999, 2001, 2003, 2005, 2007, 2008, and 2009.

[2] Information on church attendance is available for the following years: EVS: 1981; SOEP: 1990, 1992, 1994, 1995, 1996, 1997, 1998, 1999, 2001, 2003, 2005, 2007, 2008, and 2009.

using the micro level data. Due to the fact that the Socio-Economic Panel is a longitudinal survey, I divide between two variance components: the first relates to between-individual variances, which are comprised of answers from different individuals; the second variance component relates to answers for one and the same individual, who have been surveyed at different points in time. To adequately treat these two components, I use a Random Effects regression model (Wooldridge, 2002: 257 ff).

The formal setup of the regressions is as follows: church attendance is considered as the dependent variable (4-point-scale with 0=never and 3=every week). Accordingly, in the analyses I used an ordinal regression model to adequately treat this variable.[3]

The central explanatory variable of the regressions is the CrLA index as described above. However, there are two causal relationships between the engagement in consumption-related leisure activities and church attendance that I expect to be highlighted in the analyses. First, I expect the church to operate as a "foci of activity" (Feld, 1981) that enables individuals to meet and establish social relations with other persons. Once established, these relations can be expanded to a variety of other contexts. Individuals who get to know each other in a certain setting will not necessarily restrict their future-encounters to that same setting (Allan, 1979). Rather, they may move on to other contexts—among them, the areas of consumption that the market provides: "Ties to a group are created in church and carry over in daily life. Therefore, religious people may consume more culture because of their network characteristics" (Katz-Gerro and Jaeger, 2012: 217). Therefore, I assume that there will be a positive correlation on the micro level between religious attendance and engagement in consumption-related leisure activities.

In order to methodologically separate this expected (positive) causal relationship between church attendance on leisure practices from the assumed (negative) impact of the increasing engagement in consumption-related leisure activities on church-attendance, I have to insert a second version of the index into the regression. The idea is to create a variable that provides information about the development of average leisure consumption habits among the broader peer group of these individuals. If we consider consumption-related leisure activities as social practices, the decision of whether to engage in church activities should depend on the behavior of other individuals in the peer group. That is, if most individuals increasingly engage in consumption practices and accordingly enact their social relations in these settings, the relevance of the church as a focus for social activities diminishes. As a result, individuals should cease to attend the church. To treat this effect, I construct a context variable that describes for each person the mean consumption-activity level of its possible peer group which is defined as the mean CrLA index value of the birth cohort to which an individual

---

[3]   Due to the fact that the church attendance indicator has been surveyed in the SOEP only since 1990 I can use only 14 points in time in the regression analyses.

belongs, as well as the survey year. I therefore use seven birth cohorts and five-year periods.[4] The resulting measure is available for 24 macro-level units. In the analyses, I expect the measure to be negatively associated with church attendance.

Apart from these two indicators, I additionally control for further variables that other studies have found to be relevant factors in explaining church attendance differences. These are: net income, sex, age, marital status, children in the household, education level, and occupational status (cf. Halman und Draulans, 2006; Pollack and Pickel, 2007; Hirschle, 2011).

Results: descriptive analyses

The first graph in Figure 8.1 presents results for the development of net income, and the three selected leisure activities for the time span between 1980 and 2009. It becomes obvious that the trend in leisure participation is clearly correlated with the development of net income. The steep increase in income in the 1980s is accompanied by a steep increase in activity. As soon as income stagnates in the mid-1990s, leisure activity attendance rates flatten. This is true for all values, except for the values on the sports item, which continuously climbed from 1985 to 2009. Nevertheless, regression analyses on the macro level reveal that all depicted leisure activities—including sports—are substantially correlated with net income (with R-Squares ranging from 0.86 [opera, theater, museums] to 0.65 [sports]). This leads to the conclusion that engagement not only in obvious consumption-related activities such as clubbing, concerts, and theaters, but also in sports activities is governed by the market. This is to be expected given that the market provides not only sports equipment but also sports infrastructures such as fitness studios, tennis courts, climbing gyms, and bowling centers.

The second graph in Figure 8.1 shows the development of the consumption-related leisure activities index consisting of all three leisure activity items. As expected, the value of the index continually climbs—with a short drop in 1998—between 1985 and 2009. In the same graph, the development of monthly church attendance was inserted, revealing that the curves run in opposite directions. While the leisure-consumption index rises from an average rate of 3.5 in 1985 to over 4.3 in 2009, the proportion of the sample attending religious services at least monthly falls sharply from 40 percent in 1981 to around 14 percent in 2009. A bivariate regression analyses conducted on the macro level reveals that the consumption index explains for 83 percent of the variance of the church attendance indicator on the timeline.

Figure 8.2 provides an impression on the development of the involvement in consumption-related leisure activities and church attendance on the level of birth cohorts. Comparing the seven cohorts across the three age categories reveals that the steep decline in religious attendance by cohort (the earlier born, the lower

---

    [4]   Cohorts born 1950–54, 1955–59, 1960–64, 1965–69, 1970–74, 1975–79, 1980–84, and 1985–89. Year-groups: 1984–89, 1990–94, 1995–99, 2000–2004, and 2005–2009.

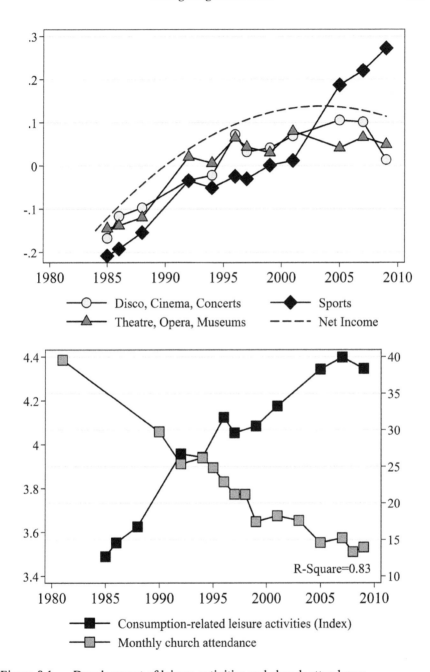

Figure 8.1   Development of leisure activities and church attendance
Data source: GSOEP 1985–2009; EVS 1981
Note: Yearly values for each consumption-related leisure activity (left graph) have been subtracted by mean values (over all years).

the average of monthly church attendance) is clearly accompanied by an increase in the mean values on the leisure consumption index. Waning engagement in religious-related activities is balanced, it seems, by an increase in engagement in consumption-related leisure activities.

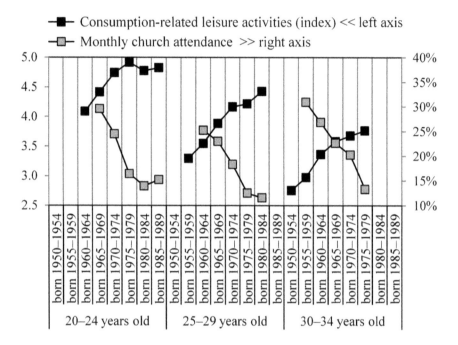

Figure 8.2   Consumption-related leisure activities and church attendance by age groups and birth cohorts

Data source: GSOEP 1985–2009

Results: random effects panel analyses

The results of the bivariate analyses show—in accordance with the consumption hypothesis—first, that the engagement in the selected leisure activities is positively correlated with increasing purchasing power; and second, that with increasing involvement in leisure activities, religious service attendance declines. In the following analyses I examine these correlations by means of panel regression analyses.

Table 8.1 presents the results from these analyses. It includes two ordinal random effects regression models with church attendance as the dependent variable. Model 1 includes all micro-level explanatory/control variables.

The results reveal a positive correlation between sex (female) and religious practice, which is well-known from the literature and cannot at this point be addressed in more detail (cf. Collett and Lizardo, 2009). Also positively correlated with church attendance is marital status (married). Because the number of couples in Germany who live together without being married has increased in recent decades (Meyer, 2006: 336), it seems reasonable to assume that those who marry are more traditionally oriented. Moreover, because the sample consists only of Catholics, those who have married have probably celebrated a church wedding, which (re) connects individuals to the church. The positive effect of the variable "children in household" can be interpreted in a similar way. Baptism and communion not only socialize the child to a particular religion, but these rites of passage also strengthen the ties of the parents to the church by prompting them to participate in religious services. The interpretation of the negative effect of higher education on religious service participation is more complicated. Certainly, it is possible to interpret this from the perspective of secularization theory as a consequence of enlightenment. On the other hand, other studies have shown that education *per se* is not necessarily negatively correlated with religiosity or church attendance (Hirschle, 2011: 278; Halman and Draulan, 2006: 279). Another explanation is that individuals with university entrance qualification (Abitur) are more likely to have moved to another region to study. As a consequence, they are removed from their place of origin, their family, and their community network, and therefore are also removed from a social milieu whereby individuals are more likely to attend religious services.

The last significant coefficient in Model 1 stems from the consumption-related leisure activities index. As expected, the CrLA index is positively associated with the dependent variable. This effect should, however, be interpreted with caution. As delineated above, one must not assume, as the formal set-up of the regression implies, engagement in consumption-oriented leisure activities will actually increase an individual's likelihood of attending church. Rather, the positive coefficient is probably a result of church attendance increasing the probability with which individuals participate in other social contexts. As scholars in the field of the study on social capital have empirically determined, the church is a source of social contacts that are extended to other activity contexts (Katz-Gerro and Jaeger, 2012: 217). Church attendance, in other words, is likely not the result, but rather the cause, of individuals' engagement in other leisure activities.

In order to treat this central question surrounding the impact and the causal relationship between church attendance and leisure consumption in more detail, I employed an additional regression model using a context-level version of the leisure-consumption index as an explanatory variable. The measure was constructed as described above: it provides information about the development of the average leisure consumption habits of the broader peer group of these individuals, operationalized on the basis of birth cohorts and the year that the survey was conducted.

Table 8.1   Random effects regressions with church attendance as dependent variable

	Model 1				Model 2			
	b	beta	se		b	beta	se	
Age	-0.007	-0.034	(0.004)		-0.034	-0.177	(0.006)	***
Sex (female=1)	0.170	0.085	(0.056)	**	0.141	0.070	(0.053)	**
Marital status (married=1)	0.313	0.152	(0.044)	***	0.289	0.141	(0.044)	***
Children under 14 in household	0.159	0.077	(0.042)	***	0.159	0.077	(0.042)	***
Education (Abitur=1)	-0.266	-0.120	(0.048)	***	-0.238	-0.108	(0.047)	***
Employment status (employed=1)	-0.025	-0.012	(0.032)		-0.043	-0.021	(0.032)	
Adjusted net household income	0.000	-0.011	(0.000)		0.000	-0.011	(0.000)	
CrLA index (micro level)	0.108	0.227	(0.008)	***	0.111	0.235	(0.008)	***
CrLA index (macro level)					-0.385	-0.232	(0.065)	***
Threshold 1	0.046				-2.281			
Threshold 2	2.082				-0.244			
Threshold 3	3.207				0.881			
Random Effects (Intercept)		0.709	(0.007)			0.708	(0.007)	
Number of observations		15,006				15,006		
Number of groups		3,533				3,533		
Average number of observations/group		4.2				4.2		
Log likelihood		-13698				-13681		

Data Source: GSOEP 1985–2009.

* p < 0.05, ** p < 0.01, *** p < 0.001.

Model 2 in Table 8.1 presents the results of the regression analyses with the additional context variable. As expected, the effect coefficient of the leisure-consumption indicator on the macro level is strongly negative and highly significant. Against the background of these results (significant positive association of the measure on the micro level and negative impact on the macro level) it seems likely that, as argued above, two causal relations are simultaneously at work: on the one hand, individuals who regularly attend churches are more likely to attend leisure activities; on the other hand, with increasing engagement of individuals in consumption-related leisure activities, the church loses its social significance as a context to meet, commune, and celebrate. As soon as the peer group discovers other settings that act as more attractive places to engage in social relations, the individual will slowly cease attending the church—or as the analyses demonstrate, it is even more likely that these individuals will simply not attend the church at all from the outset (cf. Figure 8.2). This is probably not an explicit decision against attending churches or religiosity in general; rather, consumption absorbs (and reassembles) social life (by its own means). For the individual, this results in a situation where, in order to participate in peer group activities, he has no other choice but to attend the contexts that the consumer market provides.

Conclusion

The aim of this study was to theoretically and empirically account for the impact of economic growth on religious change. I have argued that under conditions of affluence, economic development entails an increasing commodification of social activities due to an expansion and refinement of marketing techniques of companies. By adding cultural values to profane products, and by establishing infrastructures of consumption, the market incrementally provides symbolic intermediaries and opportunity structures that enable individuals to engage in social action. The participation in consumption-related leisure activities is therefore not just a hedonistic activity of pleasure-seeking, but also has (in a consumer society) become a basic practice through which to enact social relations.

Adopting this perspective ultimately traces the study of consumption back to the roots of classical sociology and Durkheim's treatise on *The Elementary Forms of Religious Life*. Durkheim analyzed the religious system as an eminently social issue, and determined, in a positivistic manner, the concrete means that set collectivity in motion. He envisioned religions mainly as providers of tangible intermediaries that enable individuals to initiate and reproduce social relations. In this sense, religion is instrumental in creating society because it catalyzes the social process from the bottom up.

Taking into account that the market provides a range of products (including infrastructures and services) that also serve as tangible intermediaries in the social process, I have argued that consumption has incrementally advanced into a market segment that was previously dominated by religious products. From this stance, the results are closely aligned to the hypothesis that waning church attendance rates are a result of the economy gaining ground in the market for symbolic and tangible social conductors. If individuals increasingly meet and commune in the various contexts that the market offers, the propensity to engage in religious activities should, in fact, gradually decline.

In the empirical part of the study, I have tested this hypothesis on a sample of German Catholics aged 18 to 35 years. Results reveal that the causal relationship between religious participation and involvement in consumption-oriented leisure activities is probably two-sided.

The bivariate analyses, relying on macro level data, revealed a significant negative correlation between leisure-consumption activities and religious attendance on the timeline between 1980 and 2009. The same was found when controlling for age across different birth cohorts. The earlier the respondents were born, the more they were engaged in consumption-related leisure activities, and the less they were involved in religious activities.

On the other hand, the panel regressions revealed a positive relation between engagement in leisure consumption and church attendance on the individual level (that is, between individuals and within the life-course of one and the same individual). While this offers an opportunity for a variety of interpretations, I suggested that this result can best be accounted for when considering that the association between the two variables is governed by two different principles. First, churches strengthen the social capital of those who attend them. Since the engagement in many consumption-related leisure activities normally require social contacts with other individuals (going to discos, vacations, concerts, theater, museums), individuals attending churches are also more likely to engage in leisure activities. Second, the push effect from attending church on participating in consumption-related leisure activities is one-sided. While individuals regularly attending churches may also engage in consumption-related leisure activities, participation in the latter activity schemes do not—for those who do not regularly go to churches—cause an increased likelihood of doing so. On the contrary, since both contexts enable individuals to participate in social interactions with increasing average engagement of the peer group in leisure consumption activities, the church incrementally loses its role as a significant setting in which to engage socially.

Chapter 9

Is There Such a Thing as Religious Brand Loyalty?

Haytham Siala

Introduction

Brand equity and brand loyalty have been cited in the extant literature as representing measures of customer loyalty towards a particular brand of products or product range (Taylor, Celuch, and Goodwin, 2004; Bloemer and Kasper, 1995). Brand equity is the value that accrues for a product that has a brand name compared with the value that it would accrue if the same product did not have a brand name and it can be measured by testing if consumers are willing to pay a premium for a branded product when a cheaper unbranded product is available. Researchers and marketing experts contend that companies often undermine the importance of a brand and that companies should consider a brand to be one of the most valuable assets of a company (Neumeier, 2006; Stolowy, Haller, and Klockhaus, 2001).

Brand loyalty, a prominent dimension of brand equity usually manifests in two different forms—*attitudinal brand loyalty and behavioral brand loyalty*—the former being a precursor to the latter (Russell-Bennett, McColl-Kennedy, and Coote, 2007; Anderson and Sullivan, 1993; Taylor, Celuch, and Goodwin, 2004; Bloemer and Kasper, 1995). Behavioral loyalty is concerned with observable actions such as repeat patronage (Ehrenberg, 2000; Anderson and Sullivan, 1993; Russell-Bennett, McColl-Kennedy, and Coote, 2007). Attitudinal brand loyalty reflects an affective attachment towards a product or brand (Bandyopadhyay and Martella, 2007; Bloemer and Kasper, 1995; Baldinger and Rubinson, 1996) that can subsequently translate into an intention to purchase a product or service (Russell-Bennett, McColl-Kennedy, and Coote, 2007; Taylor, Celuch, and Goodwin, 2004).

Group affinities and ingrained cultural values can sometimes affect consumers' lifestyles and shopping trends (Solomon *et al.*, 2007; Schiffman and Kanuk, 2009; Essoo and Dibb, 2004). Religious groups in collectivist cultures usually dictate what is an acceptable or prohibited behavior to their in-group members and the devout followers of such religious groups usually respond with strict compliance with the rules set by the group (Iannaccone, 1995; Stark and Glock, 1968; Schwartz, 1992).

The religious consumer market seems to have developed into an auspicious business venture. The Christian market in the USA is estimated to be worth

$7.5 billion (Packaged Facts, 2006) and the global Muslim market is estimated to be worth $2 trillion (A.T. Kearney, 2007). Some researchers contend that a person's extent of religious commitment to a collectivist religion could significantly affect his/her buying behavior across a broad range of products and services (Delener, 1990; Schiffman and Kanuk, 2009; Essoo and Dibb, 2004). For example, some religions impose mandatory dietary constraints on their followers (Islam and Judaism prohibit the consumption of pork to their members). This research study attempts to investigate the impact of religious commitment on the development of attitudinal brand loyalty towards religiously-compliant high-involvement products and services. High-involvement products are perceived to be high-risk items such as white goods and indemnity services that require extensive information search before a purchase decision is made (Solomon *et al.*, 2007) such as a car insurance or a life insurance (Martin, 1998).

The literature surveyed in this research study shows no signs of specific requirements or religious edicts that dictate what constitutes a "religiously conforming" high-involvement product or service in Christianity, Judaism, and other monotheistic religions. However, in Islam there is an element of a religious prescription that an indemnity service has to meet which is defined by the broader rule of *Halal* and the more specific principle of *Takaful*.

Literature Review

Religiosity

The term religiosity refers to a measure of the extent of religious commitment towards a religious group (Stark and Glock, 1968). Trust and affinity with religious groups is usually nurtured by cultural values, which are passed on and reinforced through the teachings of parents and the older generation, and the preaching of senior religious leaders such as Imams (Islam), Bishops or Reverends (Christianity), and Rabbis (Judaism). Since religious values are ingrained sacred relics and practices, devout followers of a religion are expected to conform consistently to the norms and rules dictated by their religion (Stark and Glock, 1968; Devos, Spini, and Schwartz, 2002).

Religious edicts that emanate from prominent scholars in Islam can result in boycotts of products, companies, or services. For example, a famous controversial allegation was made against the *Coca Cola* trademark that if the trademark was read in reverse it translates into the defamatory Arabic words "*No Mohammed No Mecca.*" This allegation had caused on a global scale a heated controversy in the Muslim community (Solomon *et al.*, 2007). Findings from another research study have corroborated the premise that antagonistic religious edicts issued by religious leaders can have a devastating impact on a company's revenues and market shares in the local market where it operates (Knudsen, Aggarwal, and Maamoun, 2008).

Religious centrism

Research findings from multi-disciplinary sources indicate that members of minority groups are more likely to trust salesmen (Deshpande and Stayman, 1994; Riggins, 1992) and organizations (Bonne and Verbeke, 2008) from their own ethnic or religious group and that this enhanced credibility can in turn translate into positive brand attitudes (Deshpande and Stayman, 1994; Riggins, 1992). Religious centrism (or religio-centrism) is defined as the extent to which religious identification affects a consumer's buying habits, in particular the extent to which a consumer is inclined to buy from within their own religious group (Siala, O'Keefe, and Hone, 2004).

Religious consumer segments and markets

The religious consumer market has become a lucrative and worthwhile investment. The American religious consumer market alone has attracted $7.5 billion in revenues; the product list includes religiously exclusive products such as books and audio-visual materials (Packaged Facts, 2006). The global Muslim market is estimated to be worth $2 trillion annually and the religiously exclusive Muslim financial products (banking, mortgages, insurance, etc.) in that market are estimated to be worth a whopping $400 billion with an annual growth of 15 percent (A.T. Kearney, 2007).

Despite these interesting findings and the auspicious prospects of the religious consumer market, the effect of religion on consumer behavior remains an under-researched topic. There is a paucity of articles that have explored the effect of religion on consumer interactions (Delener, 1990; Douglas and Samuel Craig, 1997) and consumer purchasing decisions (Essoo and Dibb, 2004) but there were hardly any recent articles that focus on consumers' purchasing behavior and perceptions of religiously tailored products, services, and brands.

Halal and Takaful

Halal is a Muslim religious certification that is used to endorse a product or service as being religiously compliant with the requirements and pillars of Islam (Sharia law). The concept of Takaful is a core element in defining the indemnity products and services market that is compliant with the Muslim religion. Takaful is based on a not-for-profit community insurance concept where policyholders commit to pay a subscription to help those who may suffer a loss or damage in the future. Each member is bound by an agreement to fulfill his obligation of mutual cooperation. The costs and liabilities are absorbed into the community pool and spread fairly across the community members when an accident happens to one of the fellow participants. Usurious interest rates are prohibited and uncertainty is regarded as an inevitable part of destiny.

There are already a growing number of Western and Muslim companies in various sectors that have commenced addressing the Muslim consumers' needs by launching and selling an array of Halal-compliant merchandise, brands, and indemnity services. For example, HSNC Amanah, a specialized subsidiary of HSBC plc provides Halal-based financial services to Muslim customers. Similarly, Nestlé Malaysia, the Halal-compliant arm of Nestlé has been launched in 1996 to cater for the rapidly growing Halal food-and-beverages consumer market segment (A.T. Kearney, 2007).

Brand loyalty

Brand loyalty in its behavioral form is represented by repeat purchasing behavior reflecting a conscious decision to continue buying the same brand (Ehrenberg, 2000; Anderson and Sullivan, 1993) despite situational influences and competitors' marketing attempts to switch brand-loyal consumers to another brand (Oliver, 1999; Yim and Kannan, 1999). Some researchers have asserted that the uni-dimensional model of behavioral brand loyalty to be an incomplete measure of overall brand loyalty and they suggested the addition of an attitudinal dimension to the measurement model to make it a more practical construct (Dick and Basu, 1994; Baldinger and Rubinson, 1996).

   Attitudinal loyalty is an affective commitment towards a brand (Bloemer and Kasper 1995) that manifests as a positive feeling or attitude towards a product (Dick and Basu 1994) and this positive attitude together with previous purchase satisfaction could eventually translate into repeat purchasing—i.e. behavioral brand loyalty (Russell-Bennett, McColl-Kennedy, and Coote, 2007; Anderson and Sullivan, 1993), price tolerance (willingness to pay more), and positive word-of-mouth communication about the company or brand (Srinivasan, Anderson, and Ponnavolu, 2002; Gounaris and Stathakopoulos, 2004).

Conceptual Framework and Methodology

The main objective of this study is to investigate consumers' likelihood of developing brand loyalty towards a religiously-compliant high-involvement product or service. Most religiously exclusive high-involvement products and services such as the Amanah mortgage are provided by financial institutions that are quite strict with making their customers' sensitive data available for research purposes. After conducting some extensive research for a high-involvement product and service that can be used to test the premise of religious brand loyalty, we have come across a company, Salaaminsurance.com, that claims to sell a religiously exclusive car insurance service online to Muslim customers and consequently it was selected to test the various hypotheses that are posited in this research study.

   A questionnaire was developed to conduct an online survey. The first part of the questionnaire includes demographic questions, questions assessing a participant's extent of familiarity with Internet technologies, whether they have purchased items online before on the Internet and finally, the constituent items representing the exogenous religious measurement constructs (religiosity and religio-centrism). Schisms in Islam led to the emergence of various factions and sects such as the Shia and Sunni sects. Consequently, since the results from the Muslim participants cannot be generalized on a single group, the survey questionnaire will contain a section where participants identify the Muslim sect they affiliate to. This will help the researcher in attributing any significant results to the religious sect or denomination of the participants. The second part of the questionnaire contains the constituent items representing the endogenous measurement constructs that will be tested in this study.

Research hypotheses

The relationship between the exogenous and endogenous measurement constructs represents the various hypotheses that will be tested in this research study. Figure 9.1 illustrates the conceptual model of this research study.

It is a common belief that devout followers of a collectivist religion are more likely to make purchase decisions that conform to the rules defined by their religious doctrines (Schiffman and Kanuk, 2009; Delener, 1990; Essoo and Dibb, 2004). According to Iannaccone (1995), monotheistic religions such as Islam, Judaism, and Christianity exhibit the traits of a collectivist culture. In addition, research findings from multi-disciplinary sources indicate that members of minority groups are more likely to trust salesmen or organizations from their own religious groups and this enhanced credibility can in turn translate into positive brand attitudes and loyalty (Deshpande and Stayman, 1994; Riggins, 1992). Religious commitment can be represented by two constructs: religiosity and religious centrism. Religiosity gauges an individual's extent of commitment to his/her religion for example by performing the daily prayers on a regular basis (Stark and Glock, 1968). Religious centrism looks at an individual's extent of commercial patronage towards one's religion, which is reflected by customers' exclusively buying products or services from a company that is owned or managed by someone who shares the same religion as the customer (Siala, O'Keefe, and Hone, 2004). On the basis of the aforementioned discussions we propose the following research hypotheses:

H1a: Customers who are devout Muslims will display high attitudinal loyalty towards a company selling religiously exclusive high-involvement products or services.

H1b: Customers who are highly religio-centric will display high attitudinal loyalty towards a Muslim company that sells religiously exclusive high-involvement products or services.

Although there may seem to be an apparent and natural link between being religious and being loyal towards the rules set by one's religion, the contention that H1a and H1b may be self-evident can be challenged by the following arguments 1) not all devout religious members are necessarily religio-centric; 2) religious consumers may perceive the religiously exclusive product or service that is sold online by a company as a cynical marketing ploy and therefore their trust could at best translate into brand parity instead of "religious" brand loyalty.

Attitudinal brand loyalty reflects an affective attachment or positive disposition towards a product or brand (Bandyopadhyay and Martella, 2007; Baldinger and Rubinson, 1996; Dick and Basu, 1994), which can subsequently translate into an intention to purchase a product or service (Russell-Bennett, McColl-Kennedy, and Coote, 2007; Anderson and Sullivan, 1993; Taylor, Celuch, and Goodwin, 2004). Brand loyal customers are individuals who would continuously buy a certain brand of a product even when there is an increase in the price of that product (Bandyopadhyay and Martella, 2007; Taylor, Celuch, and Goodwin, 2004; Yim and Kannan, 1999). Therefore, the following hypothesis is posited:

> H2: Customers who display high attitudinal loyalty towards a religiously-exclusive high-involvement product or service will be price tolerant (inelastic) when a cheaper "generic" substitute brand is available from a competitor.
>
> Attitudinal loyalty could eventually translate into re-purchasing behavior and positive word-of-mouth communication about the company selling the brand in question (Srinivasan, Anderson, and Ponnavolu, 2002; Gounaris and Stathakopoulos, 2004; Dick and Basu, 1994) and thus, the following hypothesis is posited:

> H3: Customers who display high attitudinal loyalty towards a company selling religiously exclusive high-involvement products or services will spread good word-of-mouth communication about the company to fellow customers.

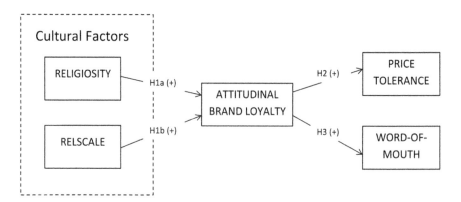

Figure 9.1   The conceptual model of this research study

Questionnaire design and measurement scales

The questionnaire consisted of 43 items in total. Items representing the various constructs were drawn from multi-disciplinary sources from the literature. Most items of the measurement constructs were based on five-point Likert scales except for the PIS construct which uses a mix of seven-point Likert scales and semantic differential scales (Mittal 1989). To counter for the response set of acquiescence, some of the Likert scale ratings and the direction of the wording of some of the items were reversed (DeVellis, 1991; Podsakoff *et al.*, 2003).

Although the number of items has slightly exceeded the recommended quota of forty for online surveys (Szymanski and Hise, 2000), the researcher hopes that the hypothetical respondents' fatigue bias effect (Szymanski and Hise, 2000) can be offset by the set of incentives that will be offered to the prospective participants. A "face validity" test was conducted on the questionnaire (Litwin and Fink, 1995), which involved presenting the questionnaire to two subject-matter experts from two British universities. The feedback from the subject-matter experts has resulted into rephrasing some of the items on the questionnaire. A paper-based version of the amended questionnaire was subsequently administered to 15 participants in a local mosque in South London and the final comments of the volunteers were noted. Although most of the participants found the time taken to complete the survey to be acceptable, the majority were reluctant in answering a question that asked the participants to note down the car insurance quotes that they got from their existing insurer and the religiously exclusive insurer. A possible explanation to the participants' reluctance to disclose the insurance premiums is that the participants might suspect that the insurance premiums reflect the number of accidents or traffic offences that they may have committed with their vehicles. Although the question represents a direct measure of price tolerance, the researcher has consequently decided to discard that question from the final version of the questionnaire.

Table 9.1 shows the various measurement constructs that were used to test the hypotheses in this research study.

Table 9.1 Measurement constructs used in this research study

Construct	Description	Sample Item
RELIG	Measures the extent of religious commitment (adapted from Glock and Stark 1965; Stark and Glock 1968).	How important is religion to your way of live and your daily decisions?
RELSCALE	Measures the extent of religious centrism (Siala, O'Keefe, and Hone 2004), which was adapted from the established measure of consumer ethnocentrism (Shimp and Sharma 1987) so that it referred to religion rather than ethnicity	I only shop from places selling religiously exclusive products and services (e.g. Halal shops).

Construct	Description	Sample Item
PIS	The Purchase-decision Involvement Scale (PIS) (adapted from Mittal 1989)	How important would it be for you to make the right choice of a car insurance?
ALOY	Measures the extent of attitudinal loyalty towards a product or service sold online (adapted from Srinivasan, Anderson, and Ponnavolu 2002). The original scale also includes a couple of items that measure consumers' purchasing intentions	I believe that this is my favorite insurance website.
WOM	The WOM (Word-of-mouth) scale measures word-of-mouth recommendations (adapted from Srinivasan, Anderson, and Ponnavolu 2002)	I will say positive things about this website to other people
PRICE	The PRICE scale measures the extent to which a customer is willing to pay more (price tolerance) for a certain brand (adapted from Srinivasan, Anderson, and Ponnavolu 2002).	Will you pay a higher price at this website if a competitor offers the same benefits?

Data Analysis and Results

Survey

The online survey was conducted in September 2009. Participants were invited by 1) e-mailing online religious community groups, and 2) placing fliers on the notice boards of various mosques in the UK. To save on commuting costs and time, mosques outside the London area were contacted via email and phone to obtain their permission for publishing the flier on their notice boards by one of their members. An incentive scheme was devised to increase the number of participants (Biner and Kidd, 1994; Hoffman *et al.*, 1998). The *pay-per-participant* charity incentive scheme was adopted for this study and a note was placed on the flier and the invitation email informing the participants that for each completed survey, a £1 donation would go to the Muslim charity of their choice. The survey was executed in separate time frames to counter the demand artifact effect (Malhotra, 2010; Podsakoff *et al.*, 2003). Participants were first asked to fill in a short questionnaire that consists of questions representing the exogenous constructs, demographic data, and the contact details of each participant (email). Three weeks later, each registered respondent was informed via email about the religiously-exclusive insurance website (salaaminsurance.com) and subsequently, a month later an email containing a URL link to the second and final part of the survey questionnaire was sent to the registered respondents, which mainly consists of items representing the endogenous measurement constructs.

Sample characteristics

The sample consists of 208 participants. Most of the participants were Asian individuals who are employed full-time, well-educated, and predominantly follow the Muslim Sunni school of thought. The age of the participants ranges between 21 and 40. Males constituted 54 percent of the sample population, while the proportion of females was 46 percent. The researcher will need to take into consideration the religious denomination bias when interpreting the results since generalizing the results to the general Muslim population could lead to inaccurate conclusions and findings.

Construct reliability

The most common test for a construct's internal reliability is Cronbach alpha (Cronbach, 1951). However, more recently composite reliability (CR) (Malhotra, 2010; Hair, 2010) and Jorekog's Rho (Jöreskog and Sörbom, 2002) have become more pertinent measures of construct reliability in research studies that utilize SEM (structural equation modeling) and CFA (confirmatory factor analysis) as part of their data analysis. There is a consensus in the literature that a score of 0.7 or higher is indicative of a construct's reliability (Hair, 2010; Nunnally, 1978; Malhotra, 2010).

A bespoke statistical Microsoft Excel plug-in tool was used in conjunction with the AMOS statistical software to calculate the CR scores for each measurement scale. Table 9.2 shows that the composite reliability scores of the measurement scales were above the threshold of 0.7 and thus all the scales were retained for subsequent data analyses.

Construct validity

A construct validity test examines the extent to which a set of items (e.g. questionnaire) of a scale measure the theoretical construct that they claim to be representing (Churchill, 1979). Testing of construct validity concentrates not only on finding out whether an item loads significantly on the factor it is measuring (convergent validity) but also on ensuring that it does not significantly load across or measure other factors (discriminant validity) (Campbell and Fiske, 1959). It is argued that the convergent significant loadings of items on a separate factor (DeVellis, 1991) and an AVE (Average Variance Extracted) score of greater than 0.5 (Hair, 2010; Malhotra, 2010) are indicative measures of a construct's convergent validity. The discriminant validity of a latent construct can be tested by checking whether the AVE score of the latent construct is greater than the squared correlation value that exists between this construct and another that it correlates with (Malhotra, 2010).

An exploratory factor analysis was performed on the constituent items representing the different constructs to see if they are valid. The Principal Components method of extraction was adopted with Direct Oblimin rotation since

Religions as Brands

the exogenous constructs are expected to be correlated (Kline, 1994). During the analysis only factors loading on three or more items were retained following the advice of Tabachnick and Fidell (2007).

The results of the factor analysis showed significant loadings of the items on separate factors. Table 9.2 shows that the AVE value of each latent construct is greater than 0.5 and that it is also greater than the squared correlation value, affirming the convergent and discriminant validity of the latent constructs. In light of these results, since the latent constructs have satisfied the criteria for both construct validity and reliability, all items representing the latent constructs were retained in the final questionnaire.

Table 9.2   Composite Reliability (CR), Average Variance Extracted (AVE) and Squared Correlation Matrix scores for the measurement scales

Construct	CR	AVE	1	2	3	4	5	6
1. RELIG	.96 (*N*=17)	.87	1					
2. RELSCALE	.89 (*N*=7)	.83	.275	1				
3. PIS	.79 (*N*=8)	.68	.036	.056	1			
4. ALOY	.97 (*N*=7)	.84	.345	.380	.030	1		
5. WOM	.92 (*N*=4)	.81	.025	.036	.016	.228	1	
6. PRICE	.91 (*N*=4)	.78	.017	.027	.004	.295	.066	1

Where *N* = Number of items

Values in the correlation matrix are the square of the original correlations

Common method bias

Common method bias (CMB) refers to a bias in a dataset that can be caused by exploratory studies using a single method to collect data from the same participants in a sample (Podsakoff *et al.*, 2003). The data for this research study was collected from one source of participants using a single method (an online survey), and therefore to test for common method bias in our dataset, a Harman's single factor test was performed in an exploratory factor analysis (Malhotra, Kim, and Patil, 2006; Podsakoff *et al.*, 2003). The result of the Harman single-factor analysis test showed that the single factor accounted for only 17.3 percent of the total variance in the solution, and thus one can assume that the effect of CMB on this study's dataset is negligible.

Car insurance as a high-involvement purchase decision

Mittal's (1989) Purchase-decision Involvement Scale (PIS) was adopted in this research study to test whether the decision to buy a Halal car insurance service is of the high-involvement type. A simple descriptive statistics test was performed on the PIS scale to test if the mean score of the sample for the PIS scale is significantly different from the expected mean of the scale. The sample mean score for the PIS scale was found to be 5.89, which is significantly higher than the expected mean value of 3.5 (the middle point of the seven point PIS scale) and thus, one can conclude that the sample considers a car insurance to be a high-involvement purchase decision.

Structural equation modeling

Malhotra (2010) contends that the minimum sample size for conducting an SEM (Structural Equation Modeling) analysis on measurement models that utilize up to five latent constructs is 200. The hypothetical model of this research study consists of five latent constructs and the sample size was 208. Since the hypothetical model of this research study meets Malhotra's (2010) criteria, AMOS 12 was used to test the goodness-of-fit of the measurement variables using the maximum likelihood estimation method. A preliminary examination for outliers, multicollinearity, homoscedasticity, heterostadicity, and normality was performed prior to the statistical analyses of the data. None of the tests have revealed anomalies in the data.

The parameter estimates of the standardized solution that were generated by the SEM test were significant at the p <.05 level. Various goodness-of-fit measures (Bagozzi and Yi, 1988) were used to test the hypothetical model and judging from the results (see Table 9.3), one can deduce that the hypothetical model has achieved an acceptable "goodness-of-fit."

Table 9.3   Goodness-of-fit and badness-of-fit measures

GFI	SEM	Criterion	Reference
Goodness-of-Fit			
Absolute fit			
GFI	.97	>.9	(Bagozzi and Yi, 1988)
AGFI	.94	>.9	
Incremental fit			
NFI	.98	>.95	(Hu and Bentler, 1999)
CFI	.96	>.95	
Badness-of-Fit			
Chi-square	1486.58		
Df	701		
p (Chi-square)	.0	>.05	(Jöreskog and Sörbom, 2002)
RMR	.013	<.05	
RMSEA	.031	<.10	(Browne and Cudeck, 1993)

Results of hypotheses testing

The three hypotheses—hypothesis 1a, hypothesis 1b, hypothesis 2 and hypothesis 3—were tested by examining the path coefficients that were calculated by the SEM analysis. All the structural path coefficients in Table 9.4 are significant and thus support the hypotheses that are posited in this study. Hypothesis 1a suggests that religiosity has a positive effect on attitudinal brand loyalty towards a company selling a religiously conforming high-involvement product or service. The coefficient that measures the relationship between the constructs in Hypothesis 1a is 0.584 with a t-value of 21.82 (significant at $p < .01$); strongly supporting hypothesis 1a. Similarly, hypothesis 1b is supported by the measured coefficient of 0.648 with a t-value of 23.97 (significant at $p < .01$) implying that religious centrism has a significant impact on the formation of attitudinal brand loyalty towards a Muslim company selling a religiously conforming high-involvement product or service. In the context of this study, since the attitudinal brand loyalty includes measures for purchasing intentions, the findings so far indicate that devout Muslim customers who display high attitudinal brand loyalty towards a company selling religiously-conforming high-involvement products or services could potentially switch to the "religious" brand that is provided by the company.

Hypothesis 2 which proposes that attitudinal brand loyalty can increase price tolerance is supported since the measured coefficient is .878 with a *t*-value of 26.36 (significant at $p < .01$). Finally, Hypothesis 3 suggests that attitudinal brand loyalty can result into positive word-of-mouth feedback from customers. The measured coefficient for the constructs representing the hypothetical relationship in hypothesis 3 is .898 with a *t*-value of 29.32 (significant at $p < .01$) and thus, hypothesis 3 is also supported.

Table 9.4   Estimates of structural path coefficients for the exogenous and endogenous constructs

Hypothesis and Effect	Proposed Effect	Coefficient	*t*-value	Is the hypothesis supported?
H1a: RELIG → ALOY	+	.584	21.82**	Y
H1b: RELSCALE → ALOY	+	.648	23.97**	Y
H2: ALOY → PRICE	+	.878	26.36**	Y
H3: ALOY → WOM	+	.898	29.32**	Y

$*p < .05$ level; $**p < .01$ level; $***p < .001$ level

Conclusion

The data analysis conducted on a sample of Muslim participants indicates that devout Muslim consumers display high attitudinal loyalty towards a company selling religiously exclusive indemnity services and that they consider the decision to buy a car insurance to be of the high-involvement type. In addition, the empirical findings of this study have shown that Muslim participants who display high attitudinal loyalty towards a company selling a religiously-compliant brand were price tolerant and they were willing to recommend the company to others. Since attitudinal brand loyalty includes measures for purchasing intentions, one can infer that this culturally induced loyalty could make religious consumers switch from an existing "generic" brand to a religiously-conforming brand.

The aforementioned results are interesting because 1) the product under investigation is a religiously commoditized product that is sold on the basis of price and the terms and conditions that are associated with the product and 2) the respondent group are technology savvy and well educated and thus are relatively capable of utilizing the Internet to search for cheaper "religionless" alternatives. Finally, due to the similarity between this research study's model and the TRA (Fishbein and Ajzen, 1975) and TRB (Ajzen, 1991) models, one can argue that the findings of this study suggest extending the TRA and TRB models by incorporating a new religious dimension to the existing attitude-intention relationship saga.

Managerial implications

The findings of this research study suggest that religion can have a significant impact on consumers' choice when purchasing a high-involvement product or service. Given the fact that religious values persist over time, there are some potential long-term benefits for companies that can identify lucrative religious consumer segments that are present in the local and global markets. The results of the SEM data analysis indicate that high attitudinal brand loyalty can induce price tolerance and good word-of-mouth feedback about a company selling a religiously-conforming brand. This implies that companies designing products or services that comply with the needs of religious consumers could end up benefiting from free "viral" word-of-mouth marketing and price tolerance as by-products.

There are some large companies (HSBC, Nestlé, etc.) who have exploited the religious market by designing and manufacturing products and services that are compliant with the needs of the Muslim consumers. However, the Muslim market is an emerging niche market and since many of the global consumer market segments are reaching their saturation points, SMEs can seize the opportunity to prosper from this emerging market by adopting the following strategies:

• Establishing a religiously compliant brand which could involve re-packaging the companies' existing products and services to make them consistent with the Muslim consumers' needs. For example, Nestlé introduced Halal certification across 100 of its product lines and it has also changed the manufacturing processes across 75 of its factories to make them Halal-compliant (A.T. Kearney, 2007). This profound approach of

non-camouflaged marketing emphasizes to consumers that the stages of production for the product are as religiously-compliant as the end product
- Identifying new products and services that can be based on religious elements which have not yet been addressed by other competitors. For example, Principle Insurance Company Limited in the UK saw an opportunity to innovate by selling a Sharia-compliant car insurance service (via its website Salaaminsurance.com) that is based on the concept of Takaful.

In general, companies that wish to cater for the religious consumer market should research meticulously on how to incorporate religious elements or attributes into their existing products and services and then proceed by promoting the customized brand through effective marketing campaigns that highlight how the product or service in question is consistent with the pillars of a religion. For example, charity is one of the five fundamental pillars of Islam and a company could introduce a Muslim charity fundraising scheme as an incentive to attract religious customers. The use of role models such as ministers of religions (Imams) in advertising a religiously exclusive product or service could suppress the doubts about the product or service in question being sold as a camouflaged commoditized brand.

Finally, the Muslim market should not only be perceived as a lucrative investment opportunity but it should also be looked after from an ethical or social perspective. Consumers' freedom of choice and product variety are important topics that are frequently cited in the literature of service marketing, consumer behavior, and other pertinent disciplines (Devlin, 2002; Mackay, 2000; Droge and Mackoy, 1995) and disregarding the special needs of a religious consumer segment can raise a moral or "egalitarian" consumerist debate.

Limitations

The relationship between the exogenous and endogenous constructs was tested using a high-involvement indemnity service—a car insurance. Despite the fact that all the hypotheses were accepted and that the relationships between the constructs were found to be positive, it is debatable whether these findings will replicate in other high-involvement product or service categories. Finally, the Muslim sample in this research study is comprised mainly of individuals who follow the Muslim Sunni school of thought and thus the findings and results should be interpreted with caution since they might not apply to the general Muslim population.

Avenues for future research

The set of hypotheses posited in this research study focused on attitudinal loyalty which includes the likelihood of a switch from the existing insurer and a potential purchase intention from Salaaminsurance.com. If a researcher can get hold of a religious customer base or sample that has actually purchased a religiously exclusive high involvement product or service from a company, a future research study could investigate the impact of religious factors on the behavioral loyalty of consumers which usually manifests in the form of actual repeat patronage (for example see Taylor *et al.* (2004) and J.M. Bloemer and Kasper (1995))

Finally, it would be quite interesting to conduct a research study about companies selling other religiously exclusive high-involvement products and services such as 1) a Halal mortgage (known as *Amana*) 2) religious tourism (for example flight package deals during the Muslim Hajj pilgrimage season). The results from these future studies would then confirm whether the research findings of the current study will replicate in a consistent manner in other industries.

Chapter 10

How Religious Affiliation Grouping Influences Sustainable Consumer Behavior Findings

Elizabeth Stickel-Minton

Introduction

Religious affiliation is well known for contributing to a consumer's core values (Fam, Waller, and Erdogan, 2004; Bailey and Sood, 1993), but research has failed to consider how religious affiliation, and more specifically religious affiliation grouping, might influence consumer behavior findings. Since the 1970s when religious affiliation was first introduced in consumer behavior literature (Cutler, 1991), religion and consumer behavior research has been dominated almost exclusively by correlational studies. These previous correlational studies are based on religious affiliation groupings that are convenient or prominent rather than theoretically-driven. The field is in need of a standard for measuring religious affiliation that is based on theoretical differences in religious doctrine (James, 1902/2004) and views toward inerrancy of the doctrine (Hoffmann and Bartkowski, 2008), thereby supporting the argument that religion is an individual difference variable.

One of the pioneering psychology and religion scholars identifies the relationship between God and nature as one of the key differences between religions (James, 1902/2004). Prior research also shows distinct differences among religious affiliations in doctrinal prescriptions regarding environmental and sustainable attitudes and behaviors (Sarre, 1995). Sustainability related prescriptions, in particular, are directly relevant to consumer behavior as spending on sustainable consumption is expected to increase from $28 billion in 2010 to $60 billion by 2014 (Chestney, 2010). With over 70 percent of people in the world adhering to one of the seven prominent world religions, understanding the theoretical relationship between religious affiliation as an individual difference variable and consumption behaviors, and more specifically sustainable consumption behaviors, is important and theoretically defensible (Hunt and Penwell, 2008).

Research specifically assessing religion's influence on consumer sustainability behaviors and attitudes is only adequately addressed in the religion and sociology literature (Wolkomir et al., 1997; Woodrum and Wolkomir, 1997). Therefore, this research seeks to fill a gap in the literature by assessing various religious affiliation grouping systems in the context of differences between religious groups on sustainable consumption variables (i.e., sustainable attitudes and behaviors).

Literature Review

Religious classification systems

Discussion of religion is found infrequently in the consumer behavior literature, partly due to religion's presence as a taboo, highly-sensitive topic (Mokhlis, 2006). However, for many people, the core tenants of religious affiliation represent the backbone of everyday behavior. An extensive review of the literature both in and outside the field of marketing led to 65 articles, three proceedings, and two chapters addressing religion as it relates to consumer behavior. Of these articles, 40 are specifically in marketing, with only eight in top tier marketing journals, ten in business journals, six in religion journals, five in sociology/psychology journals, and four in various fields such as tourism and health. Clearly, the study of religion in the field of consumer behavior is still underexplored. Because measurement of the religious variable in consumer behavior literature is extremely varied (Muhamad and Mizerski, 2010), this study's purpose is to assess different religious affiliation grouping systems using one set of consumer sustainability behavior variables.

A denominational grouping system is one method for classifying religious affiliation. Previous scholars have shown that the literalist ideology of denominations believing in an inerrant and infallible Bible drives behaviors, attitudes, and religious convictions based on doctrine (Hoffmann and Bartkowski, 2008). Denominations that believe that the Bible is inerrant, infallible, and the authoritative word for faith and conduct are Catholics, Baptists, and Pentecostals (Rhodes, 2005). In contrast, Methodists, Episcopalians, Lutherans, and Presbyterians believe that the Bible must be interpreted by the reader in light of tradition and human reason (Rhodes, 2005). This separation between denominations based on belief in the inerrancy of scripture also correlates with views on social and political issues, such as abortion and homosexuality, with inerrancy-supporting denominations much less likely to support abortion or homosexuality (Pew Forum on Religion and Public Life, 2008). Therefore, significant differences in attitudes and behaviors are expected between denominations based upon differences in inerrancy of the scripture and associated socio-political attitudes.

A fundamental classification system is similar to the denominational classification system being that both are developed according to views on social and political matters and scripture inerrancy. However, the fundamental classification system (Smith, 1990) fails to take slight differences in views among denominations into consideration. A meta-analysis of Judeo-Christian fundamentalism classifications by denomination reveals that Baptists and Pentecostals are fundamental believers; Catholics, Lutherans, non-denominational

Christians, and Methodists are moderate believers; and Jewish, Presbyterians, and Episcopalians are liberal believers (cf. Smith 1990, for further classification explanations). Smith's fundamental classification system has been used extensively in research involving Judeo-Christian denominations (Peterson and Liu, 2008).

Steensland *et al.* (2000)'s religious grouping system classifies denominations into six categories (Mainline Protestant, Evangelical Protestant, Black Protestant, Roman Catholic, Jewish, and Other) based on religious traditions and historical movements and was developed largely in response to Smith's (1990) fundamentalism classification. This new traditions-based religious grouping system is becoming a standard for research in religion and sociology research (Alwin *et al.*, 2006). Steensland *et al.* (2000) argue that this religious traditions classification system has numerous benefits over Smith's (1990) fundamentalism classification including increased attention to religious traditions, improved model fit, terminology that matches practice, and increased usefulness in studying religious trends.

Finally, very little theoretical support exists for a simple classification system consisting of Protestants, Catholics, Jews, and the non-religious, despite this classification system being the most frequently found in the consumer behavior literature. Differences between Catholics and Jews are possible due to differences in beliefs about inerrancy of the scripture, particularly for secularized Jews. However, grouping all Protestants together in one category for ease of segmentation with no theoretical base should lead to non-significant results.

Numerous other classification systems are used in religion and sociology research, although not found in consumer behavior or marketing research. For example, Bader and Froese (2005) suggest that religion should be measured on an individual level due to differences among believers within a denomination or a classification of Steensland *et al.* (2000). Bader and Froese (2005) recommend that individual "images of God" are created based on an individual's belief that God is judgmental, interested in an individual's actions, God's role in the world, and the character traits of God (e.g., motherly vs. fatherly). For the purposes of this study, only the four most used or most theoretically-defensible classification systems previously discussed will be analyzed: denominational, Smith's (1990) fundamentalism, Steensland *et al.* (2000) religious traditions, and simple religious grouping systems. Therefore:

H1: Steensland *et al.* (2000)'s religious traditions classification system and the denominational classification system will be the most significant predictor of consumption behavior in comparison to a fundamental and simple classification system. The fundamental classification system will be a significant predictor of consumption behavior third to that of Steensland *et al.* (2000)'s religious traditions classification system and the denominational classification system but still be far superior to the simple classification system. Finally, in comparison to the three theoretically supported classification systems, the simple classification system will not be a significant predictor of consumption attitudes and behavior.

Religion and sustainability

This study assesses differences in religious classification systems through views and participation in sustainable consumption. Sustainable consumption refers to the purchase and use of products and services that are environmentally-friendly (Prothero *et al.*, 2011), such as organic vegetables or chemical-free cleaning supplies, in addition to the disposal of products in an environmentally-friendly manner (Corraliza and Berenguer, 2000), such as recycling. Sustainable consumption is used to test differences between religious classification systems because views toward sustainability and sustainability-related values are discussed in religious scripture (Wolkomir *et al.*, 1997; Woodrum and Wolkomir, 1997).

Some of the earliest discussion of environmental behavior and religion goes back to the famous Lynn White thesis (1967). White's thesis analyzes Christian doctrine, specifically the book of Genesis in the Bible, identifying repetition of doctrine stating man's control over nature (e.g., man naming the animals, man exploiting nature for man's benefit) and purports that Christians are less environmentally-friendly as a result. White's thesis suggests that Christians that believe every word of the Bible to be true also believe that nature is to be used for the needs of man and that priority in everyday actions should be given to evangelizing rather than preserving the environment. Follow up studies confirm White's thesis linking inerrant belief in the Bible to less concern for the environment (Eckberg and Blocker, 1989).

Wolkomir *et al.* (1997) add to White's thesis by theorizing that denominational differences in beliefs about scriptural inerrancy lead to concern for the environment (i.e., a denomination strongly holding to inerrant beliefs of the scripture would be less likely to have concern for the environment than a denomination believing that interpretation of the Bible should be based on human reason). However, Wolkomir *et al.* (1997) conclude by stating that other measures of internal religious differentiation may be more effective than denominational affiliation in fully understanding the relationship between religion and sustainable attitudes and behaviors. Wolkomir *et al.* (1997) conclude with the same basic theory of other authors that a Judeo-Christian consumer believing in the inerrancy of the scripture should be less likely to participate in sustainable consumption practices.

However, more recent competing research shows that participation in sustainable behaviors is dependent upon personal factors, including values, with the more altruistic consumers more likely to participate in sustainable behaviors (Corraliza and Berenguer, 2000; Kollmuss and Agyeman, 2002). Additionally, values related to helping others have been found to lead to increased participation in sustainable behaviors (Kollmuss and Agyeman, 2002). Looking at the antecedents to altruism and values of helping, strong intrinsic religious beliefs have long been shown to be driving causes of altruism and helping behaviors (Johnson *et al.*, 1989). Research also shows that religious values, in general, are a primary determinant of a consumer's core values (Fam, Waller, and Erdogan, 2004), and these core values relate directly to consumer attitudes and behaviors

(Homer and Kahle, 1988). As a result, this competing research shows that highly religious consumers would actually be more likely to participate in sustainable behaviors than less religious consumers.

Even though substantial research has explored sustainable consumption (McDonald *et al.*, 2006), essentially no research has assessed how religious affiliation could act as an antecedent to participation in sustainable consumption practices. Due to prior competing findings in research on religion and sustainability, a non-directional hypothesis is developed:

> **H2:** An individual's religious affiliation will significantly influence participation in sustainable consumption practices.

Method

To assess differences between religious classification systems, a series of sustainability and environmental purchase behavior variables were analyzed using the General Social Survey 2010 dataset, which consisted of 2,044 respondents. Data were randomly sampled and collected via face-to-face, phone, and computer assisted interviews (National Opinion Research Center, 2009). Respondents have an average age of 48, are 45 percent female, have completed an average of 13 years of education, 44 percent are married, and 58 percent are self-identified as at least moderately religious.

Four different grouping systems are used based on previous research and calls for future research: religious traditions, denominational, fundamental, and simple. This study includes only Jewish and Christian religious groups due to inadequate sample sizes of other religious groups. The religious traditions classification system was developed by Steensland *et al.* (2000) and categorizes religion based on historical developments and religious traditions into six categories (Mainline Protestant, Evangelical Protestant, Black Protestant, Roman Catholic, Jewish, and Other). The denominational classification system (Smidt *et al.*, 2003) groups respondents by denominational affiliation (often including Catholic, Jewish, Baptist, Methodist, Lutheran, Presbyterian, Episcopal, Pentecost, or None). The fundamental classification system (Smith, 1990) groups respondents by strict adherence to doctrine (liberal, moderate, fundamental). Finally, the simple classification system groups respondents by broad religious group (Protestant, Catholic, Jewish, None).

To determine sustainable attitude and behavior factors, the original dataset of 2,044 respondents was split into two equal halves (1,022 respondents each). Exploratory factor analysis (EFA) was conducted on the first half, and confirmatory factor analysis (CFA) was conducted on the second half. An EFA was run using principle components analysis with varimax rotation using 13 sustainable consumption variables. Three factors were identified that explained 59.09 percent of variability in sustainable consumption: (factor 1) non-monetary sustainable behaviors, (factor 2) monetary sustainable behaviors, and (factor 3) sustainable

attitudes. See Table 10.1 for the variables composing each factor, specific wording
of each variable, and scales of variables used in this study.

Table 10.1   Variable labels *(GSS provided)*, wording, and scales

Variable	Question Wording	Scale
Construct: Religion		
relig	What is your religious preference? Is it Protestant, Catholic, Jewish, some other religion, or no religion?	NA
denom	If Protestant: What specific denomination is that, if any?	NA
other	If responding other to denom.	NA
Construct: Sustainable non-monetary behaviors		
drivless	How often do you cut back on driving a car for environmental reasons?	4 point scale, always (4) to never (1)
nobuygrn	How often do you avoid buying products for environmental reasons?	Same as above
redcehme	How often do you reduce fuel to help the environment?	Same as above
chemfree*	How often do you buy pesticide free fruits and vegetables?	Same as above
recycle*	How often do you recycle cans and bottles?	Same as above
h2oless*	How often do you save water for environmental reasons?	Same as above
Construct: Sustainable monetary behaviors		
grnprice	How willing would you be to pay much higher prices in order to protect the environment?	5 point scale, very willing (5) to not at all willing (1)
grntaxes	… to pay much higher taxes in order to protect the environment?	Same as above
grnsol	… to accept cuts in your standard of living in order to protect the environment?	Same as above
Construct: Sustainable attitudes		
carsgen	Do you think that air pollution caused by cars is …	5 point scale, extremely (5) dangerous to not dangerous (1)
indusgen	Do you think that air pollution caused by industry is …	Same as above
watergen	Do you think that pollution of America's rivers and streams is …	Same as above
chemgen*	Do you think that pesticides and chemicals used in farming are …	Same as above
Construct: Covariates		
age	Age of respondent	NA
sex	Respondent's sex	Recoded 1 = female, 0 = male

income06	Total family income	25 categories, under $1000 to $150,000 and over
marital	Are you currently – married, widowed, divorced, separated, or have you never been married?	Recoded, 1 = married, 0 = not married
educ	Highest year of school completed	0 to 20 years
polviews	Where would you place yourself on this liberal-conservative scale (respondent handed card)?	7 point scale, extremely conservative (7) to extremely liberal (1)
Construct: Covariates – Religiosity subscale		
god	Which statement comes closest to expressing what you believe about God?	6 point scale, know God exists (6) to don't believe (1)
relactiv	How often do you take part in the activities and organizations of a church or place of worship other than attending services?	11 point scale, several times a day (11) to never (1)
pray	How often do you pray?	5 point scale, recoded, several times a day (5) to never (1)
reliten	Would you consider yourself a strong [preference named in relig or denom] or a not very strong [preference]?	4 point scale, recoded, strong (4) to no religion (1)
rellife	I try hard to carry my religious beliefs over into all my other dealings in life	4 point scale, recoded, strong agree (4) to strong disagree (1)
relpersn	To what extent do you consider yourself a religious person?	4 point scale, recoded, very religious (4) to not religious (1)

* Variables included in the EFA but not the CFA or structural models due to high error terms

A CFA was then run on the second half of the dataset using the factor makeup found in the EFA. The three constructs were modeled as three correlated first-order factors. LISREL 8.8 was used, with covariances as input, to estimate the model. Four variables were removed from the CFA that had large error terms (i.e., low squared multiple correlations); see Table 10.1 for listing of removed variables. The root mean square error of approximation (RMSEA) is .046 with a p-value for test of close fit of p = .70, both measures indicating good model fit according to Hu and Bentler (1999). Additionally, the comparative fit index (CFI) is .99, again indicating good model fit, according to Hu and Bentler (1999). χ^2 is significant at 85.12(24), but this is likely due to the large sample size of 1,022 (half of the original dataset) artificially inflating the χ^2 value (Bagozzi, 2010). Other measures of model fit besides chi-square produce are less sensitive to sample size, such as CFI (West, Finch, and Curran, 1995). Therefore, the CFA has good overall fit.

Evidence of internal consistency is provided by composite reliability and coefficient alpha. Composite reliability is a LISREL-generated estimate of internal consistency analogous to coefficient alpha (Fornell and Larcker, 1981). Internal consistency is high with composite reliability ranging from .73 to .83 and coefficient alpha ranging from .72 to .84. One test of discriminant validity among factors was performed. If the square of the parameter estimate between constructs (ϕ^2) is less than the average variance extracted estimates of the two constructs, then discriminant validity is supported (Fornell and Larcker, 1981). This criterion was met across all possible pairs of constructs.

Structural equation modeling was used to test the effectiveness of the four religious classification systems in predicting sustainable non-monetary behaviors, sustainable monetary behaviors, and sustainable attitudes; see Figure 10.1 for a path diagram.

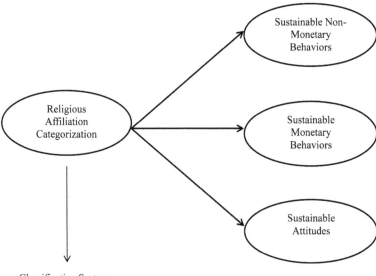

Classification Systems
- Model 1: Simple
(Protestant, Catholic, Jew, None)
- Model 2: Smith's (1990) Fundamentalism
(Liberal, Moderate, Fundamental)
- Model 3: Steensland's (2000) Religious Traditions
(Mainline Protestant, Evangelical Protestant, Black Protestant, Roman Catholic, Jew, Other)
- Model 4: Denominational
(Catholic, Jewish, Baptist, Methodist, Lutheran, Presbyterian, Episcopal, Pentecost, Non-Denominational)

Figure 10.1   Path diagram showing relationship between religious affiliation categorization and sustainable attitudes and behaviors

Literature supported individual difference variables were added as covariates and consisted of age, income, gender, years of education, marital status, and political orientation (Wolkomir *et al.*, 1997; Muhamad and Mizerski, 2007; Bailey and Sood, 1993). Religiosity was included as a covariate and consisted of a six-item composite religiosity variable with a Cronbach's alpha of .820; see Table 10.1 for descriptions of the variables composing this factor. The religiosity composite variable follows a three-dimensional model of religiosity including 1) organized religious activity, 2) non-organized religious activity, and 3) intrinsic religiosity (Chatters, Levin, and Taylor, 1992). For descriptive statistics of all variables in this study, including covariates, see Table 10.2.

Table 10.2   Means and standard deviations (continuous variables) and percentage frequencies (categorical variables)

Variable	Mean	SD	Variable	% Frequency
drivless	1.76	0.88	marital (married)	43.6%
nobuygrn	2.11	0.91	sex (femaleness)	45.4%
redcehme	2.29	0.97	Simple–Protestant	52.5%
chemfree*	2.16	0.98	Simple–Catholic	26%
recycle*	2.90	1.08	Simple–Jew	2%
h2oless*	1.90	0.96	Simple–None	19.6%
grnprice	3.08	1.22	Fund[1]–Liberal	15%
grntaxes	2.69	1.28	Fund[1]–Moderate	11.4%
grnsol	2.74	1.26	Fund[1]–Fundamental	73.6%
carsgen	3.53	0.89	RT[2]–Mainline Protestant	18.3%
indusgen	3.89	0.85	RT[2]–Evangelical Protestant	22.5%
watergen	3.96	0.88	RT[2]–Black Protestant	23.7%
chemgen*	3.65	0.90	RT[2]–Roman Catholic	30.8%
age	47.98	17.68	RT[2]–Jewish	2.4%
income06	16.37	6.00	RT[2]–Other	2.4%
educ	13.46	3.15	Denom[3]–Catholic	34.2%
polviews	4.08	1.46	Denom[3]–Jewish	2.6%
god	5.01	1.46	Denom[3]–Baptist	25.8%
relactiv	3.03	2.31	Denom[3]–Methodist	8.1%
pray	4.20	1.76	Denom[3]–Lutheran	5.8%
reliten	2.92	1.08	Denom[3]–Presbyterian	4.3%
rellife	2.86	0.95	Denom[3]–Episcopal	2.6%
relpersn	2.57	0.98	Denom[3]–Pentecost	2.6%
			Denom[3]–Non-denominational	14%

Note: N = 2044. See Table 10.1 for variable descriptions.
* Variables included in the EFA but not the CFA or structural models due to high error terms.
[1] Fund = Fundamentalism classification by Smith (1990)
[2] RT = Religious traditions classification by Steensland *et al.* (2000)
[3] Denom = Denominational classification

Results

Four religious classification systems were tested (model—simple, model 2—fundamentalism/Smith (1990), model 3—religious traditions/Steensland *et al.* (2000), and model 4—denominational), and three models were tested within each classification system (model a—base model including only religious affiliation and sustainability variables, model b—adds in religiosity, and model c—adds in all other covariates). In Tables 10.3–10.6, the results for the overall fit of the 12 structural models (4 classification systems × 3 model levels) are presented. The χ^2 is significant for all models, but this is most likely due to the large sample size of 2,044 and artificial inflation of the χ^2 valued (Bagozzi, 2010). Overall model fit for all models is less than desirable with model fit statistics falling outside the recommended cutoffs suggested by Hu and Bentler (1999). However, Browne and Cudeck (1993) suggest that CFI values of at least .90 and RMSEA values less than .08 can produce satisfactory model fit. Following these guidelines, the fundamentalism classification system is the only model that provides at least adequate model fit, though only with religious affiliation and religiosity in the model. Additionally, the denominational classification system also has adequate fit according to RMSEA, but the CFI value indicates poor model fit (Browne and Cudeck, 1993).

Table 10.3   Model 1 (simple classification): Completely standardized path estimates

	Variables	Model 1a	Model 1b	Model 1c
Protestant	SusNMbeh	–.11***	–.12***	–.13***
	SusMbeh	–.09**	–.08**	–.08**
	SusAtt	.06	–.03	–.02
Jew	SusNMbeh	.01	.02	–.01
	SusMbeh	.05	.04	.03
	SusAtt	.06*	.07*	.06*
None	SusNMbeh	.01	.04	.04
	SusMbeh	.10***	.08**	.07**
	SusAtt	.05	.07*	.07*
Religiosity	SusNMbeh		.07*	.11***
	SusAtt		*ns*	.11***
Age	SusNMbeh			.11***
Sex	SusAtt			.06*
Income	SusNMbeh			–.10**
	SusAtt			–.10***
Education	SusNMbeh			.13***
	SusMbeh			.10***

Polviews	SusNMbeh			−.22***
	SusMbeh			−.22***
	SusAtt			−.27***
Fit Statistics	χ^2	962.05	2077.35	3387.40
	df	48	57	132
	CFI	.80	.64	.54
	RMSEA	.10	.13	.11
	AIC	1046.05	2171.35	3541.40

Note: ***p < .001, **p < .01, *p < .05. Variables representing religious groups are dummy variables with Catholics as baseline group. For model c (covariates), only significant paths are listed.

Table 10.4   Model 2 (fundamentalism classification): Completely standardized path estimates

	Variables	Model 2a	Model 2b	Model 2c
Liberal	SusNMbeh	.05	.05	.02
	SusMbeh	.02	.03	.01
	SusAtt	−.01	−.01	.01
Moderate	SusNMbeh	−.05	−.04	−.06*
	SusMbeh	−.02	−.01	−.01
	SusAtt	−.12***	−.12***	−.11***
Religiosity	SusMbeh		−.12***	*ns*
Age	SusNMbeh			.09**
Sex	SusAtt			.06*
Income	SusNMbeh			−.09**
	SusAtt			−.10***
Education	SusNMbeh			.14***
	SusMbeh			.11***
Polviews	SusNMbeh			−.22***
	SusMbeh			−.22***
	SusAtt			−.27***
Fit Statistics	χ^2	455.89	476.08	1841.64
	df	40	48	117
	CFI	.90	.90	.69
	RMSEA	.07	.07	.09
	AIC	529.89	560.08	1985.64

Note: ***p < .001, **p < .01, *p < .05. Variables representing religious groups are dummy variables with Fundamentalists as baseline group. For model c (covariates), only significant paths are listed.

Table 10.5 Model 3 (religious traditions classification): Completely standardized path estimates

	Variables	Model 3a	Model 3b	Model 3c
Mainline Protestant	SusNMbeh	−.05	−.06*	−.09**
	SusMbeh	−.07*	−.05	−.05
	SusAtt	−.10***	−.09**	−.08**
Evangelical Protestant	SusNMbeh	−.02	−.03	−.01
	SusMbeh	−.10***	−.08**	−.05
	SusAtt	−.02	−.02	.01
Black Protestant	SusNMbeh	−.23***	−.14***	−.15***
	SusMbeh	−.11***	−.08**	−.08**
	SusAtt	.01	.01	−.01
Jewish	SusNMbeh	.01	.01	−.01
	SusMbeh	.03	.03	.02
	SusAtt	.06	.06	.05
Other	SusNMbeh	.01	.01	−.01
	SusMbeh	.01	.02	.01
	SusAtt	−.01	−.01	−.02
Religiosity	SusNMbeh		*ns*	.08**
	SusMbeh		-.08*	*ns*
	SusAtt		*ns*	.06*
Age	SusNMbeh			.10***
Sex	SusAtt			.06*
Income	SusNMbeh			−.10**
	SusAtt			−.10***
Education	SusNMbeh			.13***
	SusMbeh			.11***
Polviews	SusNMbeh			−.23***
	SusMbeh			−.22***
	SusAtt			−.27***
Fit Statistics	χ^2	827.56	1280.53	2701.93
	df	67	78	165
	CFI	.83	.75	.60
	RMSEA	.08	.09	.09
	AIC	931.56	1394.53	2875.93

Note: ***p < .001, **p < .01, *p < .05. Variables representing religious groups are dummy variables with Roman Catholics as baseline group. For model c (covariates), only significant paths are listed.

Table 10.6   Model 4 (denominational classification): Completely standardized path estimates

	Variables	Model 4a	Model 4b	Model 4c
Jewish	SusNMbeh	.01	.01	−.01
	SusMbeh	.04	.03	.02
	SusAtt	.06*	.06*	.05
Baptist	SusNMbeh	−.15***	−.16***	−.17***
	SusMbeh	−.11***	−.08**	−.08**
	SusAtt	.01	.01	−.01
Methodist	SusNMbeh	.01	.01	−.01
	SusMbeh	−.02	−.01	−.01
	SusAtt	−.01	−.01*	−.01
Lutheran	SusNMbeh	−.06*	−.06*	−.07*
	SusMbeh	.03	−.02	−.02
	SusAtt	−.07*	−.07*	−.05
Presbyterian	SusNMbeh	−.08*	−.08**	−.10**
	SusMbeh	−.07*	−.06*	−.07*
	SusAtt	−.09**	−.09**	−.07**
Episcopal	SusNMbeh	.01	.01	−.01
	SusMbeh	−.02	−.01	−.02
	SusAtt	.01	.01	.01
Pentecost	SusNMbeh	−.03	−.03	−.03
	SusMbeh	−.05	−.04	−.03
	SusAtt	.05	.05	.05
Non-denominational	SusNMbeh	−.01	-.01	.01
	SusMbeh	−.08**	−.06*	−.05
	SusAtt	−.03	−.03	−.02
Religiosity	SusNMbeh		*ns*	.09**
	SusMbeh		−.08**	*ns*
Age	SusNMbeh			.11***
Sex	SusAtt			.06*
Income	SusNMbeh			−.10**
	SusAtt			−.10**
Education	SusNMbeh			.13***
	SusMbeh			.11***
Polviews	SusNMbeh			−.22***
	SusMbeh			−.21***
	SusAtt			−.27***
Fit Statistics	χ^2	735.16	1008.90	2455.37
	df	103	117	222
	CFI	.85	.80	.64
	RMSEA	.06	.06	.07
	AIC	869.16	1152.90	2659.37

Note: ***p < .001, **p < .01, *p < .05. Variables representing religious groups are dummy variables with Roman Catholics as baseline group. For model c (covariates), only significant paths are listed.

All model fit statistics partially confirm H1 in showing that the simple classification system (Protestant, Catholic, Jew, None) is the poorest fitting classification system, despite it being the most frequently used classification system in the consumer behavior literature. However, contrary to H1, Smith's (1990) fundamentalism classification system provides the best fitting model (AIC = 529.89 for base model), denominational classification the next best fitting (AIC = 869.16 for base model), Steensland *et al.*'s (2000) religious traditions classification the third best fitting (AIC = 931.56 for base model), and the simple classification system the poorest fitting (AIC = 1046.05 for base model) according to AIC values. The model with the lowest AIC (Akaike's information criterion) is considered to have better model fit (Hu and Bentler, 1995).

In addition to overall model fit statistics, reviewing variance explained and the significance of specific parameters provides further information about the explanatory ability of the various religious classification systems. Completely standardized path estimates, t-values, and latent construct variance explained are provided in Table 10.3 (simple classification), Table 10.4 (Smith's (1990)/ fundamentalism classification), Table 10.5 (Steensland *et al.* (2000)/religious traditions classification), and Table 10.6 (denominational classification). For the base model (Model a), the denominational classification system accounts for the greatest amount of variance (i.e., R^2) in both sustainable non-monetary behaviors (3.4 percent) and sustainable attitudes (2 percent). Steensland *et al.*'s (2000) religious traditions classification system accounts for the greatest amount of variance in sustainable monetary behaviors (2.9 percent). In contrast, Smith's (1990) fundamentalism classification system produces the lowest explained variance in both sustainable non-monetary behaviors (.4 percent) and sustainable monetary behaviors (.1 percent), while the simple classification system explains the lowest amount of variance in sustainable attitudes (.6 percent). Despite these findings, all variance explained values are low. After including covariates (Model c), the percent of variance in sustainable variables increases to a modest 10–14 percent, with the highest variance explained in the denominational classification model for sustainable non-monetary behaviors (14.2 percent).

All classification systems in the base model (Model a) show at least some difference between religious groups in sustainable attitudes; however, Smith's (1990) fundamentalism classification does not show differences in sustainable behaviors among religious groups whereas all other classification systems do show significant differences, thereby providing partial support for H2. The simple classification system shows that Protestants are significantly less likely than Catholics to participate in sustainable behaviors, while respondents with no religious affiliation are more likely than Catholics to participate in sustainable behaviors. Both Steensland *et al.*'s (2000) religious traditions and the denominational classification systems echo the findings of the simple classification system with Mainline Protestants, Evangelical Protestants, and Black Protestants (Steensland *et al.*'s (2000) classification) as well as Baptists, Lutherans, Presbyterians, and

Non-denominational believers (denominational classification) all significantly less likely to participate in sustainable behaviors than Catholics.

As expected, the most fundamental religions (e.g., Baptists) were least likely to participate in sustainable behaviors as shown through the largest negative t-values for Baptists in the denominational classification model (t = −4.78 for sustainable non-monetary behaviors and t = −3.77 for sustainable monetary behaviors) as well as for Black Protestants in Steensland *et al.*'s (2000) religious traditions classification model (t = −4.08 for sustainable non-monetary behaviors and t = −3.87 for sustainable monetary behaviors). Interestingly, Smith's (1990) fundamentalism classification system shows no difference among religious groups in sustainable behaviors, possibly a result of having greater within variable variance in comparison to between variable variance (i.e., respondents classified as holding fundamental religious beliefs could still have many different beliefs on other issues related to sustainability that could muddy the findings).

Although the sign of the paths between specific religious groups and sustainable attitudes and behaviors is the same for most all religious groups, sustainable non-monetary behaviors most often have higher t-values and corresponding lower p-values than sustainable monetary behaviors, possibly a result of respondents' willingness to change simple behaviors before incurring large financial costs. Throughout all classification systems as well, significant relationships between religious groups and sustainable behaviors of either type are more common than significant relationships to sustainable attitudes. Interestingly, moderates in Smith's (1990) fundamental classification system and non-denominational believers in the denominational classification system have sustainable attitudes as the only significant path within the religious group. Additionally, Mainline Protestants from Steensland *et al.*'s (2000) classification had sustainable attitudes as the highest t-value for the group's sustainable attitudes and behaviors. Perhaps, non-denominational believers share many of the same beliefs as moderates and Mainline Protestants.

The addition of covariates causes model fit for all classification systems to severely deteriorate. This drop in model fit could be due to inclusion of numerous non-significant covariate paths. In all classification systems, except Smith's (1990) fundamentalism classification, the addition of religiosity to the model (Model b) increases the variance accounted for in both sustainable non-monetary behaviors and sustainable attitudes but decreases the variance accounted for in sustainable monetary behaviors. Additionally, for all classification systems, except Smith's (1990) fundamentalism classification, the only significant path for religiosity leads to sustainable monetary behaviors with respondents that are more religious being significantly less likely to participate in sustainable monetary behaviors.

In Model c (all covariates added) for all classification systems, the only covariate with no significant paths is marital status, suggesting that there is no difference in sustainable attitudes and behaviors between single respondents and married respondents. Age, sex, income, education, and political views all significantly influence at least one construct relating to sustainable attitudes and behaviors. Addition of the covariates in Model c improved the variance explained in all three outcome constructs, by almost 11 percent in some cases (e.g., for the denominational classification from 3.4 percent in Model a to 14.2 percent in Model c). Model c results show that as age increases, participation in sustainable non-monetary behaviors significantly increases. Females are significantly more likely than males to hold sustainable attitudes. Income shows a significant negative relationship with participation in sustainable non-monetary behaviors and holding sustainable attitudes (i.e., more income leads to less sustainability). More years of education leads to significantly more participation in both sustainable non-monetary behaviors and sustainable monetary behaviors. Finally, as conservativeness increases, participation in any sustainable behaviors or holding sustainable attitudes significantly decreases.

Discussion

Of the four religious grouping systems, Smith's (1990) fundamentalism grouping system provides the best overall model fit with the denominational and Steensland *et al.*'s (2000) religious traditions grouping system trailing behind, and the simple grouping system producing the poorest model fit of all grouping systems. Despite model fit being the best for Smith's (1990) fundamentalism grouping system, the amount of variance explained in the sustainable attitude and behavior outcome constructs is greatest for the denominational grouping system and Steensland *et al.*'s (2000) religious traditions grouping system. Among all methods of assessing the effectiveness of religious grouping systems, the simple religious grouping system is always the least effective, which is interesting considering that the simple religious grouping system is found most often in the consumer behavior literature.

These findings suggest that the traditional way of measuring religious affiliation in the consumer behavior literature could be adding to the perception that there are no significant differences among consumers with regards to religious affiliation (Hirschman, 1983). Following the recommendations by Alwin *et al.* (2006), multiple religious grouping systems should be used when conducting research on religion, such as Alwin *et al.*'s (2006) recommendation of using both Steensland *et al.* (2000) and a denominational classification. In this research, findings show that Smith's (1990) fundamentalism grouping system, Steensland *et al.*'s (2000) religious traditions grouping system, and the denominational grouping system could all be used as effective grouping systems.

The relationship between religious grouping system and sustainability is consistent between sustainable behaviors and attitudes (e.g., the negative relationship between being Presbyterian and participating in sustainable non-monetary as well as monetary behaviors also holds for Presbyterians having sustainable attitudes). In general, results follow previous studies showing that more liberal denominations (i.e., denominations that do not believe the Bible is inerrant and infallible) are more likely to be sustainable. However, this study provides one of the first glimpses into how religious affiliation influences sustainable consumption-related behaviors and attitudes.

Also, as research in consumer behavior frequently turns to measuring religiosity without consideration for religious affiliation, this study's findings provide support to continue to measure religious affiliation. Adding religiosity to all models only results in minimal changes to the relationship between religious classification and sustainable behaviors and attitudes. Additionally, overall model fit decreased for all models when religiosity was included in the model. Therefore, religiosity is still an important covariate to consider in religious research, but measuring religious affiliation is a necessity in all religious research to first understand the key beliefs of the respondent.

Due to the inadequate sample sizes of Muslims and other non-Judeo-Christian religions, this study is limited in the generalizability of the findings. Future studies should expand this research to include predominant world religions, such as Muslims, Hindus, Buddhists, Taoists, Confucianists, as well as denominations/sects within each of these major world religions. Future research should also consider consumer differences in areas outside of sustainability that are theoretically supported through differences in religious doctrine. In an effort to develop more accurate findings, specifically for the field of consumer behavior, future research should consider developing and distributing theoretically supported questionnaires to an internationally representative sample.

Conclusion

This study confirms previous findings that religion significantly influences consumer behavior findings; in this research specifically, sustainable consumption behaviors and attitudes. Results show that the most common religious affiliation grouping system found in the consumer behavior literature (Protestant, Catholic, Jew, None) results in the poorest model fit and is the least effective while complex grouping systems, such as denominational, Steensland *et al.*'s (2000) religious traditions, or Smith's (1990) fundamentalism, result in much better model fit, better explanation of sustainable attitudes and behaviors, and numerous significant differences between religious affiliations. Additionally, these more complex grouping systems are the only systems that are theoretically defensible through differences in religious doctrine, religious traditions, and belief in inerrancy of scripture.

These grouping systems easily lead to a segmentation base that is implementable and actionable by marketers. Religious magazines, denominational conferences, and religious social media groups are a handful of ways, among many, that these segmentation practices can be implemented by marketers in an area where targeted marketing is lacking.

PART IV
Economic Analyses of Religious Phenomena

Chapter 11

Sources of Religious Pluralism: Revisiting the Relationship between Pluralism and Participation

Roger Finke and Christopher P. Scheitle

Few recent topics in the study of religion have generated more interest and controversy than pluralism. Particularly controversial has been the proposition that religious pluralism generates higher levels of religious participation within a population. The secularization theory of religious change has long held that pluralism shatters the sacred canopy and undermines religion (Berger, 1967). In contrast, the religious economy model proposed that pluralism fosters religious activity by increasing competition and choice (Finke and Stark, 1988; 1996). This theoretical flashpoint has resulted in a heated and prolonged discussion on the outcomes of pluralism, yet few clear answers have emerged concerning the relationship between pluralism and participation.

Much of this discussion has been mired in debates over a single measure of religious pluralism, a Gini index of religious diversity, and its relationship with religious participation. Initially, debates centered on conflicting results across time and space (Chaves and Gorski, 2001; Stark and Finke, 2000: 226–7). Then in 2002 Voas, Olson, and Crockett announced that the relationship between religious pluralism and religious participation, whether negative or positive, is the result of a statistical artifact and fails to support either side of the debate. Voas *et al.* (2002) proposed that one option for future work is to look at alternative outcomes. They suggested that using measures of involvement that are independent of the participation measures used to construct the Gini index would reduce or eliminate the statistical problems of employing the religious pluralism index as a predictor.

We agree that alternative outcomes of religious pluralism should be explored, but our goal is to take a step back in the theoretical model and examine religious pluralism as an outcome. Through all of the debates there has been surprisingly little exploration of the sources or dynamics of religious pluralism or what the measures that are used to assess pluralism really mean. With attention focused on the consequences of pluralism, understanding and explaining its nature and origins has been lost. Beyond being an important stand-alone question, this is central to understanding the relationship between pluralism and participation. We cannot hope to understand a theoretical relationship until we fully understand both of the concepts involved and the indicators that are used to measure them. Our goal is to

178 *Religions as Brands*

reframe the theoretical arguments and to provide some reconciliation of previous, often contradictory, research.

Revisiting Pluralism

Peter Berger, one of the most respected contributors of writings on secularization, was one of the first to point out that religious pluralism forces religions to compete. He explained that the "pluralistic situation multiplies the number of plausibility structures competing with each other." For Berger, this pluralistic competition resulted in a "crisis of faith" (Berger, 1967: 151). The religious economy model agreed that pluralism resulted in competition but offered an opposing prediction. Rather than viewing pluralism and competition as a "crisis," Roger Finke and Rodney Stark (1988: 42) described competition as a "stimulus for religious growth and not an avenue for its demise." Despite the voluminous debate that followed, most attention centered on one question: How does religious pluralism affect religious participation in society? Or, more precisely, how does the diversity of religious involvement change religious participation?

What is interesting about all of this literature is that it has taken the existence of pluralism as a secondary phenomenon and has typically been limited to observing pluralism and participation within a single country. In the opening salvo of this debate, Finke and Stark (1988: 42) argued, that "to the degree a religious market is unregulated, pluralism will thrive." The argument here and in later work is that as regulations are lifted and religions are free to compete, religious pluralism is a given. Yet, this initial work made little effort to explain the variations across regions or local markets that exist under similar levels of regulation. Why is one area more pluralistic than another when they have similar levels of regulation? Moreover, how is this increase in pluralism related to the frequently used Gini index, and is this index a measure of religious competition, as past research has assumed?

We propose to address these questions on religious pluralism and other issues related to the larger debate in three ways. First, we provide a theoretical foundation for explaining pluralism in religious suppliers and religious consumers. We propose that in an unregulated environment, pluralism in religious suppliers is a product of two forces: the underlying pluralism of religious preferences and the number of potential adherents within an environment. This pluralism of suppliers, in turn, produces a pluralism of religious consumers. In short, when facing few external constraints, religious pluralism at the supplier and consumer levels reflects the social and cultural diversity of the area. Second, using a data source that has been drawn on for the previous debates, we offer an initial test of our theoretical model. For these tests, we move pluralism to the other side of the equation and try to understand the sources of religious pluralism instead of using pluralism as a predictor. Once again, we distinguish between two forms of pluralism: the number of religious groups (supplier pluralism) and the distribution of individuals across the religious groups (consumer pluralism). Here we refer to the match between supply and demand as *demand fulfillment*. Finally, building on the first two sections of the chapter we discuss how this clarifies previous research on religious pluralism and participation, as well as how this model of pluralism helps to explain religious change more generally and the implications it holds for religious organizations.

Explaining Organizational Pluralism

Religious economy arguments typically place emphasis on supply-side changes when explaining religious change. As a result, close attention is given to how regulations constrain the supply of religions. Whereas many scholars attempted to explain religious change in nineteenth-century America as a sudden shift in religious demand, supply-side arguments highlight the deregulation of the religious marketplace and the dramatic surge in the supply of religions that resulted (Finke, 1990; Finke and Stark, 2005). But this focus on the supply-side has led some to suggest that religious economy arguments assume there is little variation in demand. To the contrary, the argument suggests that the wide variation in religious demand is the very reason a diversity of suppliers is needed. Although it has not been directly applied to this debate, the theoretical basis for understanding variation in religious pluralism exists within the religious economies literature.

In an early publication on the topic, Finke and Stark explained that "a single faith cannot shape its appeal to precisely suit the needs of one market segment, without sacrificing its appeal to another." Later they proposed that religious economies include a set of relatively stable market niches and they defined niches as market segments of potential adherents sharing particular religious preferences (Stark and Finke, 2000: 197). Figure 11.1 was offered as a "hypothetical distribution of religious demand." But they also reviewed the religious group affiliation of over 15,000 General Social Survey respondents to illustrate how actual membership closely fit this distribution (see Table 18: 214). Just as individuals vary in their preferences for magazines, restaurants, and other products and services, they also vary in the styles of worship, beliefs, or social groups they prefer. Hence, the variety of religious groups is directly related to the distribution of religious "niches." The idea is simply that a religious supplier will not survive or be created in the first place if there are no individuals in the group's particular niche. Few will find it surprising that when the authors took a road trip across America, we didn't find any historically African-American churches in the small Midwestern rural towns devoid of African-Americans (Scheitle and Finke, 2012). Just as high-end car dealerships typically do not thrive in low-income areas and liberal newspapers do not proliferate in conservative regions, religious organizations must find a niche to serve if they are to survive.

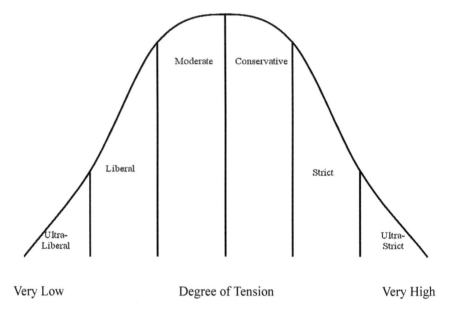

Very Low   Degree of Tension   Very High

Figure 11.1   A hypothetical distribution of religious niches
Note: Adapted from Rodney Stark and Roger Finke (2000: 197).

As we will discuss later, religious pluralism can be restrained by external forces, such as government restrictions and strong social pressures; but it can also be restrained by a lack of diverse preferences. Even when the external restraints are removed, *the number and type of religious suppliers is a product of: 1) the underlying pluralism of religious preferences and 2) the number of potential adherents within an environment.*

In short, when facing few external constraints and an adequate population in each niche, religious supply reflects the religious, social and cultural diversity of the area. When areas have more homogeneity and smaller populations, the pluralism of religious supply might be low even when competition is high.

These same forces also determine the potential size of any single religious group. Organizational size and growth are shaped by the population of the niche(s) they are serving, the number of competitors in their niche and the group's ability to effectively compete with these alternative suppliers. For a group to grow they must have market potential within the niche they serve and they must serve that niche more effectively than their competitors. For example, a few of the reasons that most new religious movements have so little potential for growth is that they are serving a small market niche, there is an abundance of new competitors, and many of the new movements aren't very effective at appealing for adherents.

These same ideas have been addressed in greater detail and tested far more rigorously by organizational ecologists and economists. But the conclusions are often quite similar. Regardless of the organizations studied, they have found that suppliers of goods and services tend to form around different taste dimensions or niches (Hannan, Carroll, and Polos, 2003). Using the vocabulary of organizational ecologists, supplier pluralism is a product of the number of taste dimensions and the supply of resources available. For religious markets the number of taste dimensions refers to variation in religious preferences and the resources refer to the potential number of adherents in each market niche. Together they set the upper limits for religious diversity, just as taste dimensions and the supply of resources sets the diversity limits for organizations in any market.

This same line of research also helps to explain why a single organization or supplier cannot serve all market preferences. Organizational ecologists find that to the extent that an organization attempts to serve a wider range of preferences, often covering multiple niches, they will be less effective than a specialized organization appealing to a narrower group of preferences (Hannan and Freeman, 1977). This is clearly evident with religious organizations. Christerson and Emerson (2003) report that multiracial congregations seldom serve all racial and ethnic groups equally and they struggle to integrate all groups into the life of the congregation. As a result, multiracial congregations with a majority racial group tend to predominantly serve that group, leaving out the minority groups and often serving them less effectively than an organization specializing in their preferences.

Organizational ecologists also point to another challenge for groups attempting to serve diverse preferences: a lack of social homophily. The pressure for social homophily makes it difficult for organizations serving a wide market segment to fully integrate individuals into the organization (McPherson, Smith-Lovin, and Cook, 2001). Because individuals want to form relationships and networks with individuals similar to themselves, a heterogeneous population makes it difficult for individuals to create these relationships. That is, the more generalist an organization, the more it contains individuals who are "on the edge" of the organization or "in between" the organization and its competitors (Popielarz and McPherson, 1995). These less integrated flanks of the group's niche base are at risk for dropping out or being taken away by competing groups that provide a product more tailored to the individual. This means that broad organizational niches are of particular concern to voluntary or social organizations that rely on relationships between members.

Yet, despite the advantages of religious organizations specializing and serving only a single market niche, many religious groups seek to be generalists, serving multiple religious niches. The success of these generalist religious organizations to survive and even grow relies on multiple factors. First, despite being generalists at the national or regional level, they must find ways of being specialists at the local congregational level. For example, the Catholic immigrants to America in the late nineteenth and early twentieth century formed national parishes that were organized by ethnicity and the remaining parishes were organized by geographic proximity. This resulted in congregations that were homogeneous at the local level, but varied widely in language, social groups and worship styles. Large Catholic congregations and Protestant mega-churches are often forced to become multiple sub-congregations within the larger congregation.

Generalist organizations might also thrive when they serve as the primary organizational vehicle for resisting the state or leading social conflict. For example, the Catholic Church of Quebec in the mid-twentieth century or of Poland in the 1980s and 90s attained extremely high levels of member commitment as the Church served as the organizational and symbolic force for organizing against outside rulers. Once local political control was attained, however, the level of commitment displayed a sharp decline.

Finally, the most common way for generalists to serve a diverse range of market niches is through government support. As we will review in greater detail below the state's support for one religion and restrictions on others serves to increase both the entry and ongoing operating costs of other religions. When these restraints are lifted, however, we expect the diversity of religious suppliers to more closely match the diversity of religious preferences.

The U.S. offers one example of how religious pluralism increases as religious preferences become more diverse, the population swells, and market constraints are lifted. In 1776, the number of religious groups in the 13 colonies was limited to approximately thirty to forty, and much of this diversity resided within the socially diverse and religiously tolerant Pennsylvania colony. By 1890, the Census Office found 143 different religious groups, multiple new groups arising because of racial and ethnic boundaries. With an increasingly diverse population following the turn of the nineteenth century, the Bureau of the Census tally rose to 213 different religious groups in 1926. Today, Gordon Melton's *Encyclopedia of American Religions* (2009) reports information on more than 2,300 different groups. Although religious freedoms help to explain the rich pluralism found in the United States, they don't explain the sharp increases over time or the variations across regional units.

This model has many implications for individual organizations, as well as the market as a whole, but we want to begin by focusing on two propositions explaining the sources of supplier pluralism. First, *the more pluralistic the religious preferences are in an area, the higher is the pluralism in religious suppliers.* A diversity of preferences results in multiple market niches, each opening the door for a new group of suppliers. Second, *regardless of the pluralism in preferences, the size of the population (absolute resources) will be positively related to the pluralism of religious suppliers.* Whether we are talking about automobile companies or religious groups, few suppliers have a complete monopoly over their niche. When the resources within a niche increase, there are opportunities for multiple suppliers. Because the primary resource of any religious group is the membership, these propositions point to the importance of understanding the size and diversity of the population. How many people are available for membership? To what extent do the people have diverse religious preferences that represent different market niches?

This discussion also proposes that the pluralism of religious suppliers should be closely related to the pluralism of religious consumers. This latter pluralism is what has typically been referred to as religious pluralism in previous research and has been measured by a Gini index or a Herfindahl index of market concentration. Although attempting to measure religious competition, the index is in fact measuring the probability that any two congregants are members of the same religious group. In other words, *the Gini index used in past research is measuring the pluralism of religious consumers.*

Figure 11.2 illustrates the theoretical model. Both the preference pluralism (diversity of religious preferences) and the number of potential adherents available (population) explain the number of different religious suppliers present, and the number of suppliers has a direct effect on the pluralism of religious consumers. Notice, however, that preference pluralism and the total population do not have a direct relationship with consumer pluralism. We expect the presence of different niches and the size of the population to increase the number of suppliers in the geographic area. However, these variables do not necessarily have any *direct* relationship with the distribution of consumers among those suppliers.

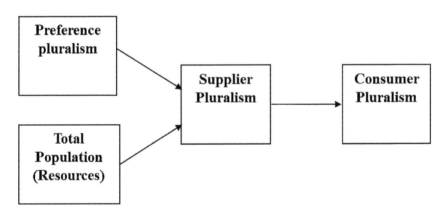

Figure 11.2   Theoretical model explaining supplier and consumer pluralism

Beyond the variation in their niche size, religious groups also vary in their competitive advantages (e.g., time of entry into the market, historical or cultural ties to an area, effective evangelism or marketing, etc.) and other factors. The result is that multiple religious groups in a single niche can divide membership in many different ways. They may each have an equal share, or one may dominate. All we can be sure of is that the creation of new niches and the addition of more population creates opportunities for more suppliers, and the existence of more suppliers will increase consumer pluralism. The size and pluralism of the population increase the number of religious groups competing for members but do not determine their success or failure unless there is only one supplier occupying a particular niche. Quite simply, the availability of a large population in a market niche does not ensure success.

When translated into the terminology of religious economies, this model suggests that to the extent that religious markets are unregulated, religious supply will eventually reflect demand. Pluralism in suppliers will vary according to the pluralism of market niches and the potential adherents available in each niche. Thus, much of the variation in consumer pluralism across markets is explained by the distributions within the market.

Examining the Model

To examine the model, we need data that will offer four key measures for multiple religious markets: 1) the total population size, 2) the diversity of preferences in the population, 3) the number of different religious suppliers, and 4) the distribution of consumers among those suppliers. To fulfill these requirements, we use the 1865 Census data for New York counties (Hough, 1867). The Census includes a wide range of social, political, and economic indicators, as well as measures for fifty-three religious denominations. These data have been used several times in previous research on pluralism.

For the consumer pluralism, or the distribution of people across suppliers, we begin with the standard Herfindahl index of market concentration. This is computed by taking the percentage of total attenders in a county held by a denomination and squaring it. This is done for each denomination; then all of these values are summed. The maximum potential value is 1, which represents the situation in which one organization holds all of the county's attendees. To make this a measure of pluralism, we subtract the Herfindahl index from 1, so higher numbers represent a greater spread of the population across organizations, and lower numbers indicate that the population is more concentrated in one or only a few groups. We know that much controversy has surrounded this measure, but the controversy has been focused on its use as a predictor of religious participation. We will not be conducting such an analysis, so those issues are not relevant to the analysis.

The measure for supplier pluralism is the number of different religious organizations in the county. This measure is the sum of indicators in which 1 indicates that a denomination had at least some seating capacity in the county and 0 indicates that they had no presence in the county. This measure ranges from 2 to 22, and the mean is 13. Our measure for the number of potential adherents is simply the county's total population.

Finding a measure of preference pluralism, however, proved far more difficult. Although a direct measure is lacking, we attempt to tap into the diverse preferences of the population by using a measure of income. It has long been recognized that social class is one attribute that distinguishes a religious group's resource niche (Demerath, 1965; Niebuhr, 1929). Socioeconomic status has remained a consistent predictor of the type of religious group an individual joins or is raised in (Davidson and Pyle, 2011; Kiester, 2011; Smith and Faris, 2005), although it is clear that religious groups help to reproduce these inequalities as well (Darnell and Sherkat, 1997). The theoretical explanations have varied, but they often argue that more strict or conservative religions appeal to the lower classes because they offer supernatural compensation for a lack of worldly success (e.g., Iannaccone, 1988: 260–61; Stark and Bainbridge, 1987). Ultimately, the source and causal nature of the link between socioeconomic status and religion are not important for our purposes. It is important only that religious groups were differentiated on this dimension in nineteenth-century New York.

The 1865 Census contains information on monthly wages for employed males in the county. We computed a Herfindahl index based on the distribution of wages in nine categories ($0 to $20, $21 to $30, $31 to $40, $41 to $50, $51 to $60, $61 to $70, $71 to $80, $81 to $90, and $91 to $100). As with the distribution of religious resources, a value of 1 on this index means that the wages are concentrated entirely within one of these categories. Lower values mean that there is more diversity of wages in the county. To make this a measure of resource diversity instead of resource concentration, we subtracted the score from 1 so that higher numbers represent more resource diversity and lower numbers represent less resource diversity. The mean for this measure is .64, and the range is .11 to .84.

We use AMOS 5.0 to create a structural equation model mirroring the theoretical model presented above. The results with standardized coefficients are shown in Figure 11.3. The data fit the model extremely closely. The *p*-value for the close fit test is .211, meaning that we cannot reject the null hypothesis that the model fits the data well. Other model fit scores lead to similar conclusions (e.g., normed fit index = .960; comparative fit index = .984). The model, although simple, explains 32 percent of the variation in supplier pluralism and 54 percent of the variation in consumer pluralism.

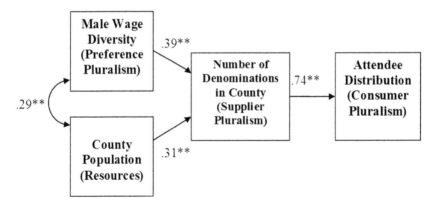

Figure 11.3   Testing the religious pluralism and diversity model

Most important, the measures are related to each other as expected. Preference pluralism, as measured by wage distributions, positively increases the number of religious suppliers in a county, as it creates opportunities for groups serving particular niches to enter the market. Similarly, the total size of the population increases the number of suppliers, as increased size provides more opportunities for the sharing of niches. In turn, an increase in the number of different religious suppliers in a county creates a wider spread of religious consumers among those suppliers. In the language of previous research, the number of religious groups increases a county's level of religious pluralism.

These results strongly support our argument that the number of religious groups is a product of diverse market niches and the size of the population available in these niches. As predicted, pluralism of preferences and population size have strong direct effects on the number of suppliers but have no direct effects on consumer pluralism. Moreover, supplier pluralism and consumer pluralism are closely related, though not identical. To slightly rephrase the findings, the results suggest that equilibrium will develop over time. *As the number of religious suppliers reflects the pluralism of preferences and population size, the consumption of religion will eventually reflect demand.*

Implications for Past Debates

The theory and analysis presented here have important implications for how religious markets operate and for the organizations within those markets. We will explore several of these implications, but we begin by returning to the question that has caused so much debate in the literature: Does religious pluralism, what we refer to as consumer pluralism, increase participation rates?

Observed versus expected pluralism

In the analysis and discussion above, we distinguished among three types of pluralism. We showed that the pluralism of religious consumers is a product of supplier pluralism, which is itself a product of pluralism in underlying religious preferences and the size of the population.

For instance, two counties with the same level of pluralism may differ greatly in the pluralism that would be expected given their differences in population size and underlying pluralism in religious preferences. This can be thought of as the difference between *observed pluralism* and *expected pluralism*. A county with an observed level of religious pluralism that equals its potential pluralism is very different from one that has a large gap between the two. The former has suppliers serving most or every existing niche, while the latter has niches that are underserved.

The above discussion and analysis require that we rethink the reasoning behind this question. If observed levels of pluralism simply reflect underlying pluralism of religious preferences, then there would be no reason to assume a relationship between religious pluralism and participation. Areas that are very pluralistic have an underlying pluralism of demand, and the observed level of pluralism simply reflects that demand.

However, if the observed pluralism is serving as a proxy for the extent to which the areas have reached their full potential for pluralism based on underlying religious demand, then there are reasons to expect a relationship between religious pluralism and participation.

This might help in explaining some conflicting findings in this area. As noted earlier, statistical problems have plagued most of the research on pluralism and participation. But work by James Montgomery (2003) avoided the statistical pitfalls outlined by using an alternative measure of competition. Yet, Montgomery found conflicting results using the nineteenth-century New York data and the 1990 data for U.S. counties. In the former, Montgomery found a positive relationship between pluralism and participation. In the latter, however, he did not find support for such a relationship. He concluded that the difference might be explained by demand-side variations that past models were not addressing. Our results suggest that the differences between the nineteenth-century and twentieth-century data should be expected. We agree with Montgomery that variation in demand does occur and should be acknowledged, but rather than stressing the homogeneity or heterogeneity of demand we focus on the gap between the pluralism of demand and the pluralism of supply. When demand fulfillment is relatively high across all cases, such as counties or states in the contemporary United States, the variation in religious pluralism is an indicator of social pluralism rather than demand fulfillment or religious competition. In contrast, because supply was failing to meet demand in New York counties in the nineteenth century, the pluralism index served as a crude proxy for the extent to which counties were reaching their full potential for pluralism.

This raises a question that we want to address more fully: When will supply fail to meet demand? In particular, what are the constraints that will prevent supply from meeting the diversity of preferences?

Constraining demand fulfillment

The literature identifies two primary sources of constraint on religious supply, although others may exist. First, as noted earlier, government or other institutional restraints may prevent certain groups or all groups from moving into an area. This creates a gap between demand and supply, with the suppliers in the area failing to reflect the population's religious preferences. Second, there may be a significant population upheaval due to immigration, migration, or general population growth. This could produce a diverse population that is not being equaled by the supply of religious groups in the area. Given time, the imbalance could fade as new groups respond to the demand, but achieving this balance requires both time and freedom from constraints. Whether the constraint is government restrictions or

188 Religions as Brands

demographic changes, the result is that supply will fail to match the preferences of the population.

Numerous historical examples illustrate the dramatic rise in supply when government constraints are removed. The best-documented case is the rise of religious pluralism in the United States (Finke, 1990; Mead, 1963), but many other examples could be offered. In Latin America, Anthony Gill (1998), Andrew Chesnut (2003), and others have documented that the recent surge of new evangelicals was a response to the lifting of government constraints. In Japan, after religious restrictions were lifted and Shintoism was disestablished following World War II, the new religions were described as arising "like mushrooms after a rainfall" (quoted in McFarland, 1967: 4). More recently, when Taiwan's 1989 Law on Civic Organizations allowed all religions to exist and removed multiple prohibitions, there was a well over twelvefold increase in the number of different religious groups in Taiwan (from 83 in 1990 to 1,062 in 2004), and the total number of temples and churches more than doubled (Lu, 2008). A similar surge in supply was evident in post-Soviet nations when controls were briefly removed from virtually all religions (Froese, 2001; Greeley, 1994). The reduced regulations and surge in religious supply is also related to religious involvement. Using an extensive cross-national data collection, Jonathan Fox and Ephraim Tabory recently concluded that religious restrictions are "significantly and negatively correlated" with religious participation.

This returns us to our earlier point. The central theoretical concept affecting outcomes such as participation rates might not be absolute or realized pluralism but the gap between the unit's expected or potential pluralism. With this in mind, it makes sense that studies using direct measures of regulation instead of using pluralism as a proxy for regulation would find more of an effect between pluralism and participation. Regulation produces wide gaps between the distribution of the population and the distribution of suppliers, preventing underlying demand from being met.

Even when suppliers face no constraints from the government, there are other mechanisms that can produce a gap. Returning to nineteenth-century New York offers such an example. Following rapid expansion in the western and northern frontiers, heavy immigration in eastern cities, and the Civil War, which affected all areas, religious supply often failed to meet the diversity of demand. Excluding towns with no church attendance reported, Table 11.1 shows that 86 of 900 New York towns reported only one religion, and another 233 towns reported minimal religious diversity. As expected, the lowest levels of church attendance were reported in towns with no diversity (the town has only one denomination), and the largest difference in attendance is between towns with no diversity and towns with some diversity. The percentage of people attending church weekly more than doubles when moving between those two scenarios, illustrating the consequences of having at least some diversity in religious supply.

Table 11.1   Pluralism and weekly church attendance in 900 New York State
towns, 1865

Pluralism Index Score	Percent Who Attend Weekly	Number of Towns
0	10.6%	86
.001–.549	22.9%	233
.550–.699	29.9%	293
.700–.799	33.6%	231
.800 and over	33.9%	57

Adapted from Rodney Stark and Roger Finke (2000: 226).

Conclusions, Implications, and Questions

One of the primary goals of this chapter has been to propose and test a theoretical model of pluralism that helps to clarify the relationship between religious pluralism and religious participation. As just discussed, the proposed model helps clarify the relationship between religious pluralism and religious participation in several areas. Distinguishing between the concepts of preference pluralism, supplier pluralism and consumer pluralism, the model explains that consumer pluralism is a product of religious supply and religious supply is explained by the diversity of religious preferences and the size of the population. Our initial test of the model offered strong confirmation.

This model also helps us to better understand what the frequently used diversity index is measuring. Rather than serving as an indicator for variation in religious competition, it is often serving as measure of the diversity of religious preferences. To the extent that external market constraints are low and "demand fulfillment" is high, consumer pluralism will measure preference diversity rather than different levels of competition.

But the proposed model has implications that go far beyond the narrow debate on pluralism and participation. Some are related to the market as a whole. For example, this model highlights the importance of constraints on religious markets. To the extent that constraints are placed on religious organizations, demand fulfillment will be reduced. Conversely, the absence of constraints will result in a higher level of demand fulfillment. In short, constraints restrict the ability of religious supply to meet demand.

But the proposed model also holds many implications for the religious organizations operating in the market. Below we list a few propositions that we have addressed in our previous research.

1. To the extent that religious organizations appeal to different niches over time, their potential for growth is altered by the size of the new niche, the number of new competitors, and their ability to compete (Finke and Stark, 2005; Stark and Finke, 2000).

2. To the extent that people unite or interact on the basis of homogeneity, a decrease in homogeneity in one area (e.g., social class) will be met by an increase in homogeneity in another area (e.g., religious beliefs) (Scheitle, 2007).
3. To the extent that religious organizations straddle market niches, they must find ways to allow for homogeneity in subgroups (Stark and Finke, 2000).
4. To the extent that competition is high within niches, niche overlap will tend to reduce the ability of religious organizations to retain members outside of their primary niche (Scheitle, 2007).
5. Religious competition within niches will tend to reduce the growth of any single organization, but will increase overall participation in the religious market (Finke and Stark, 2005; Scheitle, 2007).

The implications and propositions reviewed here are only a first step in this discussion. There are many questions and issues that need far more attention. Some are related to measurement. How do we measure demand fulfillment? In other words how do we measure the gap between observed vs. expected pluralism? We offered a very crude indicator of religious preference, but far better measures should be developed.

Likewise many questions could be raised about market constraints and why these constraints have a greater impact on some religious niches and organizations than others. For example, previous work suggests that during times of social upheaval the more established religions lose support and new religions arise. How are these changes related to the various market niches and how do these changes play out both within market niches and across them? We also need to better understand government and social constraints on religious markets (Grim and Finke, 2011; Finke and Harris, 2012). Sects and cults are the most frequent targets of government restrictions, but how do the constraints targeted for one niche constrain the activities of other niches? And, are some niches better equipped to cope with the restrictions than others? We know that Jehovah's Witnesses continue to organize and even proselytize wherever they go, but what about the religious groups in religious niches where less commitment is required?

With attention narrowly focused on the relationship between pluralism and participation, we have often failed to explore the sources and consequences of this pluralism. The simple model proposed in this chapter offers an initial step in this exploration.

Chapter 12

Authority and Freedom: Economics and Secularization

Steve Bruce

Introduction

Economics has always had a place in the study of certain peripheral aspects of religious organization and behavior. For example, the fortunes of religious organizations—in the metaphorical sense—are obviously tied to their fortunes in the literal sense. Churches have prospered along with their congregations. The English Cotswolds and East Anglia have a number of "wool churches": magnificent fifteenth-century buildings that were a by-product of a local boom in the wool trade. The statistical returns of Methodist chapels in County Durham offer many examples of the other extreme.[1] The quarterly report of membership figures from the Thornley Primitive Methodist circuit in 1886 includes the following plaintive note: "our circuit is still suffering much from the total stoppages of the Thornley, Wheatley Hill and Ludworth collieries. We have taken from the roll books the unusually large number of 319 names for the year; many who were members with us at the time when the collieries stopped have had no employment since and in consequence have ceased to meet with us" (Thornley, 1886).

Churches have not been simply passive victims or beneficiaries of economic change. Some religious organizations have been large enough to influence the economy. The great European monasteries were agricultural as well as spiritual powerhouses. Most religions have some sort of resource that has to be managed. The Church of Christian Science protects and promotes the works of Mary Baker Eddy. The Church of Scientology puts considerable effort into protecting the copyright of L. Ron Hubbard's writings. They may have particular principles that constrain them—nineteenth-century Methodist chapel trustees, for example, would not hire out their halls for social events that involved drinking alcohol or gambling—but like any secular organization, churches have to deal with matters that fall into the remit of economics. The most common subject debated by the trustees of Methodist chapels was not the advance of Methodism or the spiritual needs of the people: it was the cost of repairing or replacing the heating system.

[1] My research on Methodism was conducted while I was in receipt of a Leverhulme Senior Research fellowship, for which I am eternally grateful. I would also like to thank the staff of Durham Record Office and Durham University Library for their assistance.

Furthermore, the language of economics regularly features in religious life because business has always provided a stock of metaphors. Ever since people bought and sold anything, the language of trade has provided a way of talking about other aspects of life. Squeamish believers have regarded such metaphors as inappropriate for God's work but most church people have periodically used them. Some have seen them as a way of challenging inhibiting conservativism. American mass evangelists such as Dwight Moody and Billy Graham, for example, particularly revelled in the application of business language to their operations because they hoped it would attract to their work young men previously alienated by the effete nature of the churches and because it implied that that the mainstream churches were not trying hard enough (Evenson, 2003).

What concerns me in this chapter is something quite different to the traces of economics we find in the above examples. Since the 1990s a small but highly productive and influential group of American sociologists and economists has argued, not that economics can explain the economic concerns of religions, but that the principles which explain economic behavior can also explain perfectly well the core issues of religion that concern sociologists. I have previously presented an extensive critique of the work of Roger Finke, Rodney Stark, and Laurence Iannaccone (Bruce, 1999). Here I will present enough of a critique to show why I reject the economistic version of rational choice theory before trying to be clear about the circumstances in which such an approach to religion would be viable.

A Critique of Rational Choice

The sociological explanation of purposive action generally involves creatively alternating between two very different tasks. We try to find regular patterns of difference in evidence about behavior and we try imaginatively to construct the reasons behind the actions that produce such patterns. Neither interpreting data nor accounting for action on its own is sufficient. Without the patterns in the data we have no evidence; without a plausible account of why people should behave in this way we have no explanation. A crucial element of a plausible account is reasonableness. I do not mean that an action must seem sensible to us; I do mean that if we imagine that we share the values and beliefs of the actors in question and put ourselves in their position then what we think they are doing must be minimally rational (Wallis and Bruce, 1983). As Alfred Schutz put it: "What makes it possible for a social science to refer at all to events in the life world is the fact that the interpretation of any human act by the social scientist might be the same as that by the actor" (1943: 147).

I have problems with the application of economic principles to religious behavior on both fronts. First, many of the propositions derived from the foundational principles of economistic rational choice are not uniquely well supported by the data. That "uniquely" is important. While some rational choice claims are apparently refuted by the evidence, others (especially those derived from human capital models) fit the data all too easily because while the hypotheses seem at first sight to be quite specific they are actually very broad. And the same data generally fit other explanations equally well or better. Second, many of the accounts of individual action that are offered to explain such patterns as are found in the evidence ring false. In some cases an illustration is offered that sounds implausible. In others, when we try to "unpack" the explanation we find that it rests on assumptions about people's motives and intentions that we would not apply to ourselves in similar circumstances. Of course it is not an infallible test but the practical application of Schutz's observation—does it sound like the kind of explanation I would apply to myself?—offers a generally useful way of proceeding. As I will show, the imagined "homo economicus" of the rational choice theorists rarely seems plausible (Bryant, 2000).

Interpreting data

Rodney Stark, Larry Iannaccone, and Roger Finke and a few colleagues believe that differences in patterns of religious behavior should not be explained (as they traditionally have been) as the result of differing levels of demand for, or interest in, religion but as a consequence of market structures and other externalities that influence the supply of religious goods and services (Young, 1997; Finke and Stark, 1992; Finke, 1990; Stark and Iannaccone, 1994). The best known and most powerful of their propositions is that religious diversity (usually coupled with an absence of state interference) is associated with increased participation in religious activities. As Alexis De Tocqueville noted in his later nineteenth-century comparison of France and America, a variety of churches competing in a free market for religious goods attracted more adherents and greater commitment than a single hegemonic church (De Tocqueville, 1969). We may well challenge De Tocqueville's observations on the grounds that the diversity he noted for America as a whole was far less a feature of the religious life of any particular town or village. Edwin Gaustad's detailed religious geography shows that "there were in 1950 amazingly few counties that were not dominated by one or another ecclesiastical bodies ... in approximately one-half of the counties of the nation, a single religious body accounts for at least 50 percent of all the membership in the county" (1962: 159). Although the United Kingdom is often presented as an exemplar of hegemonic state religion, my calculations from the 1851 Census of Religious Worship show a very similar degree of domination (Bruce, 1991).

But there are two much bigger reasons for being skeptical of this key supply-side claim: it fails the general test of wider international comparison and it even more obviously fails the test of change over time. Any review of comparative degrees of secularity across the whole range of European societies shows that the most religious are also the most religiously homogenous. Lithuania is more religious than its more diverse neighbors Latvia and Estonia. Overwhelmingly Catholic Republic of Ireland is more religious than religiously diverse England. Poland, Italy, Spain, and Portugal are more religious than Germany. The supply-side claim also fails the test of comparisons across time within single countries. Even allowing for the murder of the Jews, almost every European state is more religiously diverse now than it was in 1900. And almost every European state is less religious than it was in 1900. If diversity was positively correlated with religiosity the UK should be much more religious now than it was in the Middle Ages. It patently is not.

In brief the supply-side model's interpretation of the data fails at the societal level. Interestingly, Iannaccone recognizes as much when he says that the supply-side model does not work for Catholic cultures, which, given the large number of Catholic cultures in Europe, is much the same as saying that it does not work at all (Iannaccone, 1991).

Accounting for action

The economistic approach is even less convincing in producing accounts of action. I will give two examples to illustrate the problem.

The explanation for the superiority of free markets in religion is complex. One element rests on the "Heinz 57 varieties" proposition that the religious needs of a diverse people are better satisfied by a multiplicity of different churches than by outlets of a single hegemonic church (Finke, 1992). Another concerns the willingness of the clergy to work hard to attract and retain a following. Stark argues that clergy who are paid out of taxation will work less hard than clergy who are paid out of congregational donations. He specifically says that, in contrast to the American position where Lutherans have to raise a congregation in order to raise an income, Lutheran pastors in Germany will prefer to have fewer people in their congregations because that way they maximize their utility: they get paid more for doing less (Stark, 1997). There have been periods in the histories of most state churches that fit that bill: the novels of Jane Austen or Anthony Trollope provide many examples of indolent Anglican clergymen more concerned to flatter their ecclesiastical masters or the landed gentry who controlled lucrative patronage than they were to serve the needs of their parishioners. But the same funding structure did not inhibit the many curates and priests who worked sacrificially to bring both religious offices and social improvement to the lives of their charges. What is plausible as an observation about some cases becomes implausible when it is raised to the level of a general assumption about human behavior. This is apparent if we apply the same logic to university professors. To maximize his utility, Stark should give bad lectures and be rude to his students. Fewer people will take his courses and, until his university sacks him, he will get the same money for less work. I have known hundreds of academics; I know of only two or three who would reason like Stark's imagined Lutheran priest. Of course the clergy are not immune to financial inducements but of all occupations, this one seems less likely than most to attract the utility-maximizing *homo economicus*.

My second example comes from Iannaccone's explanation of why couples who share a common religion tend to be more religiously active than mixed religion couples. One of his reasons is that it is cheaper to be religious if a couple share the same religion. "A household can produce religious commodities more efficiently when both husband and wife share the same religion. Single-faith households benefit from 'economics of scale': the same car drives everyone to church" (1990: 301). Does that really sound plausible? In the nineteenth century Christians in the Scottish highlands thought nothing of walking 20 miles to church and back. Is it really likely that the price of petrol is a primary consideration in whether to attend church or not?

Conditions for Maximizing Utility

Initially my disagreement with the rational choice theorists was *ad hoc* but the frequency with which I found myself at odds with their claims led me to search for the common foundations of the separate arguments. I gradually became convinced that rational choice treatments of specific issues in the sociology of religion were flawed because religion was itself not a suitable realm for utility maximizing. Appropriately my main guide to that conclusion was Gary Becker, the Nobel-prize-winning Chicago economist who was at the forefront of the imperialistic expansion of economics. In a brief essay in a collection on rational choice edited by Jon Elster, Becker presented a handy summary of the basic principles of the economic model of human action (Becker, 1986).

According to Becker, a basic requirement for maximizing utility is that we be able to compare alternatives. In choosing between brands of soap powder, we can compare the strength of the powders and decide which offers the greatest return. Instead of experimenting ourselves, we can subscribe to the reports of a consumer association which performs such tests for us. But how can we compare the value of being a Jehovah's Witness, a Jew and a Jesuit? We can decide which faith has the nicer buildings or the more-uplifting songs but that is like being able to compare only the packaging of rival soap powders. As the veracity of the core claim made by competing religions—the ability to provide life after death—can only be known after death, in this life we have no way of knowing which, if any, is correct.

There is a related problem which is important for my conclusion. When I compare wash powders Sudso and Osdus, I suppose that I am comparing similar chemicals and that my choice of one over the other could easily be reversed, for example, if the weaker of the two is increased in strength. But the Muslim does not view Christianity as a very similar product that with a bit of tweaking could be every bit as attractive. The Strict Baptist One does not suppose that the Church of Rome is a viable alternative that just falls short of being as good as his own faith. The religion to which one adheres is the truth: the religion one rejects is the work of the devil. In contemplating a choice between a Ford and a Volvo, I suppose that both are motor cars and that although I choose one of them, the other still exists. Traditionally religion is not like that. While the neutral observer may see all religions as being similar, adherents see them as categorically different and incomparable. My religion is the true one. The others are the work of Satan: falsehoods designed to trap the unwary. Believers cannot compare religions in the way they compare cars because to the extent that they believe in one religion, the others are not viable alternatives.

Another way of making the same point is to consider the origins of religion. Religions are in one sense obviously a human construct. We can often name the people who invented or significantly developed them: Paul, Gautama Buddha, Guru Nanak, Joseph Smith. But unlike secular productions such as literature or music, the authorship of which is acknowledged and copyrighted, religion is routinely reified (Berger and Luckmann, 1967). It is a constitutive feature of all major religions (and most minor ones) that the human authorship is denied. Adherents to any one religion will always accuse *other* religions of being social constructions but their faith is the one true unchanging religion delivered by God which they had no choice but to accept. If that is an accurate understanding of how most adherents view religion, then we have to say that the comparison of alternatives which, according to Becker, is an essential pre-condition for rational choice, is not a common feature of the realm of religion.

A second requirement for economizing, Becker says, is the ability to compare costs. The price of different soap powders is expressed and exacted in a common currency. My box of Sudso conveniently tells me how many machine loads I can wash with its contents at particular temperatures; it also tells me the price. My supermarket also aids price comparison by listing under the packages of various sizes, the price per standard unit of weight. I can thus readily see the relative costs of Sudso and Osdus. But the costs of being a Jew, Jesuit, Jehovah's Witness, or Jain are almost as obscure as the benefits. Selling enlightenment is common among purveyors of New Age spirituality (and I will return to the significance of that fact) but it is anathema to the major religious traditions. One of the key complaints of the Protestant reformers was that the Church was selling God's mercy. The problem is not solved by substituting the "shadow price" of time for money. How costly is time spent on some activity depends on the extent to which we find that passage of time pleasant or otherwise. An hour of third rate Christian rock music is suffering to me; it is patently a pleasure to members of charismatic fellowships. This is not just a difference of taste. It is also an unavoidable consequence of the alternation that takes place around the point of belief. Drinking cheap wine and eating stale bread and consuming the blood and flesh of Christ may to all outward appearances be the same activity but for the unbeliever and the believer the mass are two quite different things. As the "cost" of attending mass is quite different for the believing Catholic and the skeptical observer, it is difficult to see how the costs of belief can be compared.

A third requirement is the opportunity to choose between alternatives. For most of recorded history, religious affiliation has not been a matter of choice. For most people now living, religious affiliation has not been a matter of choice. Religion identity is generally a matter of destiny. People acquire religion in the same way they acquire language: by being born in a particular time and place. As with language, they adhere to it because everyone else does. And with time and generations, the faith acquires the additional authority of history and tradition.

Here we come to the crux of the matter. The believer's freedom to choose is constrained psychologically by the assumption that one religion is right and the others wrong. The task is to identify God's will, not our preferences. The three capacities that Becker posits as essential to economizing all require that people objectively have the chance to choose and subjectively believe that they have the right to make such judgments. Even when religious people do make choices (which for reasons I will elaborate is rarely), they do not believe themselves to be doing so. They have been called by God. Conventionally religious cultures suppose that there is a God (or a divine principle with the power of moral judgment) and that our job is to conform to his demands. Religion is authority.

The freedom to choose is further constrained by *social pressure*. If all the people of a certain territory belong to the same religion, that pressure is considerable. Adding an element of diversity increases the pressure if competing religious identities are associated with competing ethnic or national identities. And precisely because the spread of any new religion often follows ethnic (especially linguistic) fault lines, religion is often closely associated with other equally powerful sources of group identity. In Pakistan, Sunni Muslim terrorists kill Shia Muslims because they are religious deviant; they also kill them because they are ethnic minority Persian-speaking Hazaras. After owning five Vauxhall Vectras, I bought a Ford Mondeo. No one tried to kill me for my apostasy. In Iran and Pakistan apostasy is punishable by death. During the break-up of the former Yugoslavia, inter-faith couples were ostracized, exiled or murdered.

Even when religious affiliation is not closely tied to some secular identity which commands loyalty, that religions tend to have ethnic bases and associations is a constraint on choice. One of the most curious failings of Stark *et al.*'s research into the effects of religious diversity is that in measuring how diverse is any particular place, they count ethnic variants of the same denomination as alternatives. To a Swedish speaker, adding a German Lutheran church to a town that already has a Swedish Lutheran church is hardly increasing the options. The point is even more telling when applied to race. Even now American church life is heavily segregated; very few white people attend black churches. Having black and white Pentecostal churches gives more diversity than having just one or the other but it does not increase choice.[2]

---

[2]   A generally unremarked weakness of much research on the effects of religious diversity is that it uses the Herfindahl index of difference, which produces a score between 0 and 1, where the higher number represents greater diversity. If a town has five equally popular churches, it scores 0.80. But if it has one large church to which half the people belong, three each with 10 percent and four others each with 5 percent of the population, it will score only 0.61. The first case will be counted as more diverse than the second, even though the second offers a greater range of choices.

That until very recently the distribution of religions usually coincided with ethnic, national, or state boundaries reminds us that such changes in the religious landscape as do occur are seldom the result of shifts in individual preference. Or at least we can only shoe-horn such change into the language of individual utility-maximizing by saying that the late fifteenth-century Iberian Jews who converted to Christianity on the threat of death had an individual preference not to be killed: true but trite. The spread of Islam around the Mediterranean was the result of military conquest. France is not a Catholic country because millions of individual Frenchmen severally decided to prefer Catholicism. When Clovis converted in the sixth century he imposed his decision on his nobles who in turn used force and persuasion to bully and hector their people into conformity.

To summarize, there are three reasons why it is difficult to regard religion as an appropriate field for the exercise of choice. First, there is the empirical observation that most people inherit rather than choose a religion. Second, religious people do not generally think of themselves as having the right to choose; God chooses them rather than the other way round. Third, where religion is popular and socially important, it is usually associated with other bases of social identity which prevent, constrain or inhibit choice to an extent that is not found with the sorts of consumer goods and services that conventionally occupy the time of economists.

I could continue to work through the list of Becker's basic principles of economics but this brief consideration of the above three—the ability to compare outcomes, to compare costs, and to make choices—is enough to make the point that religion, as it has been traditionally conceived and practiced, is not treated by its adherents as a field of opportunities to maximize utility. It has not been a consumer good.

Secularization

I use the past tense in the previous sentence because two important facets of secularization are the decline in obedience to divine authority and the decline in the use of social power to enforce religious conformity. As religion has lost social significance it has become more like a consumer good. The secularization paradigm is considerably more complex than the straw man its critics like to demolish but it can be summarized in three related changes: the differentiation of the secular sphere from religious institutions and norms; the marginalization of religion to the private sphere; and the decline in popularity of religious beliefs and practices (Casanova, 2006: 12). Although Bryan Wilson used indices of decline to illustrate secularization, he defined it by the first two changes. It is generally the relationship between those first two and the third that is at the root of most arguments. Peter Berger, for example, initially offered the most articulate explanations of why the first two changes led to the third but later recanted and argued that social differentiation and privatization need not erode the plausibility of religion (Berger, 2011). I think his recantation unnecessary and continue to argue that that differentiation and marginalization, by weakening the social authority of religion and reducing the impact of religious institutions on the lives of most people, decreases its salience and weakens the mechanisms by which it is successfully transmitted from generation to generation (Bruce, 2011). Stark's supply-side story is in effect a reversal of the conventional connections: structural differentiation strengthens religion by allowing churches to concentrate on their core business; marginalization removes government interference; the free market does the rest.

My argument in this chapter does not require the bigger arguments over secularization to be settled. It is enough to note that whatever its cause, there has been a notable decline in levels of religious belief and practice in the modern industrial liberal democracies of the West and that includes the USA. The current "culture wars" should not distract us from the fact that, between the middle of the twentieth century and its end, the proportion of the American people that is regularly church-going declined from around 40 percent to about 20 percent. But almost more important than the decline in popularity of organized religion in the West is the shift in its ethos from church and sect-like certainty and dogmatism to denominational and cultic ecumenism, liberalism, and syncretism. We do not have to accept all three elements of the secularization paradigm. We need only accept the first two and take them as the cause of a fundamental change in the way that societies see religion and then add that most mainstream denominations (and the sort of alternatives described as "New Age") have colluded with the change by making their faith more this-worldly than other-worldly in orientation, more inclusive than exclusive in attitude to alternatives, and more therapeutic than God-pleasing in primary purpose. Let us call this "secularization." We can now go back through Becker's pre-requisites for utility-maximizing and see how secularization changes their applicability to religion.

First, there is the issue of comparing outcomes. The this-worldly, therapeutic, and ecumenical ethos of most mainstream churches makes comparison easier because it removes the need to work out which faith has the unique access to salvation. In what amounts to *de facto* universalism, most churches now accept that most others will also provide salvation. At the same time, most have become rather quiet about just what salvation actually means. Hell has generally fallen off the agenda and mentions of heaven have become either vague or rare. However much religious leaders may in private wish it different, they now act as if most churches are similarly good at delivering the primary object of religion and thus leave potential members to compare the secondary elements. For the last five years I have been fairly systematically sampling the range of Christian churches on offer in the UK and where possible engaging attenders in conversation about their reasons for choosing one church over another. Not one person has explained his or her choice by reference to the major theological or ecclesiastical differences that created our current denominational landscape. To illustrate the point I will summarize the main appeal of the charismatic "new churches": easy road access and parking, comfortable buildings with toilets, soft chairs rather than pews, after-service coffee and snacks, crèches, and lively worship styles.

The abandonment of claims to unique access to salvation is even more stark in the world of New Age, alternative, or holistic spirituality. In this realm there is no authority greater than the individual. If there is a divine power, it resides in all of us and we simply have to discover it. With truth reduced to "what works for me" and conflict removed by the relativistic assumption that what works for me may not necessarily work for you, then it is possible for people to compare between alternatives. More than that, they feel comfortable selecting elements from a wide variety of religious traditions and combining them. The active seeker may learn to meditate with the Hindu-inspired Transcendental Meditation, take "Mindfulness" courses at a Tibetan Buddhist monastery, and adopt some of the principles of Chinese necromancy in decorating their house according to their understanding of Feng Sui. The modern spiritual person can maximize his or her utility by sampling a variety of religions.

It remains difficult to compare costs because, New Age spirituality aside, religion continues to resist monetization. Nonetheless it is only in a largely secular culture that people think about religion in those terms. Only the self-aggrandizing consumer would claim the right to even contemplate the price of religion let alone decline to follow the path of righteousness because it was too expensive. When Margaret Fell, an early English Quaker, wrestled with the question of whether she should outwardly conform to the state church and take communion in the Church of England, she did not consider the price of her actions (or inaction). She prayed for God's will to be made clear to her (Glines, 2003).

Although the complexity of the causes makes it difficult to demonstrate the causal connections, an important element of the secularization paradigm concerns the combined effects of increased individualism and the growth of science and technology. The religion of the Middle Ages was hierarchical and authoritarian: the power of the Creator being mirrored in the power of his earthly representatives. The proper attitude of the laity was unquestioning obedience. By making every person individually responsible for his or her salvation, by removing the clergy's role as intermediary, and by encouraging literacy, the Reformation inadvertently gave a considerable boost to the importance of the individual over against the community. Although the individualism was initially one of responsibility, it eventually became one of rights. Science and technology greatly increased our control over our environment. The combined result was what David Martin has called an increased sense of "mastery over fate": "the general sense of human power is increased, the play of contingency is restricted, and the overwhelming sense of divine limits that afflicted previous generations is much diminished" (1969: 30). Compared to their medieval ancestors, modern people are simply more questioning and more assertive. They may still find it hard to compare the costs of competing religions but they now have the right attitude for such comparisons.

I earlier mentioned that most New Agers are quite comfortable buying and selling spiritual goods and services. In part this is because they appreciate that the providers are not backed by a church with historically accumulated resources and need to be paid for their work. In part it is because the cash nexus is a way of expressing the right to determine costs. Traditional religion offers its services freely but then exerts considerable pressure on the adherent to conform to its demands. Because you pay to attend Experience Week at the Findhorn community, you remain in control of your commitment. If after the third day, you decide that it is not working for you, you can walk out. Because you buy the Osho dynamic meditation DVD, you decide when you are going to meditate.

The largely secular society clearly allows Becker's third pre-requisite. In the sixteenth century, British monarch Queen Mary had the Archbishop of Canterbury and two other leading bishops burnt to death in public—the equivalent of having them shot on prime-time television—because they would not accept her interpretation of God's will. Many objected to Mary's decision but few objected to the principle that the state should use its power to enforce the correct religion. It is precisely part of what we mean by secularization that modern societies not only a) allow people to worship the wrong God but b) also actively protect our right to be religiously wrong. It is now almost two hundred years since the British government accepted that citizenship rights could no longer be coupled to religious affiliation and allowed Catholics the vote. It has now gone further and passed an equality act which severely curtails the rights of religious people to discriminate against those who do not share their principles. For example, no matter how strong their convictions, conservative Protestant hoteliers can no longer refuse to rent a room to a homosexual couple. Religious affiliation has largely been de-coupled from other forms of social identity. Some historical ethnic connections remain. A working class Northern Ireland Catholic who married a Protestant would still be wise to move to one of the province's mixed cosmopolitan areas but even in Northern Ireland the notion of religious liberty is sufficiently well-embedded that politicians such as Ian Paisley, who built his career on religio-ethnic conflict, ended it making speeches in favor of religious freedom (Bruce, 2009: Ch. 9). The insistence of some Greek politicians that Greek national identity should continue to be co-terminus with Greek Orthodox Christianity or the decision of the Hungarian Fidesz party government to reduce the number of officially-recognized religions from 300 to 14 are widely condemned as infringements of human rights.

The change in the nature and status of religion has, of course, not gone unopposed. One suspects that many religious leaders privately yearn for a return to the days of power and domination. I am fairly sure that when he is at home in the Vatican, the Pope still thinks that the Catholic Church alone has the ear of God and everyone else is wrong. In its public presentations, Transcendental Meditation denies that it is a religion, offers its meditational techniques to all comers, and tells potential customers that no change of belief is required. But it has its Siddhis program for advanced meditators and in that inner core, TM is not just one religion among others but the best religion. Clearly some members of fundamentalist churches that support the Christian right in the USA would like to see a return to a world in which their values and patterns of behavior occupied a position of social honor. But even such traditional believers are forced to accept the modern rules of engagement. The US Christian Right does not argue that abortion should be banned because God says so; it argues the secular case that abortion infringes the right to life of the unborn child. It does not argue that gay marriage offends the God who sorted out Sodom and Gomorrah; it argues the social functional case that heterosexual marriage offers the best environment for the raising of children. Darwinian evolution is no longer rejected, as it was by William Jennings Bryan in the famous Scopes trial, on the grounds that "The Rock of Ages is more important than the age of rocks"; instead it is claimed that the scientific evidence better favors an "intelligent design" model (De Camp, 1968). In brief, even those who wish to return to theological imposition are compelled to defend their ambitions in secular terms and to make their case in secular arenas such as elections and law courts.

In the first part of this chapter, I argued that religion, as it has been conceived and practiced in the past (and as it is still conceived and practiced in large parts of the globe), is not amenable to rational choice explanations because such religion does not allow what Becker regards as the pre-requisites for economizing behavior. If people do not, or are unable to, compare benefits and costs and do not, or are unable to, choose their religion, there is little point in trying to analyze their behavior with the intellectual tools of economics. In the second part, I tried to show that changes in the nature and status of religion in the western world over the last two centuries have removed some of the psychological and social obstacles to economizing.

The conclusion of this line of reasoning, if it is accepted, is profoundly ironic. Stark and his associates have been at the forefront of the application of the principles of economics to religious belief and behavior. They have also been the most vociferous deniers of secularization. The two things are not necessarily connected. It would be possible to argue that some of their supply-side explanations work equally well for all levels of religious demand. For example, were it true, the claim that the state-support for religion depresses uptake could work in settings where there was high and low implicit demand for religion. However, as well as asserting that societal differences in levels of religious take-up are a consequence of characteristics of the religious market (that is, a supply-side phenomenon), Stark, Finke, and Iannaccone have committed themselves to the view that the demand for religion is stable and enduringly high. Stark offers two reasons for this. In the compensators and rewards theory he developed with William S. Bainbridge he argued that religions were superior to secular ideas in providing plausible compensators because they could invoke the next life as well as this one (Stark and Bainbridge, 1987). In his attempt to explain why women are more religious than men, he offered Blaise Pascal's wager in the new guise of "risk-aversion." Women are more religious than men because, as they show by committing fewer crimes, they are less likely to take risks (Miller and Stark, 2002). He does not spell out just what is the risk in being religiously indifferent but we have to presume he means that the irreligious run the risk of getting hell instead of heaven. Both arguments have been criticized extensively elsewhere and need not concern us beyond appreciating that Stark and his colleagues think that, while particular expressions of religious sentiment may rise and fall, in the long-run secularization is impossible because the stable implicit demand will find some new outlet.

The grand irony is that it is only when attitudes to religion change in ways most of us are happy to call "secularization" that it becomes possible to apply the principles of economics to religious behavior. In conventionally religious cultures, the ideas of the rational choice approach are irrelevant. Only in largely secular societies, which Stark and his colleagues deny exist, is it possible for ordinary people to treat religion in a utility-maximizing manner and hence for analysts to explain their behavior in terms of economistic rational choice ideas. It is only when religion loses its supernatural authority and is marginalized as a matter of personal preference over which the community and the state has no right of judgment, that it becomes a consumer good like cars and toothpaste. Only in a largely secular society is religion a matter of personal preference.

Conclusion

There is a crucial turning point in the social development of religion in the West when most people stopped believing in an authoritative God who had to be obeyed and started to think of themselves as having the ability and the right to choose their Gods. That change in attitude was accompanied by a fundamental change in the social status of religion. Although the roads to religious freedom were many and tortuous, most modern states now regard religious affiliation as a private matter. As religion has declined in popularity, ties between religious affiliation and other social forms of identity have weakened. The major Christian churches in the West have accepted that they can no longer impose on the people in the manner of the sociological "church" and many sects have also evolved in a denominational direction. Our new forms of religion, exemplified by the world of holistic spirituality, are sociological cults. Migration has brought to the West sizeable populations of Muslims, many of whom maintain a traditional authoritarian, dogmatic, and impositionist view of religion but even they are now accommodating. The tiny numbers of jihadists attract the most attention but a far greater number are coming to the view that religious affiliation and commitment should be matters of personal preference.

The rational choice theorists often cite Adam Smith's *An Inquiry Into the Nature and Causes of the Wealth of Nations* for its defense of the market free from state interference. They miss its more germane message: the claim for an economic sphere free from the influence of such non-economic considerations as religious precepts. Smith can as well be seen as a proponent of structural differentiation as of Chicago economics. What I have argued is that so long as religion is traditionally conceived, it is not a realm for utility-maximizing. Although this may sound somewhat paradoxical, it is the recent freeing of religion from traditional religious considerations that now allows people to treat their faith as a matter of personal choice and preference. It is secularization that allows us to self-consciously select our Gods and thus allows the possibility that, insofar as people engage in utility-maximizing in this field, the application of principles from economics may be illuminating. However, the freedom to choose Gods is also the freedom to choose none and the Gods that we self-consciously choose to worship will never be as powerful as those we felt obliged to obey on fear of eternal death. Precisely because it permits choice, modern religion is of low salience.

In so concluding I have no wish to denigrate the work of my colleagues who are interested in the branding and marketizing of religion. Doubtless there is much of value to be learnt by applying concepts from economics and business studies to religion in the modern world. I would only add this reservation. The same change that makes such a novel disciplinary focus worthwhile also explains why relatively few people are interested in religion.

Chapter 13

The "Business Model" of the Temple of Jerusalem: Jewish Monotheism as a Unique Selling Proposition

Philippe Simonnot

I am Abraham's servant. The Lord has greatly
blessed my master, and he has become wealthy;
he has given him flocks and herds, silver and gold,
male and female slaves, camels and donkeys.

Genesis 24: 34–5

A single place of worship of a single God for a single people: such is the Unique Selling Proposition in the form of a "trinity" that prevailed in ancient Judaism, from the tenth century B.C. to the destruction of the temple of Jerusalem by the Roman troops in the year 70 of our era. This model made the Jewish temple the most important financial center of that time, after Rome. The accumulation of capital reached such a level in the first century B.C. that the Roman general Crassus in 54 could draw from it more than 10,000 talents (60 million *denarii*), a gigantic sum if we consider that the tribute that the Romans imposed on Judea when they conquered it was in the order of 700 talents per year. This "business model" did not cease to haunt the two other religions come from the Bible, Christianity and Islam, without either one of them ever managing to reproduce it completely, whereas not an insignificant part of Judaism and of modern evangelicalism continues to imagine or to hope for the reconstruction of the famous temple.

Apparently, nothing in the original Hebrew religion is predisposed to such monopolization. When Abraham arrives in Canaan, he appropriates the already existing holy places: the Oak of Moreh at Shechem, the Oak of Mamre at Hebron, the altar at Bethel (situated ten km north of Jerusalem), Mount Moriah (the future Jerusalem). The "Covenant Code" between God and the chosen people, in Moses' version, goes as far as to legitimate the multiplicity of the sanctuaries: "You need make for me only an altar of earth and sacrifice on it your burnt-offerings and your offerings of well-being, your sheep and your oxen; in every place where I cause my name to be remembered I will come to you and bless you."[1] The Ark of the Covenant, conceived in the desert of Exodus, is eminently mobile. Even David, who would set it up in Jerusalem, took it with him when he had to flee

---

[1] Exodus 20: 24.

the Holy City occupied by Absalom, his rebellious son. Only when Solomon built the temple would the Ark find its definitive place in the Holy of Holies in the tenth century B.C. It was thus necessary to adapt the Covenant Code for the monopolistic trend of the cult to make headway. More especially as this trend would be naturally contradicted by the very multiplicity of the "high places" and the political, economic, religious, and social interests with which they are inevitably associated.

We must, therefore, explain how Judaism evolved from multi-polarity to the extreme centralization that has been its leading form for centuries. Economic reasoning, it seems, opens the way to understanding not only the reasons for such a process, but also its financial, social, and political consequences. For this we must first answer the question: supposing that religion is an economic good, to which category does it belong?

Religion as an Economic Good

Of the different ways to categorize economic goods, we will look at three, which appear to us the most pertinent for classifying religion: *according to the degree of information of the consumer, according to the appropriability, and finally according to the mode of payment.*

According to the degree of information of the consumer, we distinguish three types of goods: 1) "inspection" goods, whose quality we can measure by sight (apples or fish on display), 2) "experience" goods, which reveal their quality only after being experienced (the meal served to you in a restaurant), and 3) "credence" goods, whose quality rests on the confidence that you have in their producer: you will never know, if you are healed, if you owe the healing to your doctor or to nature or to good luck; similarly, if you win or lose a trial, you will not be able to verify the part attributable to your lawyer; if your banker makes a fortune for you, you can always claim that he had nothing to do with it. For "credence" goods, it is not by chance that special orders and distinctive clothing have been instituted (the Order of physicians, the Order of architects, the Order of lawyers, etc.)[2] so as to furnish a mark of quality that can reduce the asymmetry of information between the producer and the consumer, much greater than in the first two categories.

Within the credence goods category, we can further differentiate goods of "pure credence," where the asymmetry of information is both maximal and bilateral. Maximal because the result of religious practice is both unverifiable and un-falsifiable, to return to the well-known categories of Popper (we can verify neither that the result is true, nor even that it is false), especially if is situated in "another life," *post mortem.* It is bilateral because "clients" cannot verify the quality of the "product" served to them and because, at the same time, the "producers" cannot

---

[2]   Many people are aware of the attempt at regulation that has targeted psychoanalysis these past few years in France.

appreciate, either, the sincerity of the "clients" except to probe their kidneys and their heart. Certainly, they sometimes have recourse to "inquisitions," but their result, as we know, is hardly convincing. Hence the importance of rituals, dietary restrictions, clothing, vows, pilgrimage duties, creeds and orthopraxy—a vain race for evidence of a genuine faith that can never be produced.

We can also explain the enormous investments that certain religions pour into their sanctuary—investments all the more costly as they are not recoverable. So it was for the gigantic Temple of Jerusalem. So it was, for the immense Gothic cathedrals.[3] So it was, once again, for the monumental Saint Peter's Basilica in Rome. Every time, it is a question of reinforcing popular belief and fervor by the magnificence of the places of worship. Just like the banks that cover their offices and facades with marble to reassure the customers.

If there is order, then, for physicians, lawyers, bailiffs, and bankers, there is all the more reason for us to expect to find order in religion, and that is in fact what we observe in most cases. That is saying that in this domain, we must expect to see some distrust towards the competition and a trend to cartelization, or even to monopolization. The value of a pure credence good depending entirely on the credibility of its provider, we can expect that the latter will tolerate with difficulty the presence of rival competitors who will necessarily want to implicate this credibility in order to enhance their own.

We can also explain by these characteristics the way in which a religion enters the "market." It must appear as very new, of course, to attract new "clients," but also very old, to reassure them, great age appearing as a guarantee of quality in this domain. If generations have believed in such and such a god for centuries or even for "centuries of centuries" to use a time-honored phrase, it is because that particular god has a good chance of existing. Thus, first-century Christianity, although new, claimed precedence over Judaism by referring directly to Abraham. And Islam performed exactly the same operation six centuries later. An exercise rarely successful in history and whose difficulty reinforces the monopolistic tendencies of the religious "market."

Second criterion of classification: appropriability, or the quality of a good of being appropriable.[4] Here economists distinguish individual goods from collective goods. Individual goods can be appropriated individually; collective goods cannot. This hat, if it is on my head, will not be on yours. It is an individual good. The air that I breathe is a collective good. It is not appropriable. Contrary to appearances, many goods and services have this characteristic. When you grow roses along the border of your property, passers-by that you will never see again, and from whom you cannot obtain any tolls, benefit from their beauty and their scent. If I smoke

---

[3]   The art historian Henry Kraus maintains that donations for building the cathedrals were easier to obtain when the threat of the plague was imminent. Cf. Kraus, H. (1979).

[4]   Readers may refer to our *Économie du droit*, tome 2: *Les personnes et les choses*, Paris, Les Belles lettres, 2004.

a cigarette in public, I make unknown third parties "benefit" from the smoke that I exhale.

The collective good has a very remarkable and almost miraculous property, which is of concern to the economy of religion in that it recalls the miracle of the multiplication of loaves in the Gospels or again of manna in Exodus: the fact that an additional individual is enjoying its advantages does not reduce the amount available to everyone else who is already doing so. In the language of the economists, this property is called "non-rivalry." Thus a collective good is such that the fact that an individual is consuming it does not prevent at least one other person from consuming it at the same time. Religion would thus have the appearances of a collective good, while providing individual satisfaction.

It is quite obvious that the State will tend to take an interest in collective goods because the very fact of their being collective makes them difficult to finance.

The collective good has a second characteristic that is of concern to the economic analysis of religion, that of being "non-enclosable."[5] We say that a good is "enclosable" when, in the state of our technical knowledge, there is an economic means of preventing people from consuming it once it is produced. By opposition, a good is said to be "non-enclosable" when the means of preventing people from consuming it comes at a prohibitive cost. I cannot prevent the bees from my neighbor's hive from gathering pollen in my garden, except by building protections that are outrageously expensive and ultimately ridiculous.

We must realize that the possibility of enclosing depends on the state of technology. A television broadcast over the airwaves was apparently non-enclosable until the day when scrambling processes were invented that can exclude television viewers who are not equipped with decoding devices. In general, individual goods are in appearance more easily enclosable than collective goods are. However, enclosable collective goods do exist. A performance that takes place in the street is certainly not enclosable. But if it is produced in a closed space, it is enclosable. And people can be made to pay to attend it. Access to a place of worship can be prohibited to non-Muslims, as has been the case for mosques in France for the past few years[6] and in Mecca since Mohammed. On Christmas Eve, the basilica of the Vatican, which is enclosable, is enclosed, and its entry limited to those who have a pass. It would be easy to charge for this pass. We could say the same thing about all places of worship. The temple of Jerusalem was eminently enclosable—only the High Priest could enter the Holy of Holies once a year.

On the other hand, access to a religion is generally free; it is enough to believe in it (that is what is called conversion) on the condition, in some cases, of undergoing

---

[5]   The French scholarly literature employs the term "*non-excluable*," taken from the even worse-sounding English word "*non-excludable*," which is less expressive than non-enclosable. Accordingly, we replace excludable by enclosable in the remainder of the text, while asking readers to please excuse all this jargon.

[6]   We could also cite cases of auto-exclusion. I tried to show a Muslim friend around the Cathedral of Notre Dame in Paris. She obstinately refused to set foot in it.

certain rites. Thus, access to Judaism is limited, for men, to the circumcised.[7] Now, circumcision horrified the Greeks or the Romans. Some religions or sects go much further in excluding, purposely erecting barriers to entering in different forms: completely shaving one's head or else never shaving one's beard, wearing clothing of a certain color, covering women's heads with a veil, prohibiting a particular food or a particular marriage, duties of fasting, praying, going on pilgrimages, abstaining from any sexual relations on certain occasions or even for one's entire life, viewing homosexuality as an "abomination" punishable by death,[8] considering abortion a crime, accepting polygamy or not, prohibiting loans with interest, attending Mass daily (*Opus dei*), doing nothing every seven days, etc. As many ways to make enclosable a good that is not so by nature, and thus to avoid the problems associated with the impossibility of enclosing. All these rules and prohibitions at the same time increase the "access cost" of the religious good.

Due to its characteristics, the collective good incites people to adopt the behaviors of "free riders." This poses a very major problem for the financing of religion.

The passer-by who walks by your flowering hedge enjoys a "free ride." Without spending anything whatsoever, he benefits from your efforts to plant rosebushes. Similarly, a salaried person can benefit from the union action in his company even if he is not a member and is not paying any dues.

Since religion has some aspects of a collective good, we can expect to see problems of "free riding" in its domain. For example, if a belief has beneficial effects on living in society because it teaches love for one's neighbor, respect for keeping one's word, repulsion for crime, or merely rules of public or private hygiene, even the unbeliever will enjoy these benefits without paying the price, that is, without having to undergo the rites and paying the tithes associated with this belief. Another example: if a particular religion provides aid to the poor, assistance to the sick, education to children, and justice, these are as many "collective goods" from which disbelievers benefit just as much as believers do. In every historical period, Machiavellians, cynical to varying degrees, have advocated the support of religion for reasons of a social and/or political nature.

A good share of religious services is conducive to the exercise of free riding. These "Sunday parishioners" who remain content with Sunday Mass, rarely opening their purses, or, even worse,[9] those for whom it is enough to make their "Easter duty," benefit from the services of the parish priest no less than the pious faithful who take part fully in parish life. Free riding is also manifest in the temporal distribution of works of piety. Often succeeding a carefree and sinful youth is an

---

[7]   "It remains almost impossible for a non-Jew to convert to the religion of Israel," writes even Paul Veyne in his most recent book (2007).

[8]   "You shall not lie with a male as with a woman; it is an abomination." Leviticus 18: 22. "If a man lies with a male as with a woman, both of them have committed an abomination; they shall be put to death; their blood is upon them" Leviticus 20: 13.

[9]   Worse from the viewpoint of the church in question and of its funding.

old age narrowly confined to devotion and prepared to pay dearly to "redeem one's sins" and to secure the salvation of one's soul. What would happen to the accounts of Social Security, already in a very bad way, if we paid our contributions only at an advanced age?[10] It is true that the young are in general less rich than the elderly, a fact that compensates for the financial effect of their lesser piety.

An ordinary trade exchange enables us to calculate the preferences of the partners by the price that is paid in kind or in money. Free consumption reveals no preference. We certainly suspect that the good in question fulfills a demand, but we are unable to establish a "function" for this demand, that is, to know what quantities are demanded for what price. In these conditions, it is very difficult for a private business to launch into the production of such a good. Hence the attempted intervention of state control already mentioned.

The question becomes complicated because of "network effects," sometimes called in the scholarly literature "club effects" from which religion benefits. This means that the value that a consumer attributes to a good depends on the number of users of this good. Just as an isolated train track can function only when connected to the network, so the people whose computers and software programs are no longer compatible with those of most other users see their investment devalued. The strongest are further reinforced and the weakest weakened. As is said in the Gospels: "For to all those who have, more will be given, and they will have an abundance; but from those who have nothing, even what they have will be taken away."[11]

Network effects are well known to the transportation and communications industries, where the competition between businesses is achieved by extending the networks and where the value of a network increases considerably if it can be connected to other networks. In these domains, the intention is to extend the network over the entire planet.

Similarly, a religion has all the more "value" for the believer as it has believers. The televised spectacle of crowds thronging Saint Peter's Square in Rome for the beatification of John Paul II, for example, or circling the Ka'aba in Mecca, has a considerable publicity value.

The network effect also explains the sudden spread of new sects, as is the case today in Latin America and in Africa where the Evangelicals have conquered "markets" at a rapid rate. But also, we are not surprised to note a trend to cartels, or even monopolies, so great is the difficulty for the "religious SME" to survive for long amid these giants.

---

[10]   In the Christianity of the first centuries, one could resolve this problem by receiving baptism *in articulo mortis*. As a pagan, one cannot commit any sins. By receiving baptism at the moment of death, one was assured of ascending straight to heaven. That is what Constantine the Great did (272–337). Fortunately for the Church, the Roman emperor assigned enormous sums for its funding well before his baptism. The origin of the capital that the papacy still has at its disposal comes from his donations. Cf. Simonnot (2005).

[11]   Matthew 25: 14–30.

The collective good aspect thus reinforces the trend of religion towards monopoly.

Third criterion of classification, pertinent for religion: the mode of payment, which can be either mandatory (taxation), or voluntary. Within the latter, we make a distinction between exchanges and donations. Here a fact comes into play that can be observed at all times and in all places: people have a need to give. Even in our societies said to be dominated by the market economy, the share of donation remains considerable. First, we see it in the flow of everyday life, punctuated by birthdays, anniversaries, all sorts of commemorations, which are as many opportunities to give presents to parents and to friends. But there are also extraordinary events, either caused by natural catastrophes: earthquakes, floods, tsunamis; or artificially created by appeals on radio and television for worthy causes: the fight against cancer, leprosy, AIDS, etc., which can trigger a mass outpouring of public generosity.

Thus, underlying every society, there would be a financial deposit constituted of sums, great or small, which good people are ready to give for the salvation of their soul or their mental health or for any other purpose—a deposit of "potential blessed share."[12] Economists, let us remember, do not have to concern themselves with the psychology or the philosophy of the economic agent. It is enough for them to note that the need to give exists. Each one of the faithful, in principle, gives what he wants, and by this very gift reveals not only his preference but the intensity of his preference, which is, moreover, extremely variable. Sometimes, this is sufficient to finance the collective good in question.

Aided by the division of labor, "companies" are constituted to explore, drill and exploit the deposit of "blessed share." The latter is not indefinitely extensible, even if it is indefinitely renewable on condition of not touching the capital. Every place of worship, even the humblest parish, can thus be considered as a sort of derrick erected there to draw up, if possible, the most from the "blessed share" that there is in the wealth of each person, even in the case of the most impoverished. Every religion tries to tap into this fabulous deposit, and if it can do so, to gain its monopoly over a given territory.

We observe a dynamics of giving, sometimes very powerful. And the call to generosity in certain circumstances proves very efficient and even overly efficient. Let us remember that at the time of the Asian tsunami in 2004, Doctors Without Borders had to ask people to stop sending donations for which there was no longer any use. Similarly, Moses, if we believe the Bible story, had to put an end to the fund-raising initiated to build the sanctuary of Yahweh, which was then no more

---

[12] "Blessed share" by antiphrasis to the *Accursed Share* by Georges Bataille (1947). In this well-known work, the Surrealist poet believes he has discovered in the economic process a permanent trend to excess that can be reabsorbed only by "consummation"—as opposed to mere consumption—that is, by sacrifices, donations, festivals, games, waste, war, destruction, etc.

than the Tent of Meeting.[13] Very quickly, the situation had come about that: "The people are bringing much more than enough for doing the work that the Lord has commanded us to do. So the people were restrained from bringing; for what they had already brought was more than enough to do all the work."[14] This scene that takes place in the far reaches of the desert is obviously implausible. It only tells us that even in a desert, there still lies under the feet of any human community a deposit of "blessed share" that can be explored and exploited.

Moreover, donating is somehow contagious, as we see during the televised broadcasts where a sort of contest as to who will give the most is organized. The prophet Haggai, when he was encouraging the exiled of Babylon to rebuild the Temple of Jerusalem, held out the prospect to them of their gifts to the sanctuary generating a world movement of capital towards Zion. "I will shake all the nations, so that the treasure of all nations shall come, and I will fill this house with splendor, says the Lord of hosts. The silver is mine, and the gold is mine, says the Lord of hosts."[15]

It will thus be a matter of exploring, then of exploiting, this deposit of "blessed share"—in the sense that we said above—and then of transporting its products. Such an "industry," as the history of mining indicates, naturally tends to become a monopoly for well-known reasons of economies of scale and of vertical integration.

Since it is indeed necessary to have intermediaries between the gods and the people, "pontiffs" (etymologically, "bridge makers"), that is, kings, priests, rabbis, monks, imams, etc., the sacrificial offerings are not lost for everyone. The philosopher Rémi Brague said with regard to the Mohammedan god: "Allah: it pays off,"[16] but this rather blunt expression could be applied just as well to the two other religions come from the Bible. Religion would thus be a method of predation all the more efficient as it is based on donations from the faithful and other tithes;[17] it would have invented the oxymoron that is voluntary taxation, subsequently degraded by the State, that pseudo-Church, into a mandatory contribution.

There happens to be a truth too often forgotten by today's economists: there are no monopolies in nature. Monopoly can exist only through intervention of the State, which alone in principle has the power to erect and enforce barriers to entering a market (customs duties, trading licenses, patents, marketing authorizations, etc.). And in fact, in history, all religious monopolies have relied on public authority, or else have appropriated it. For example, the first temple of Jerusalem was built, as

---

[13] The Tent of Meeting would be set up by Joshua at Shiloh after the Hebrews entered the Promised Land. David would transfer it to Jerusalem.
[14] Exodus 36: 4–7.
[15] Haggai 2: 7–8.
[16] Brague (2005).
[17] Unless otherwise stated, we reserve the term "tithe" for voluntary contributions. It would often happen that tithes were made mandatory. They then lose their characteristic of being gifts.

we have just seen, by King Solomon. The second would be constructed upon the return from Exile thanks to the support of the Great Persian King. Coming into play at this point is the well-known dialectic of Pilate and Caiaphas, the Army and the Church, the throne and the altar, the Red and the Black. With the risk that the religious monopoly, like any monopoly, abuses its position as Adam Smith has so perceptively remarked, who explained the abuses that he observed as much among the Catholics as the Anglicans. This is because the Catholic church, like the Anglican church, each on its own territory, avoids competition, and thereby increases its "fees" while the quality of its product is deteriorating; at the same time, from the fact of its position, each one can apply "discriminatory"[18] fees on its "clients"—in ordinary language, fees depending on whether they like the look of you. Again, in nineteenth-century France, there were nine distinct classes of funeral, the first class costing 122 times more than the ninth and involving 22 priests and six cantors; for seats in church, there was the choice of 19 types of subscription and 87 price categories! This is something that has become impossible, as the merchants of religion know very well, since the Church is no longer in a position of monopoly.

Religious monopoly, once successfully established by means of State aid, nevertheless encounters a difficulty coming from the diversity of the religious demand—a difficulty greatly surpassing the mere problems of generation already mentioned. If the majority of the "clientele," presumably, is satisfied with an average quality at an average price, at the two ends of the scale of religious preferences, we find at the "top" end the very pious "consumers" who would be ready to pay a much higher price for a "better quality product," and at the "bottom," on the contrary, "clients" who would be content with a mediocre product at a lower price. This diversity of tastes and demands compels the monopoly, if it wants to survive, to practice a "wide differential" in order to satisfy everyone. The task is not beyond reach as is shown by the example of the Catholic Church when it was in the situation of monopoly. Severe and rigorous monastic orders ensured the satisfaction of the most demanding clients, while the "Sunday parishioners"

---

[18]   We must remember that in principle in a competitive market there is only a single price for a particular category of merchandise. Relative to this price imposed on them by the interplay of competition, some consumers would be willing to pay more. The difference between this higher price and the price really paid constitutes the basis of what is called "consumer surplus" in the jargon of the economists. The consumer will use this surplus either to increase savings or to buy other products. In the case of a discriminatory monopoly, which in order to maximize its profits would manage to practice a price scale corresponding exactly to the various intensities of its clients' desires, all the "consumer surpluses" would, in some sense, be confiscated by the monopolizer. It is very obvious that such discrimination is possible only on two conditions. The first is that the monopoly must be solidly established; otherwise, the "overtaxed" consumer would obtain the merchandise in question from another producer. The second is that this same merchandise must not be resalable, or else the "under-taxed" consumer would have such an advantage in reselling it at a profit to the overtaxed consumer that there would be a gradual return to the single price.

could limit themselves to making "Easter duty"—that is, going to confession and communion once a year, and taking part just as infrequently in the funding of worship. But as soon as the religious "market" is open to competition, then this wide differential is harder to keep up and the old monopoly is attacked at both ends of its "market." At the bottom of the scale, obscure belief systems try to hijack the "Sunday parishioners" with bogus religions or philosophies.

At the top end of the scale, sects come along offering newer, more rigorous and exacting "products," which they succeed in selling at full price, and the "price," that is, the requisite sacrifices of time and of money, even becomes a guarantee of quality, like in art or in fashion. Subsequently, these sects, once settled into their niche, will try to extend their "clientele" by lowering both their prices and their demands. All do not succeed in this, of course. But those who manage to extend become churches in their turn, trying to profit from the monopolistic tendencies of the economy of religion. The birth of Christianity was in keeping, if we dare say, with this "business model." The sect became a church. But we can also conceive that churches re-become sects by letting go of the fringe groups composed of the most lax members of their "clientele" and by concentrating on the most conservative or fundamentalist members.

When the monopoly supported by the State abuses its position, competitors will emerge, either inside the church in question—they are called reformers, schismatics, or heretics (first-century Essenes, sixteenth-century Protestants)—or outside the church, with the appearance of new religions (Christianity, Islam).

From here on we could even imagine, in the manner of the well-known "business cycles," a sort of religious "cycle" that would reproduce itself indefinitely: in a market open to competition, a religion tends to monopoly; this monopoly must be supported by the State; once supported by the State, it abuses its position; the "product" deteriorates; other religions appear and we find once again the situation of competition; and so forth.

Economics of Monotheism

Now if we investigate what type of religion will most easily obey the monopolistic trend, a trend, let us repeat, that is in the very nature of religion, we will find that monotheism is in a good position since, in principle, it attributes the monopoly of divinity, if we dare say, to a single god and this god will have nothing but contempt for the multiple gods of monotheism, challenging even their divine nature.

Immediately obvious to the casual observer is that a single god acts more easily as a financial medium for those who serve him than do a multitude of gods that are in competition. In the first place because the single god provides an easier resolution to the central problem of any religion, namely, that of its credibility. The god that appears in the Bible, certainly, reveals himself as often cruel, terrible, partial, and jealous, but he is less unpredictable and more reliable than the capricious and immoral gods who are on the "market" at the same time. No doubt it was reasonable to offer occasional sacrifices on the "pagan" altars from which the priests took their share, but people could choose among several divinities and if they did not get what they wanted, they could change cults. In monotheism, it is always the same god with which you are dealing—a god, moreover, who is universal; whose look can follow you everywhere on earth. You cannot escape him.[19]

Furthermore, the gods do not appear to be concerned with human affairs except in function of their own interests, while the god of the Bible is constantly preoccupied with "his people." Worship of the gods is usually proportionate to the benefits that people expect to gain from them or to avoiding the miseries that the gods can cause. If need be, people can change gods. The 'love of God' for humanity is a concept that is difficult to imagine in polytheism. It is almost inseparable from monotheism. The single and almighty god cannot not be "merciful," except to condemn humanity to despair.

The next phase, as we may guess, will be to proceed from a single god to a single cult. Then, people will strive to move up to a higher level of monopolization by decreeing that to a single god, a single form of worship must be celebrated in a single place. In the jargon of the economists, we will say that this monotheism has been a "maximize" of the religious income.

As it happened, Judaism has followed these three phases of monopolization very exactly.

Hence the expansion of Jewish monotheism in Antiquity. At the beginning of our era, paganism, in crisis, was fragmented into a multitude of cults, and Judaism had become the first religion of the Roman Empire—penetrating into the social elite through the women, who did not have to undergo the ordeal of circumcision to Judaize. Poppaea, the wife of Nero, is a good example of this. Besides, this same empire needed, in order to consolidate, a monotheism that was not Jewish. Christianity exactly fulfilled this demand, notably when Paul broke free of the requirement for male circumcision.

Consequences of the Monopoly of the Temple of Jerusalem

The centralization of the cult in Jerusalem would lead to the destruction of the competing temples of biblical inspiration, notably the one erected by the Samaritans on Mount Gerizim. It generates an organization of the priestly class in two levels: the priests properly said and the Levites. The mining metaphor can again be used to account for these two levels of exploitation of the "blessed share": the Levites would have the concessions to those deposits granted by the priests of Jerusalem who would have the monopoly of them; the Levites thus have access to the revenues drawn from the deposits that they have permission to exploit, and

---

[19]   We all remember the verse from Victor Hugo: "L'œil était dans la tombe et regardait Caïn." [The eye was in the grave and was gazing at Cain.]

they must pay the priests royalties for this exploitation, that is, tithes of tithes. What complicates the scheme is that the priests on their side have a direct access to the resource.

The exploitation of the "blessed share" is extended to the Jews as a whole, and as the diaspora expands geographically notably for demographic[20] reasons, which require Israel at this period to be a country of emigration, deposits of the blessed share will be exploited all over the world—which will raise problems of transporting revenue to Jerusalem. Obviously the further away one is from the center of the system, the more essential converting the tithes into monetary cash will become, for reasons of convenience and conservation of the value of the transported good.

Thus we see right away that for this centralized system to work, it is necessary for the Jews of the diaspora to refuse to sacrifice locally and to obtain permission to send funds in gold or silver to Jerusalem: two exorbitant privileges at a time when it is evidence of civic-mindedness to honor the gods of the local place and where it is generally prohibited to take out monetary cash. The citizens of Athens could almost have accepted that Jews did not worship the goddess Athena, but what they could not understand is that they would turn down the invitation to honor their god Yahweh in the temple of the city. Not to mention how repugnant they found circumcision.

These privileges were obtained from time to time, but being exorbitant, and thus very visible, they were fragile and likely to be challenged. In other terms, the monopoly of the Temple, by its existence and its functioning, resulted in making life difficult for the Jews of the diaspora, condemned as they were to being imperfect citizens if they had obtained that dignity.

For the Temple of Jerusalem, this influx of money coming from the whole diaspora made it one of the principle financial powers of the period. No other temple attained this level of wealth, because none other was in a situation of monopoly. It was an entirely liquid wealth; the Temple of Jerusalem being endowed with no landed estates unlike all the other temples of Antiquity—and the papacy itself would accumulate immense landed estates. Such liquidity is of a nature to attract a great deal of covetousness, and in fact this Temple of Jerusalem was regularly pillaged, notably by Crassus, as we have said, and of course at the time of its destruction in 70 A.D.

Of course, we observe disfunctioning in the system. Either the priests are not paid enough and have to desert the Temple to be able to survive,[21] or conversely greedy priests steal more than their share. The sons of the priest Eli, priests themselves, take their share from the cauldron while it is still boiling.[22] The first-century Jewish historian Flavius Josephus tells us that under the reign of Agrippa, in the 50s, the high priests had such boldness and impudence that they sent slaves

---

[20]   Everything is arranged in the Jewish religion to ensure the maximum birth rate.
[21]   Nehemiah 13: 10.
[22]   I Samuel 2: 12–17.

to gather the tithes due to the priests with the result that the poorest priests starved to death.[23]

The prophets were not last to castigate the greed of the priests[24] and even of the prophets:

> For from the least to the greatest of them,
> everyone is greedy for unjust gain;
> and from prophet to priest,
> everyone deals falsely.[25]

We are approaching the model of pure theocracy of the second Jewish temple so well described by the great Mommsen in his celebrated *History of Rome*, that is to say, a "religious college directed by a high priest, supported by foreign domination [Persian, then Egyptian, then Greek and finally Roman], and renouncing any political power, in order to preserve the originality of the people and to dominate them, under the foreigner's protection."[26]

The model of the temple of Jerusalem would only be partially "copied" by the two other religions for better and for worse. Thanks to the papacy, Christianity would succeed at least until the Reformation in a financial centralization that would recall that of Jerusalem at the time of its splendor to the point that the Sistine Chapel has the same dimensions as the Holy of Holies of the Jerusalem Temple, without thereby instituting a monopoly of sacrifice, since the Mass can be said on any blessed stone. The papacy has become at certain times, like the temple of Jerusalem, one of the greatest financial powers of the world, attracting the most influential bankers: the Medicis, Fugger, and Rothschild, to mention only the most prominent names. Of course this gigantic monopoly was contested and finally destroyed. Islam, on its side, having built what it thought was a copy of the Temple (the Dome of the Rock) on the site that Solomon had chosen,[27] would

---

[23]   Flavius Josephus, Antiquities of the Jews, 20: 181.

[24]   Micah 3: 11.

[25]   Jeremiah 6: 13; 8: 10

[26]   Mommsen, *The History of Rome*, book VI, chapter XI. The Jewish historian Flavius Josephus, already cited, employs this term himself to describe what he considers as the political innovation of Israel: "Innumerable are the differences in the particular customs and laws among all humankind, but we can summarize them as follows: some legislators have permitted their governments to be under monarchies, others put them under oligarchies, and others under a republican form. Our legislator [Moses] did not consider any of these governments; he has instituted – if we may use such a strained expression—a Theocracy, by ascribing the authority and the power to God." (*Contra Apionem*, II, 164–6.)

[27]   When they arrived in Jerusalem in 1099, many Crusaders thought that it really was the Temple of Solomon. As for Arafat, he said he was convinced that there had never been any temple in that location, that the only Jewish temple had been built on Mount Gerizim, and that consequently Islam had the monopoly of that sacred site in Jerusalem. Cf. Montefiori (2011), pp. 217 and 509.

retain a sort of religious monopoly, in the form of the pilgrimage to Mecca, with all its abuses that we know, without ever succeeding in durably establishing a financial centralism. Today, the Islamic banks weigh altogether one hundred times the financial weight of the Vatican, but they are in competition with one another.

Bibliography

A.T. Kearney, *Addressing the Muslim Market: Can You Afford Not To?* http://imaratconsultants.com/wp-content/uploads/2012/10/Addressing-Muslim-Market.pdf (accessed January 31, 2013).

Abreu, Madalena, "The Brand Positioning and Image of a Religious Organisation: An Empirical Analysis," *International Journal of Nonprofit and Voluntary Sector Marketing*, 11 (2) (2006): 139–46.

Ajzen, Icek, "The Theory of Planned Behavior," *Organizational Behavior and Human Decision Processes*, 50 (1991): 179–211.

Akerlof, George A.: "The Market for Lemons: Quality, Uncertainty and the Market Mechanism," in *Quarterly Journal of Economics*, 84 (1970): 488–500.

Albrecht, Daniel, "Rites in the Spirit: A Ritual Approach to Pentecostal/Charismatic Spirituality," *Journal of Pentecostal Theology Studies*, 17 (1999): 1–280.

Allan, Graham, *A Sociology of Friendship and Kinship* (London: Allan & Unwin, 1979).

Altermatt, Urs, "Schweizer Katholizismus von 1945 bis zur Gegenwart: Abschied vom 'katholischen Milieu,'" *Politisches Studien*, 32 (1981): 53–62.

Alwin, Duane, F., J.L. Felson, E.T. Walker, and P.A. Tufiş. 2006. "Measuring Religious Identities in Surveys," *Public Opinion Quarterly*, 70 (4) (2006): 530–64.

Amghar, Samir, "Le salafisme en France: de la révolution islamique à la révolution conservatrice," *Critique internationale*, no. 40, (2008): 95–113.

Anderson, Benedict, *Imagined Communities: Reflections on the Origin and Spread of Nationalism*, Rev. Ed. (London: Verso Book, 1983 [2006]).

Anderson, Eugene W., and M.W. Sullivan, "The Antecedents and Consequences of Customer Satisfaction for Firms," *Marketing Science*, 12 (2) (1993): 125–43.

Andritzky, Walter, *Alternative Gesundheitskultur. Bestandsaufnahme und Teilnehmerbefragung* (Berlin: VWB— Verlag für Wissenschaft und Bildung, 1997).

Appadurai, Arjun, "Disjuncture and Difference in the Global Cultural Economy, in Mike Featherstone (ed.), *Global Culture: Nationalism, Globalization and Modernity*, 295–310 (London: Sage Publications Ltd., 1990).

Babik, Milan, "Nazism as a Secular Religion," *History and Theory*, 45 (3) (2006): 375–96.

Bader, Christopher, and P. Froese, "Images of God: The Effect of Personal Theologies on Moral Attitudes, Political Affiliation, and Religious Behavior," *Interdisciplinary Journal of Research on Religion*, 1 (11) (2005): 2–24.

Baggini, Julian, "Assembly Required. The Astonishing Scenes at the Opening of a Branch of Ikea Yesterday Were a Kind of Religious Frenzy, Says Julian Baggini, but Worshipping at the Altar of Mammon Needn't Be All Bad," *The Guardian*, February 11, 2005.

Bagozzi, Richard P., "Structural Equation Models are Modelling Tools with Many Ambiguities: Comments Acknowledging the Need for Caution and Humility in Their Use," *Journal of Consumer Psychology*, 20 (2) (2010): 208–14.

Bagozzi, Richard. P., and Y. Yi, "On the Evaluation of Structural Equation Models," *Journal of the Academy of Marketing Science*, 16 (1) (1988): 74–94.

Bailey, Edward, "The Implicit Religion of Contemporary Society: Some Studies and Reflections," *Social Compass*, 37(4) (1990): 483–97.

Bailey, Jessica M., and J. Sood, "The Effects of Religious Affiliation on Consumer Behavior: A Preliminary Investigation," *Journal of Managerial Issues*, 5 (3) (1993): 328–52.

Baldinger, Allan. L., and J. Rubinson, "Brand Loyalty: The link Between Attitude and Behavior," *Journal of Advertising Research*, 36 (6) (1996): 22–34.

Bandyopadhyay, Subir, and M. Martella, "Does Attitudinal Loyalty Influence Behavioral Loyalty? A Theoretical and Empirical Study," *Journal of Retailing and Consumer Services*, 14 (1) (2007): 35–44.

Barker, Eileen, *The Making of a Moonie. Brainwashing or Choice?* (Oxford: Basil Blackwell, 1984).

Barna, George, *Marketing the church. What they never taught you about church growth* (Colorado Springs: Navpress, 1990).

Barnes, Sandra L., "Religion and Rap Music: An Analysis of Black Church Usage," *Review of Religious Research*, 49 (3) (2008): 319–38.

Barro, Robert J., J. Hwang, and R. McCleary, "Religious Conversion in 40 Countries," *Journal for the Scientific Study of Religion*, 49 (1) (2010): 15–36.

Barth, Claudia, *Esoterik. Die Suche nach dem Selbst. Sozialpsychologische Studien zu einer Form moderner Religiosität* (Bielefeld, 2012).

Barth, Karl, "Quousque tandem," *Zwischen den Zeiten*, 8 (1930): 1–6.

Baudrillard, Jean, *The Consumer Society: Myths and Structures* (London: Sage, 2009).

Beaudoin, Thomas M., *Consuming Faith: Integrating Who We Are with What We Buy* (Lanham, MD: Sheed & Ward, 2007).

Beck, Guy L., *Sacred Sound: Experiencing Music in World Religions* (Ontario, Canada: Wilfrid Laurier University Press, ed. 2006).

Beck, Ulrich, *Risk Society: Towards a New Modernity* (London: Sage, 1992).

Becker, Gary, "The Economic Approach to Human Behavior," in Jon Elster (ed), *Rational Choice*, 108–22 (Oxford: Basil Blackwell, 1986).

Becker, Gary S., "The Economic Approach to Human Behavior," in ders. (ed.), *The Economic Approach to Human Behavior*, 3–16 (Chicago: The University of Chicago Press, 1990 [1976]).

Becker, Gary S., *The Economic Approach to Human Behavior* (Chicago: Chicago University Press, 1976).

Becker, Judith, *Deep Listeners: Music, Emotion, and Trancing*. Bloomington, IN: Indiana University Press, 2004.

Beckert, Jens, "Vertrauen und die performative Konstruktion von Märkten," *Zeitschrift für Soziologie*, 31 (2002): 27–43.

Belk, Russell W., "Wolf Brands in Sheep's Clothing," in Jane Pavitt (ed.), *Brand. New*, 68–9 (London: V & A Publications, 2000).

Belk, Russell. W., and G. Tumbat, "The Cult of Macintosh," *Consumption Markets & Culture*, 8 (3) (2005): 205–17.

Belk, Russell. W., M. Wallendorf, and J.F. Sherry, "The Sacred and the Profane in Consumer Behavior: Theodicy and the Odyssey," *Journal of Consumer Research*, 16 (1) (1989): 1–39.

Bellah, Robert. N. *et al.*, *Habits of the Heart: Individualism and Commitment in American Life* (California: University of California Press, 1985).

Berger, Peter L., *The Sacred Canopy: Elements of a Sociological Theory of Religion* (New York: Anchor, 1967).

Berger, Peter L., "Epistemological Modesty: An Interview with Peter Berger," *Christian Century*, 114 (1997): 972–75, 978.

Berger, Peter L., *Adventures of an Accidental Sociologist* (Amherst: Prometheus Books, 2011).

Berger, Peter L., B. Berger, and H. Kellner, *Das Unbehagen in der Mordernität* (Frankfurt am Main: Campus, 1995).

Berger, Peter L., and T. Luckmann, *The Social Construction of Reality: A Treatise in the Sociology of Knowledge* (Harmondsworth, Middx: Penguin, 1967).

Biner, Paul M., and H.J. Kidd, "The Interactive Effects of Monetary Incentive Justification and Questionnaire Length on Mail Survey Response Rates," *Psychology and Marketing*, 11 (5) (1994): 483–92.

Blacking, John, *How Musical Is Man?* (Seattle: University of Washington Press 1973).

Bloch, Jon P., *New Spirituality, Self, and Belonging. How New Agers and Neo-Pagans Talk about Themselves* (Westport: Praeger, 1998).

Bloemer, José M.M., and H.D.P. Kasper, "The Complex Relationship Between Consumer Satisfaction and Brand Loyalty," *Journal of Economic Psychology*, 16 (2) (1995): 311–29.

Bonne, Karijn, and W. Verbeke, "Muslim Consumer Trust in Halal Meat Status and Control in Belgium," *Meat Science*, 79 (1) (2008): 113–23.

Book, Betsy, "Virtual World Business Brands: Entrepreneurship and Identity in Massively Multiplayer Online Gaming Environments," 2005, available at SSRN: http://ssrn.com/abstract=736823 or http://dx.doi.org/10.2139/ssrn.736823.

Boubakeur, Dalil, *Charte du culte musulman en France* (Paris: Éditions du Rocher, 1995).

Bourdieu, Pierre, "Genèse et structure du champ religieux," *Revue française de sociologie* XII (1971): 295–334.

Bourdieu, Pierre, *La Distinction. Critique Sociale du Jugement* (Paris: Minuit, 1979).

222 *Religions as Brands*

Bourdieu, Pierre, *Questions de sociologie* (Paris: Minuit, 1984).
Bourdieu, Pierre, *Die feinen Unterschiede. Kritik der gesellschaftlichen Urteilskraft* (Frankfurt am Main, 1992).
Bourdieu, Pierre, *Rede und Antwort* (Frankfurt am Main, 1992).
Bourdieu, Pierre, and J.-C Passeron, *La Reproduction. Éléments pour une théorie du système d'enseignement* (Paris: Minuit, 1970).
Brague, Rémi, *La loi de Dieu: Histoire philosophique d'une alliance* (Paris: Gallimard, 2005).
Brewer, Stephanie M., J.J. Jozefowicz, R.J. Stonebraker, "Religious Free Riders: The Impact of Market Share," *Journal for the Scientific Study of Religion*, 45 (3) (2006): 389–96.
Brinitzer, Ron, *Religion. Eine institutionenökonomische Analyse* (Würzburg, 2003).
Brinkerhoff, Merlin B., and J.C. Jacob, "Mindfulness and Quasi-Religious Meaning Systems: An Empirical Exploration within the Context of Ecological Sustainability and Deep Ecology," *Journal for the Scientific Study of Religion*, 38 (4) (1999): 524–42.
Brown, Callum G., *The Death of Christian Britain. Understanding Secularisation 1800–2000* (London: Routledge, 2001).
Browne, Michael W., and R. Cudeck, "Alternative Ways of Assessing Model Fit," in K.A. Bollen and S.J. Long (eds), *Testing Structural Equation Models* (Newbury Park, CA: Sage, 1993).
Bruce, Steve, "Pluralism and Religious Vitality," in Steve Bruce (ed.), *Religion and Modernization: Sociologists and Historians Debate the Secularization Thesis*, 170–94 (Oxford: Oxford University Press, 1991).
Bruce, Steve, "The Truth about Religion in Britain," *Journal for the Scientific Study of Religion*, 34 (1995a): 417–30.
Bruce, Steve, "A Novel Reading of Nineteenth Century Wales: A Reply to Stark, Finke and Iannaccone," *Journal for the Scientific Study of Religion*, 34 (1995b): 520–22.
Bruce, Steve, *Choice and Religion. A Critique of Rational Choice Theory* (Oxford: Oxford University Press, 1999).
Bruce, Steve, "The Supply-Side Model of Religion: The Nordic and Baltic States," *Journal for the Scientific Study of Religion*, 39 (1) (2000): 32–46.
Bruce, Steve, *God is Dead: Secularization in the West* (Oxford: Blackwell, 2002).
Bruce, Steve, "Les limites du 'marché religieux,'" *Social Compass*, 53 (1) (2006): 33–48.
Bruce, Steve, "The Social Limits on Religious Markets," in Jörg Stolz (ed.), *Salvation Goods and Religious Markets*, 81–100 (Berne: Peter Lang, 2008).
Bruce, Steve, *Paisley: Religion and Politics in Northern Ireland* (Oxford: Oxford University Press, 2009).
Bruce, Steve, *Secularization* (Oxford: Oxford University Press, 2011).
Bruce, Steve, and D. Voas, "Vicarious Religion: An Examination and Critique," *Journal of Contemporary Religion*, 25 (2) (2010): 243–59.

Bruhn, Manfred, et al., *Oekumenische Basler Kirchenstudie. Ergebnisse der Bevölkerungs- und Mitarbeiterbefragung* (Basel: Römisch-Katholische Kirche Basel-Stadt Evangelisch-Reformierte Kirche Basel-Stadt, 1999).

Bryant, Joseph M., "Cost-Benefit Accounting and the Piety Business: Is Homo Religiosus, at bottom, a Homo Economicus?," *Method & Theory in the Study of Religion*, 12 (4) (2000): 520–48.

Buchanan, James, *The Demand and Supply of Public Goods* (Chicago: Rand McNally, 1968).

Buchanan, James, "The Constitution of Economic Policy," *American Economic Review*, 77 (1987): 243–50.

Callon, Michel, "Is Science a Public Good?," *Science, Technology, & Human Values*, 19 (4) (1994): 395–424.

Campbell, Colin, "The Cult, the Cultic Milieu and Secularization," *A Sociological Yearbook of Religion in Britain*, 5 (1972): 119–36.

Campbell, Donald T., and D.W. Fiske, "Convergent and Discriminant Validation by the Multitrait-Multimethod Matrix," *Psychological Bulletin*, 56 (2) (1959): 81–105.

Carrette, Jeremy, and R. King, *Selling Spirituality: The Silent Takeover of Religion* (London; New York: Routledge, 2005).

Carrick Coleman, B., "Appealing to the Unchurched: What Attracts New Members?," *Journal of Nonprofit & Public Sector Marketing*, 10 (1) (2008): 77–91.

Chatters, Linda M., J.S. Levin, and R.J. Taylor, "Antecedents and Dimensions of Religious Involvement among Older Black Adults," *Journal of Gerontology*, 47 (6) (1992): 269–78.

Chaves, Mark, "All Creatures Great and Small: Megachurches in Context," *Review of Religious Research*, 47 (2006): 329–46.

Chaves, Mark, and P.S. Gorski, "Religious Pluralism and Religion Participation," *Annual Review of Sociology*, 27 (2001): 261–81.

Chen, Chiung H., "Marketing Religion Online: The LDS Church's SEO Efforts," *Journal of Media and Religion*, 10 (4) (2012): 185–205.

Cherak, Fatima Z., "Anthropologie de 'l'exorcisme' en islam: représentations et pratiques de la rouqya en Algérie, en Egypte et en France," thèse non publiée (Aix-en-Provence, Université de Provence, 2007).

Chesnut, R. Andrew, *Competitive Spirits: Latin America's New Religious Economy* (Oxford: Oxford University Press, 2003).

Chestney, Nina, "U.S. Sustainability Spending Seen Doubled by 2014," *Reuters*, October 6, 2010.

Chevalier G., "Genèse et structure du champs religieux," *Revue française de sociologie*, 7 (1981): 295–334.

Chevènement, Jean-Pierre. 2000. Déclaration de M. Jean-Pierre Chevènement, ministre de l'intérieur, sur l'organisation du culte musulman en France dans le cadre de la laïcité et de la loi de 1905 sur la séparation de l'Église et de l'État,

Paris le 28 janvier 2000. http://discours.vie-publique.fr/notices/003000469. html (accessed July 6, 2011).

Christerson, Brad, and M. Emerson, "The Costs of Diversity in Religious Organizations," *Sociology of Religion*, 64 (2003): 163–81.

Churchill, Gilbert A. Jr., "A Paradigm for Developing Better Measures of Marketing Constructs," *Journal of Marketing Research*, 16 (1) (1979): 64–73.

Coase, Ronald H., "The Nature of the Firm," *Economica* (New series) 4 (16) (1937): 386–405.

Collett, Jessica L., and O. Lizardo, "A Power-Control Theory of Gender and Religiosity," *Journal for the Scientific Study of Religion*, 48 (2) (2009): 213–31.

COMOR (Commission organisation de la Consultation des musulmans de France), 2000. Principes et fondements juridiques régissant les rapports entre les pouvoirs publics et le culte musulman en France. http://www.lecfcm. fr/?p=2599 (accessed July 1, 2011).

Corraliza, José A., and J. Berenguer, "Environmental Values, Beliefs, and Actions," *Environment and Behavior*, 32 (6) (2000): 832–48.

Cova, Bernard, "Community and Consumption. Towards a Definition of the 'Linking Value' of Product or Services," *European Journal of Marketing*, 31 (3/4) (1997): 297–316.

Cronbach, Lee J. "Coefficient Alpha and the Internal Structure of Tests," *Psychometrika*, 31 (1951): 93–6.

Cutler, Bob D., "Religion and Marketing: Important Research Area or a Footnote in the Literature?," *Services Marketing Quarterly*, 8 (1) (1991):153–64.

Cutler, Bob D., and W.A. Winans, "What Do Religion Scholars Say About Marketing? Perspectives from the Religion Literature," *Journal of Professional Services Marketing*, 18 (2) (1999): 133–45.

Darnell, Alfred, and D.E. Sherkat, "The Impact of Protestant Fundamentalism on Educational Attainment," *American Sociological Review*, 62 (1997): 306–45.

Dassetto, Felice, *L'Iris et le Croissant. Bruxelles et l'islam au défi de la co-inclusion* (Louvain-la-Neuve: Presses Universitaires de Louvain, 2011).

Davidson, James D., and R.E. Pyle, *Ranking Faiths: Religious Stratification in America* (Lanham: Rowman and Littlefield Publishers, Inc., 2011).

Dawson, Andrew, "Consuming the Self: New Spirituality as 'Mystified Consumption,'" *Social Compass*, 58 (3) (2011): 309–15.

Day, Jonathon, S. Skidmore, and T. Koller, "Image Selection in Destination Positioning: A New Approach," *Journal of Vacation Marketing*, 8 (2) (2002): 177–86.

de Camp, Lyon Sprague, *The Great Monkey Trial* (New York: Doubleday, 1968).

De Graf, N. D., *Secularization: Theoretical Controversies Generating Empirical Research* (2012).

Deacy Christopher, and E. Arweck, *Exploring Religion and the Sacred in a Media Age* (Burlington: Ashgate Publishing Company, 2009).

Delener, Nejdet, "The Effects of Religious Factors on Perceived Risk in Durable Goods Purchase Decisions," *Journal of Consumer Marketing*, 7 (3) (1990): 27–38.

Demerath, Nicholas J., *Social Class in American Protestantism* (Chicago: Rand McNally, 1965).

Deshpande, Rohit, and D.M. Stayman, "A Tale of Two Cities: Distinctiveness Theory and Advertising Effectiveness," *Journal of Marketing Research*, 31 (1994): 57–64.

Deshpande, Rohit., K. Herman, and A. Lobb (2011). "Branding Yoga," *Working Paper, Harvard Business School Marketing Unit Case No. 512–025.*

Deutscher Bundestag, *Endbericht der Enquete Kommission, Sogenannte Sekten und Psychogruppen. Neue religiöse und ideologische Gemeinschaften und Psychogruppen in der Bundesrepublik Deutschland* (Bonn: 1998)

DeVellis, Robert F., *Scale Development: Theory and Applications* (London: Sage Publications, 1991).

Devlin, James F., "An Analysis of Choice Criteria in the Home Loans Market," *International Journal of Bank Marketing*, 20 (4/5) (2002): 212.

Devos, Thierry, D. Spini, and S.H. Schwartz, "Conflicts Among Human Values and Trust in Institutions," *British Journal of Social Psychology*, 41 (2002): 481–94.

Dick, Alan S., and K. Basu, "Customer Loyalty: Towards an Integrated Framework," *Journal of the Academy of Marketing Science*, 22 (2) (1994): 99–113.

Dinnie, Keith, "Place Branding: Overview of an Emerging Literature," *Place Branding and Public Diplomacy*, 1 (1) (2004): 106–10.

Djupe, Paul A., "Religious Brand Loyalty and Political Loyalties," *Journal for the Scientific Study of Religion*, 39 (1) (2000): 78–89.

Dobbelaere, Karel, *Secularization: An Analysis at Three Levels* (Bruxelles: Peter Lang, 2002).

Douglas, Susan P., and C. Samuel Craig, "The Changing Dynamic of Consumer Behavior: Implications for Cross-Cultural Research," *International Journal of Research in Marketing*, 14 (4) (1997): 379–95.

Droge, Cornelia, and R.D. Mackoy, "Postconsumption Competition: The Effects of Choice and Non-Choice Alternatives on Satisfaction Formation," *Advances in Consumer Research*, 22 (1) (1995): 532–6.

Dulleck, Uwe, and R. Kerschbamer, "On Doctors, Mechanics, and Computer Specialists—The Economics of Credence Goods," *Journal of Economic Literature*, 44 (2006): 5–42.

Durkheim, Émile, *Le Suicide: Étude de Sociologie* (Paris: PUF, 1986).

Durkheim, Émile, *The Elementary Forms of Religious Life* (Oxford: Oxford University Press, 2008).

Eckberg, Douglas L., and T.J. Blocker, "Varieties of Religious Involvement and Environmental Concerns: Testing the Lynn White Thesis," *Journal for the Scientific Study of Religion*, 28 (4) (1989): 509–17.

Ehrenberg, Andrew S.C., "Repeat-Buying: Facts, Theory and Applications," *Journal of Empirical Generalisations in Marketing Science*, 5 (2000): 392–770.

Einstein, Mara, *Brands of Faith. Marketing Religion in a Commercial Age* (New York: Routledge, 2008).

Einstein, Mara, "The Evolution of Religious Branding," *Social Compass*, 58 (2011): 331–8.

Ekelund, Robert B., F.G. Mixon, and R.W. Ressler, "Advertising and Information: An Empirical Study of Search, Experience and Credence Goods," *Journal of Economic Studies*, 28 (1995): 33–43.

Ekelund, Robert B., R.F. Hébert, and R.D. Tollison, *The Marketplace of Christianity* (Cambridge: Massachusetts Institute of Technology Press, 2006).

Essoo, Nittin, and S. Dibb, "Religious Influences on Shopping Behaviour: An Exploratory Study," *Journal of Marketing Management*, 20 (7–8) (2004): 683–712.

Evans, Mark, *Open Up the Doors: Music in the Modern Church* (London: Equinox Publishing Ltd., 2006).

Evenson, Bruce J., *God's Man for the Gilded Age: DL Moody and the Rise of Modern Mass Evangelism* (Oxford: Oxford University Press, 2003).

Fam, Kim S., D.S. Waller, and B. Zafer Erdogan, "The Influence of Religion on Attitudes Towards the Advertising of Controversial Products," *European Journal of Marketing*, 38 (5/6) (2004): 537–55.

Fath, Sébastien, *Dieu XXL. La révolution des megachurches* (Paris: Editions Autrement, 2008).

Favre, Olivier, *Les Eglises évangéliques de Suisse* (Genève: Labor et Fides 2006).

Favre, Olivier, "Les évangéliques: des chrétiens convaincus dans un monde de plus en plus secularise," in Martin Baumann, and Jörg. Stolz (eds), *La nouvelle Suisse religieuse, risques et chances de sa diversité*, 134–50, Religions et modernité (Genève: Labor et Fides, 2009).

Featherstone, Mike, "Lifestyle and Consumer Culture," *Theory, Culture & Society*, 4 (1987): 55–70.

Featherstone, Mike, *Consumer Culture and Postmodernism* (London: Sage, 2010).

Feld, Scott L., "The Focused Organization of Social Ties," *American Journal of Sociology* 86 (5) (1981): 1015–35.

Finke, Roger, "How the Upstart Sects Won America: 1776–1850," *Journal for the Scientific Study of Religion*, 28 (1989): 27–44.

Finke, Roger, "Religious Deregulation: Origins and Consequences," *Journal of Church and State*, 32 (1990): 609–26.

Finke, Roger, "An Unsecular America," in Steve Bruce (ed.), *Religion and Modernization: Sociologists and Historians Debate the Secularization Thesis*, 145–69 (Oxford: Oxford University Press, 1992).

Finke, Roger, A.M. Guest, and R. Stark, "Mobilizing Local Religious Markets: Religious Pluralism in the Empire State, 1855 to 1865," *American Sociological Review*, 61 (1996): 203–18.

Finke, Roger, and J. Harris, "Wars and Rumors of Wars: Explaining Religiously Motivated Violence," in Jonathan Fox (ed.), *Religion, Politics, Society and the State* (Boulder, Colorado: Paradigm Publishers, 2012).

Finke, Roger, and L.R. Iannaccone, "Supply-Side Explanations for Religious Change," *Annals of the American Academy of Political and Social Science*, 527 (1993): 27–40.

Finke, Roger and Christopher P. Scheitle, "Understanding Schisms: Theoretical Explanations for Their Origins. In Sacred Schisms. How Religions Divide," in James R. Lewis and Sarah M. Lewis (eds), 11–33 (Cambridge: Cambridge University Press, 2009).

Finke, Roger, and R. Stark, "Religious Economies and Sacred Canopies: Religious Mobilization in American Cities, 1906." *American Sociological Review*, 53 (1988): 41–9.

Finke, Roger, and R. Stark, *The Churching of America, 1776–1990: Winners and Losers in our Religious Economy* (New Brunswick: Rutgers University Press, 1992).

Finke, Roger, and R. Stark, *The Churching of America, 1776–2005: Winners and Losers in our Religious Economy, Second Edition* (New Brunswick: Rutgers University Press, 2005).

Finney, R. Zachary, R.A. Orwig, and D.F. Spake, "Lotus-Eaters, Pilgrims, Seekers, and Accidental Tourists: How Different Travelers Consume the Sacred and the Profane," *Services Marketing Quarterly*, 30 (2) (2012): 148–73.

Fischer, Johan, "Halal, Haram, or What? Creating Muslim Space in London," in J. Pink (ed.), *Muslim Societies in the Age of Mass Consumption: Politics, Culture and Identity between the Local and the Global* (3–22) (Newcastle: Cambridge Scholars Publishing, 2009).

Fishbein, Martin, and I. Ajzen, *Belief, Attitude, Intention and Behavior: An Introduction to Theory and Research* (London: Addison-Wesley, 1975).

Fligstein, Neil, "A Political-Cultural Approach to Market Institutions," *American Sociological Review*, 61 (1996): 656–73.

Fornell, Claes, and D.F. Larcker, "Evaluating Structural Equation Models with Unobservable Variables and Measurement Error," *Journal of Marketing Research*, 18 (1) (1981): 39–50.

Fournier, Susan, "Consumers and Their Brands: Developing Relationship Theory in Consumer Research," *The Journal of Consumer Research*, 24 (4) (1998): 343–73.

Fox, Jonathan, and E. Tabory, "Contemporary Evidence Regarding the Impact of State Regulation of Religion on Religious Participation and Belief," *Sociology of Religion*, 69 (2008): 245–71.

Freie Gesundheitsberufe (o.J.): Alternative Lebens- und Gesundheitskultur. Eine empirische Studie über Angebotsstrukturen im Sektor "Freie Lebensberatung und Gesundheitsförderung," http://www.frankfurter-gespraeche.de/ download/ Zusammenfassung.pdf (accessed March 15, 2011).

Friess, Sonja, "Marktförmige Inszenierung und leibsozialisatorische Massnahmen," in Susanne Schaaf and Matthias Mettner (eds), *Religion zwischen Sinnsuche, Erlebnismarkt und Fundamentalismus* (Zürich: Schriftenreihe infoSekta, 2004).

Froese, Paul, "Hungary for Religion," *Journal for the Scientific Study of Religion*, 40 (2001): 251–68.

Galbraith, John K., *The Affluent Society* (London: Penguin, 1975).

Gaustad, Edwin S., *Historical Atlas of Religion in America* (New York: Harper and Sons, 1962).

Gauthier, François, T. Martikainen, and L. Woodhead, "Introduction: Religion in Consumer Society," *Social Compass*, 58 (3) (2011): 291–301.

Gebhardt, Winfried, M. Engelbrecht, and C. Bochinger, "Die Selbstermächtigung des religiösen Subjekts. Der 'spirituelle Wanderer' als Idealtypus spätmoderner Religiosität," *Zeitschrift für Religionswissenschaft*, 13 (2005): 133–52.

Geisser, Vincent, "L'UOIF, la tension clientéliste d'une grande fédération," *Confluences Méditerranée*, 57 (2006): 83–101.

Gest, Alain, and J. Guyard, *Rapport fait au nom de la commission d'enquête sur les sectes*, 1996, http://www.assemblee-nationale.fr/rap-enq/r2468.asp (accessed July 8, 2011).

Giddens, Anthony, *Konsequenzen der Moderne* (Frankfurt am Main, 1996).

Gill, Anthony, *Rendering Unto Caesar: The Roman Catholic Church and the State in Latin America* (Chicago: University of Chicago Press, 1998).

Gill, Anthony, "Lost in the Supermarket: Comments on Beaman, Religious Pluralism, and What it Means to be Free," *Journal for the Scientific Study of Religion*, 42 (3) (2003): 327–32.

Gilmore, James H., and B.J. Pine II, *Authenticity: What Consumers Really Want* (Boston, MA: Harvard Business School Press, 2007).

Glines, Eliza, *Undaunted Zeal: The Letters of Margaret Fell* (Richmond: Friends United Press, 2003).

Glock, Charles Y., and R. Stark, *Religion and Society in Tension* (Chicago: Rand McNally & Company, 1965).

Goldner, Colin, *Die Psycho-Szene* (Aschaffenburg: Alibri Verlag, 2000).

Gordon, James S., *The Golden Guru. The Strange Journey of Bhagwan Shree Rajneesh* (Lexington: The Stephen Greene Press, 1987).

Gounaris, Spiros, and V. Stathakopoulos, "Antecedents and Consequences of Brand Loyalty: An Empirical Study," *Brand Management*, 11 (4) (2004): 283–306.

Greeley, Andrew, "A Religious Revival in Russia?," *Journal for the Scientific Study of Religion*, 33 (1994): 253–72.

Greil, Arthur. L., and T. Robbins, "Introduction: Exploring the Boundaries of the Sacred," in dies. (ed.), *Religion and the Social Order. Between Sacred and Secular: Research and Theory on Quasi-Religion vol. 4*, 1–26 (Connecticut: Jai Press Inc., 1994).

Greil, Arthur. L., and D.R. Rudy, "On the Margins of the Sacred," in T. Robbins and D. Anthony (eds), *In Gods We Trust. New Patterns of Religious Pluralism in America. Second Edition, Revised and Expanded*, 219–32 (New Brunswick Transaction Publishers, 1990).

Grim, Brian J., and R. Finke, *The Price of Freedom Denied: Religious Persecution and Violence* (Cambridge University Press, 2011).

Gruber, Jonathan, and D.M. Hungerman, "The Church vs. the Mall: What Happens When Religion Faces Increased Secular Competition?," *NBER Working Paper Series, Working Paper 12410* (http://www.nber.org/papers/w12410—accessed January 31, 2013) (2006): 1–35.

Gruber, Jonathan, and D.M. Hungerman, "The Church vs. the Mall: What Happens When Religion Faces Increased Secular Competition?," *Quarterly Journal of Economics*, 123 (2008): 831–62.

Gugutzer, Robert, *Thesen zur "Entgrenzung" von Religion, Sport und Körperpraxis, Tagung "Körper, Kult und Konfession"* (Frankfurt: Goethe-Universität, 2010).

Haddorff, David W., "Religion and the Market: Opposition, Absorption, or Ambiguity?," *Review of Social Economy*, 58 (4) (2000): 483–504.

Haenni, Patrick, "L'économie politique de la consommation musulmane," Institut Religioscope, Etudes et analyses, no. 18, 2008.

Haenni, Patrick, "The Economic Politics of Muslim Consumption," in J. Pink (ed.), *Muslim Societies in the Age of Mass Consumption: Politics, Culture and Identity between the Local and the Global* (327–42) (Newcastle: Cambridge Scholars Publishing, 2009).

Hair, Joseph F., *Multivariate data analysis*. 7th ed. (Upper Saddle River, NJ: Prentice Hall, 2010).

Haley, Eric, C. White, and A. Cunningham, "Branding Religion: Christian Consumers' Understanding of Christian Products," in D.A. Stout and J.M. Buddenbaum (eds), *Religion and Popular Culture*, 269–88 (Ames: Iowa State University Press, 2001).

Halman, Loek, and V. Draulans, "How Secular is Europe?," *The British Journal of Sociology*, 57 (2) (2006): 263–88.

Hamès, Constant, "La notion de magie dans le Coran," in Constant Hamès (ed.), *Coran et talismans: textes et pratiques magiques en milieu musulman*, 17–48 (Paris: Karthala, 2007).

Hamilton, Malcom, "Eating Ethically: 'Spiritual' and 'Quasi-Religious' Aspects of Vegetarianism," *Journal of Contemporary Religion*, 15 (1) (2000): 65–83.

Hanlon, Patrick, *Primal Branding: Create Zealots for Your Brand, Your Company and Your Future* (New York: Simon & Schuster Ltd., 2006).

Hannan, Michael T., and J. Freeman, "The Population Ecology of Organizations," *American Journal of Sociology*, 82 (1997): 929–64.

Hannan, Michael T., G.R. Carroll, and L. Polos, "The Organizational Niche," *Sociological Theory*, 21 (2003): 309–40.

Harrison, Ted, *Elvis People: Cult of the King* (London: Fount, 1992).

Heelas, Paul, *Spiritualities of Life. New Age Romanticism and Consumptive Capitalism* (Oxford and Cambridge (Mass.), 2008).

Heelas, Paul, and L. Woodhead, *The Spiritual Revolution: Why Religion is Giving Way to Spirituality* (WileyBlackwell, 2004).

Hell, Daniel, "Die Seele ist tot. Es lebe das Seelische! Erlebniskultur als Gegenbewegung zur vorherrschenden Rationalisierung," in Susanne Schaaf and Matthias Mettner (eds), *Religion zwischen Sinnsuche, Erlebnismarkt und Fundamentalismus* (Zürich: Schriftenreihe infoSekta, 2004).

Hero, Markus, "Auf dem Weg zum religiösen Markt? Neue Religiosität und Esoterik," in: ders., V. Krech and H. Zander (eds.), *Religiöse Vielfalt in Nordrhein-Westfalen. Empirische Befunde und Perspektiven der Globalisierung vor Ort* (Paderborn, 165–78, 2008a).

Hero, Markus, "Religious Pluralization and Institutional Change. The Case of the Esoteric Milieu," *Journal of Religion in Europe*, 2 (2008b): 200–226.

Hero, Markus, *Die neuen Formen des religiösen Lebens. Eine institutionentheoretische Analyse neuer Religiosität* (Würzburg: Ergon Verlag, 2010).

Hero, Markus, "Vom Guru zum religiösen Entrepreneur. Neue religiöse Experten und die Entstehung eines alternativreligiösen Marktes," in W. Damberg, and L. Hölscher (eds): *Soziale Strukturen und Semantiken des Religiösen im Wandel. Transformationen in der Bundesrepublik Deutschland 1949–1989*, 35–49 (Essen: 2011).

Hervieu-Léger, Danièle, *La religion en miettes ou la question des sectes* (Paris: Calmann-Lévy, 2001).

Hill, Jonathan P., and D.V.A. Olson, "Market Share and Religious Competition: Do Small Market Share Congregations and Their Leaders Try Harder?," *Journal for the Scientific Study of Religion*, 48 (4) (2009): 629–49.

Hirschle, Jochen, "The Affluent Society and its Religious Consequences: An Empirical Investigation of 20 European Countries," *Socio-Economic Review*, 9 (2) (2011): 261–85.

Hirschman, Albert O., *Rival Views of Market Society* (New York: Viking, 1986).

Hirschman, Elizabeth C., "Religious Affiliation and Consumption Processes: An Initial Paradigm," *Research in Marketing*, 6 (1983): 131–70.

Hoffman, Sandra C., A.E. Burke, K.J. Helzlsouer, and G.W. Comstock, "Controlled Trial of the Effect of Length, Incentives, and Follow-Up Techniques on Response to a Mailed Questionnaire," *Am. J. Epidemiol*, 148 (10) (1998): 1007–11.

Hoffmann, John E., and J.E. Bartkowski, "Gender, Religious Tradition and Biblical Literalism," *Social Forces*, 86 (3) (2008): 1245–72.

Höhn, Hans-Joachim, *Zerstreuungen, Religion zwischen Sinnsuche und Erlebnismarkt* (Düsseldorf: Patmos, 1998).

Höllinger, Franz, and T. Tripold, *Ganzheitliches Leben. Das holistische Milieu zwischen neuer Spiritualität und postmoderner Wellness-Kultur* (Bielefeld: 2012).

Holt, Douglas B., "Jack Daniel's America: Iconic Brands as Ideological Parasites and Proselytizers," *Journal of Consumer Culture*, 6 (3) (2006): 355–77.

Homer, Pamela M., and L.R. Kahle, "A Structural Equation Test of the Value-Attitude-Behavior Hierarchy," *Journal of Personality and Social Psychology*, 54 (4) (1988): 638–46.

Hough, Franklin B., *Census of the State of New York for 1865* (Albany, NY: Van Benthuysen, 1987).

Hu, Li-tze, and P.M. Bentler, "Cutoff Criteria for Fit Indexes in Covariance Structure Analysis: Conventional Criteria versus New Alternatives," *Structural Equation Modeling: A Multidisciplinary Journal*, 6 (1) (1999): 1–55.

Hunt, John, and D. Penwell, *AMG's Handi-Reference World Religions and Cults* (Chattanooga, TN: AMG Publishers, 2008).

Hunt, Stephen, "The Alpha Programme: Some Tentative Observations of State of the Art Evangelism in the UK," *Journal of Contemporary Religion*, 18 (1) (2003): 77–93.

Iannaccone, Laurence R., "A Formal Model of Church and Sect," *The American Journal of Sociology*, 94 (1988): 241–68.

Iannaccone, Laurence R., "Religious Practice: A Human Capital Approach," *Journal for the Scientific Study of Religion*, 29 (3) (1990): 297–314.

Iannaccone, Laurence R., "The Consequences of Religious Market Structure. Adam Smith and the Economics of Religion," *Rationality and Society*, 3 (2) (1991): 156–77.

Iannaccone, Laurence R., "Religious Markets and the Economics of Religion," *Social Compass*, 39 (1) (1992): 123–31.

Iannaccone, Laurence R., "Sacrifice and Stigma: Reducing Free-Riding in Cults, Communes and Other Collectives," *Journal of Political Economy*, 100 (1992): 271–92.

Iannaccone, Laurence R., "Why Strict Churches Are Strong," *American Journal of Sociology*, 99 (5) (1994): 1180–212.

Iannaccone, Laurence R., "Risk, Rationality and Religious Portfolios," *Economic Inquiry*, 33 (2), (1995): 285–95.

Iannaccone, Laurence R., "Voodoo Economics? Reviewing the Rational Choice Approach to Religion," *Journal for the Scientific Study of Religion*, 34 (1) (1995): 76–89.

Iannaccone, Laurence R., "Strictness and Strength Revisited—Reply," *American Journal of Sociology*, 101 (1996): 1103–8.

Iannaccone, Laurence R., "Introduction to the Economics of Religion," *Journal of Economic Literature*, 36 (3) (1998): 1465–95.

Iannaccone, Laurence R., R. Finke, and R. Stark, "Deregulating Religion: The Economics of Church and State," *Economic Inquiry*, 35 (1997): 350–64.

Illouz, Eva, *Consuming the Romantic Utopia: Love and the Cultural Contradictions of Capitalism* (Berkley: University of California Press, 1997).

Izberk-Bilgin, Elif, "Infidel Brands: Unveiling Alternative Meanings of Global Brands at the Nexus of Globalization, Consumer Culture, and Islamism," *Journal of Consumer Research*, 39 (2012): 663–87.

James, William, *The Varieties of Religious Experience* (New York: Touchstone, 1902/2004).

Jelen, Ted G., *Sacred Markets, Sacred Canopies. Essays on Religious Markets and Religious Pluralism* (Lanham, Boulder, New York, Oxford: Rowman & Littlefield Publishers, 2002).

Johnson, Ronald C., G.P. Danko, T.J. Darvill, S. Bochner, J.K. Bowers, Y.H. Huang, J.Y. Park, V. Pecjak, A.R.A. Rahim, and D. Pennington, "Cross-Cultural Assessment of Altruism and its Correlates," *Personality and Individual Differences*, 10 (8) (1989): 855–68.

Jones, Charles B., "Marketing Buddhism in the United States of America: Elite Buddhism and the Formation of Religious Pluralism," *Comparative Studies of South Asia, Africa and the Middle East*, 27 (1) (2007): 214–21.

Jones, Steve, *Brand Like a Rock Star: Lessons from Rock "n" Roll to Make Your Business Rich & Famous* (Austin, TX: Greenleaf Book Group LLC, 2012).

Jöreskog, Karl G., and D. Sörbom, *LISREL 8.53* (Lincolnwood, IL: Scientific Software International, Inc., 2002).

Just, Wolf-Dieter, and B. Sträter, *Kirchenasyl. Ein Handbuch* (Karlsruhe: Loeper Literaturverlag, 2003).

Kaptchuk, Ted J., and D.M. Eisenberg, "The Persuasive Appeal of Alternative Medicine," *Annals of Internal Medicine*, 129 (12) (1998): 1061–5.

Katz-Gerro, Tally, and M. Meier Jaeger, "Religion, Religiosity, and Cultural Stratification: Theoretical Links and Empirical Evidence," in: Lisa A. Keister, John McCarthy, and Roger Finke (eds), *Religion, Work and Inequality* (Research in the Sociology of Work, vol. 23), 337–66, 2012.

Keller, Kevin L., "Conceptualizing, Measuring, and Managing Customer-Based Brand Equity," *Journal of Marketing*, 57 (1) (1993): 1–22.

Kelley, Dean M., *Why Conservative Churches Are Growing. A Study in Sociology of Religion.* (#, Trans.), (Macon, Georgia: Mercer University Press (1986 (1972)).

Kepel, Gilles, *Les banlieues de l'Islam. Naissance d'une religion en France* (Paris: Seuil, 1987).

Kepel, Gilles, *La République et l'islam*, Le Monde, April 27, 1988.

Khedimellah, Moussa, "Une version de la ruqiya de rite prophétique en France. Le cas d'Abdellah, imam guérisseur en Lorraine," in Constant Hames (ed.), *Coran et talismans: textes et pratiques magiques en milieu musulman*, 385–408 (Paris, Karthala, 2007).

Kline, Paul, *An Easy Guide to Factor Analysis* (London: Routledge, 1994).

Knoblauch, Hubert, "Einleitung: Soziologie der Spiritualität," *Zeitschrift für Religionswissenschaft*, 13 (2005): 123–31.

Knoblauch, Hubert, *Populäre Religion, Auf dem Weg in eine spirituelle Gesellschaft* (Frankfurt am Main: Campus-Verlag, 2009).

Knudsen, Kjell, P. Aggarwal, and A. Maamoun, "The Burden Of Identity: Responding To Product Boycotts In The Middle East," *Journal of Business & Economics Research*, 6 (11) (2008): 17–26.

Koch, Anne, "Spiritualisierung eines Heilwissens im lokalen religiösen Feld? Zur Formierung deutscher Ayurveden," *Zeitschrift für Religionswissenschaft*, 13 (2005): 21–44.

Kollmuss, Anja, and J. Agyeman, "Mind the Gap: Why Do People Act Environmentally and What are the Barriers to Pro-Environmental Behavior?," *Environmental education research*, 8 (3) (2002): 239–60.

Kopytoff, Igor, "The Cultural Biography of Things: Commoditization as Process," in Arjun Appadurai (ed.), *The Social Life of Things, Commodities in Cultural Perspective*, 64–91 (Cambridge, Cambridge University Press, 1986).

Kotila, Heikki, "Die Thomasmesse: Eine finnische Volksbewegung zur Erneuerung des gottesdienstlichen Lebens," *Jahrbuch für Liturgik und Hymnologie*, 38 (1999): 65–87.

Kotler, Philip, and S.J. Levy, "Broadening the Concept of Marketing," *Journal of Marketing*, 33 (1) (1969), 10–15.

Kraus, Henry, *Gold was the Mortar: The Economics of Cathedral Building* (London: Routledge and Kegan Paul, 1979).

Kunz, Ralph, "Von der Zucht zur Wucht, in: Religion zwischen Sinnsuche, Erlebnismarkt und Fundamentalismus," Susanne Schaaf and Matthias Mettner (eds) (Zürich: Schriftenreihe infoSekta, 2004).

Kunz, Ralph, "Grenzen der Vermarktung—Marketing zwischen Oekonomisierung und Gemeindeaufbau," in C.R. Famos, and R. Kunz (eds), *Kirche und Marketing. Beiträge zu einer Verhältnisbestimmung*, 29–46 (Zürich: TVZ, 2006).

Kuscynski, Liliane, "Variations sur le retour de l'aimé. Consultations maraboutiques parisiennes," C. Hames (ed.), *Coran et talismans: textes et pratiques magiques en milieu musulman*, 347–84 (Paris: Karthala, 2007).

Kuzma, Andrew, A. Kuzma, and J. Kuzma, "How Religion has Embraced Marketing and the Implications for Business," *Journal of Management and Marketing Research*, 2 (2009): 1–10.

Kuzma, Ann T., A.J. Kuzma, and J.R. Kuzma, "How Religion has Embraced Marketing and the Implications for Business," *American Society of Business and Behavioral Sciences*, 15 (1) (2008): 933–9.

Lam, Pui-Yan, "May the Force of the Operating System Be with You: Macintosh Devotion as Implicit Religion," *Sociology of Religion*, 62 (2) (2001): 243–62.

Lienhard, Susanna, *Die Bedeutung der Zugehörigkeit zum "International Christian Fellowship" (ICF). Identitätskonstruktionen und -verhandlungen von ICF-Mitgliedern* (Lizentiatsarbeit, Universität Freiburg, 2009).

Lindstrom, Martin, *Brand Sense: How to Build Powerful Brands Through Touch, Taste, Smell, Sight and Sound* (London: Kogan Page, 2005).

Lipset, Seymour M., "American Exceptionalism Reaffirmed," In B.E. Shafer (ed.), *Is America Different? A New Look at American Exceptionalism*, 1–45 (Oxford: Clarendon Press, 1991).

Litwin, Mark S., and A. Fink, *How to Measure Survey Reliability and Validity* (London: Sage, 1995).

Loi du 9 décembre 1905 concernant la séparation des Églises et de l'État. http://www.legifrance.gouv.fr/affichTexte.do?cidTexte=LEGITEXT000006070169&dateTexte=20110704 (accessed July 4, 2011).

Loveland, Matthew T., "Religious Switching: Preferences Development, Maintenance, and Change," *Journal for the Scientific Study of Religion*, 42 (1) (2003): 147–57.

Lu, Yunfeng, *The Transformation of Yiguan Dao in Taiwan: Adapting to a Changing Religious Economy* (Lanham, MD: Lexington Books, 2008).

Luckmann, Thomas, *The Invisible Religion* (New York: MacMillan, 1967).

Luhmann, Niklas, "Formen des Helfens im Wandel gesellschaftlicher Bedingungen," in Hans-Uwe Otto, and Siegfried Schneider (eds), *Gesellschaftliche Perspektiven der Sozialarbeit*, 21–43, (Neuwied: 1973).

McCarthy, Jerome E. (1975), *Basic Marketing: a Managerial Approach*, Homewood, Richards D. Irwin Inc., Fifth Edition.

McDaniel, Stephen W., "Church Advertising: Views of the Clergy and General Public," *Journal of Advertising*, 15 (1) (1986): 24–9.

McDonald, Seonaidh, C.J. Oates, C.W. Young, and K. Hwang, "Toward Sustainable Consumption: Researching Voluntary Simplifiers," *Psychology & Marketing*, 23 (6) (2006): 515–34.

McFarland, H. Neill, *The Rush Hour of the Gods: A Study of New Religious Movements in Japan* (New York: Macmillan 1967).

McGraw, A. Peter, J.A. Schwartz, and P.E. Tetlock, (2012) "From the Commercial to the Communal: Reframing Taboo Trade-Offs in Religious and Pharmaceutical Marketing," *Journal of Consumer Research*, 39 (1) (2012): 157–73.

McIntyre, Elisha H., "Brand of Choice: Why Hillsong Music Is Winning Sales and Souls," *Australian Religion Studies Review*, 20 (2) (2007): 175–94.

Mackay, Stuart, "Marketers Must Manage Choice Not Meet Needs," *Marketing (00253650)*, 26 (2000).

McKenny, Leesha, Money Christmas: Hillsong Ensures Show in Tune with Spirit of the Season. *The Sydney Morning Herald*. Online edition. December 11, 2011. http://www.smh.com.au/entertainment/about-town/money-christmas-hillsong-ensures-show-in-tune-with-spirit-of-season-20111218-1p0vd.html (accessed June 8, 2012).

McLeod, Hugh, *The Religious Crisis of the 1960s* (Oxford: Oxford University Press, 2007).

McLuhan, Marshall, *The Medium is the Massage: An Inventory of Effects* (New York: Bantam Books, 1967).

McMillan, Andrew. 2011. The Power in Grooving for God. *The Australian*. Online edition. October 28, 2011. http://www.theaustralian.com.au/arts/music/the-power-in-grooving-for-god/story-fn9d2mxu-1226178790943 (accessed June 8, 2012).

McPherson, Miller, L. Smith-Lovin, and J.M. Cook, "Birds of a Feather: Homophily in Social Networks," *Annual Review of Sociology*, 27 (2001): 415–44.

Malhotra, Naresh K., *Marketing Research: An Applied Orientation*, 6th ed. (London: Prentice Hall, 2010).

Malhotra, Naresh K., S.S. Kim, and A. Patil, "Common Method Variance in IS Research: A Comparison of Alternative Approaches and a Reanalysis of Past Research," *Management Science*, 52 (12) (2006): 1865–83.

Manning, Paul, "The Semiotics of Brand," *Annual Review of Anthropology*, 39 (2010): 33–49.

Maréchal, Brigitte, *Les Frères musulmans en Europe: Racines et discours* (Paris: PUF, 2009).

Marica, George, *Emile Durkheim. Soziologie und Soziologismus* (Jena: Fischer, 1932).

Marmor-Lavie, Galit, P.A. Stout, and W.-N. Lee, "Spirituality in Advertising: A New Theoretical Approach," *Journal of Media and Religion*, 8 (1) (2009): 1–23.

Martin, Charles L., "Relationship Marketing: a High-Involvement Product Attribute Approach," *Journal of Product and Brand Management*, 7 (1) (1998): 6–26.

Martin, David, *The Religious and the Secular* (London: Routledge and Kegan Paul, 1969).

Maslow, Abraham, *Motivation and Personality* (New York: Harper, 1954).

Mauss, Marcel, (1924), "Essai sur le don. Forme et raison de l'échange dans les sociétés primitives," *l'Année Sociologique*, seconde série, 1923–24.

Mayer, Jean-François, "Salvation Goods and the Religious Market in the Cultic Milieu," in Jörg Stolz (ed.), *Salvation goods and religious markets: theory and applications*, 257–74 (Bern: Peter Lang, 2007).

Mayzaud, Yves, "Historique et enjeu de la notion d'Erlebnis," *Phénice*, 2 article 8 (2005).

MDG, *Milieuhandbuch. "Religiöse und kirchliche Orientierungen in den Sinus-Milieus 2005"* (München, 2005).

Mead, Sidney E., *The Lively Experiment* (New York: Harper and Row, 1963).

Meier, Urs, "Kirche und Lifestyles. Milieu-Typologien in Religionssoziologie und Kirchenmarketing," in C.R. Famos, and R. Kunz (eds), *Kirche und Marketing. Beiträge zu einer Verhältnisbestimmung*, 217–28 (Zürich: TVZ, 2006).

Melton, J. Gordon, *The Encyclopedia of American Religions*, 8th Edition (Detroit: Gale Research, 2009).

Mervin, Sabrina, *Histoire de l'islam. Doctrines et fondements* (Paris: Flammarion, 2000)

Merz-Benz, Peter-Ulrich, "Salvation Goods and Culture Goods: An Interpretation of Max Weber," in Jörg Stolz (ed.) *Salvation Goods and Religious Markets. Theory and Applications* (Bern: Peter Lang, 2008).

Meyer, Thomas, "Private Lebensformen im Wandel," in: Rainer Geißler (ed.), *Die Sozialstruktur Deutschlands*, 331–57 (Wiesbaden: VS Verlag, 2006).

Miller, Alan S., and R. Stark, "Gender and Religiousness: Can Sociological Explanations Be Saved," *American Journal of Sociology*, 107 (2002): 1399–423.

Mission d'information sur la pratique du port du voile intégral sur le territoire national. 2009. Rapport d'information fait au nom de la mission d'information sur la pratique du port du voile intégral sur le territoire national n° 2262 déposé le 26 janvier 2010 (mis en ligne le 27 janvier 2010 à 0 heure 30). http://www.assemblee-nationale.fr/13/dossiers/voile_integral.asp (accessed July 23, 2011).

Mitchell, Tony (ed.) *Global Noise: Rap and Hip Hop Outside the USA* (Middletown, CT: Wesleyan University Press, 2001).

Mittal, Banwari, "Measuring Purchase Decision Involvement," *Psychology and Marketing*, 6 (2) (1989): 147–62.

Miviludes Le Risque sectaire. http://www.miviludes.gouv.fr/IMG/pdf/RAPPORT_MIVILUDES_2004.pdf (accessed July 8, 2011).

Montefiori, Simon S., *Jerusalem, The Biography* (London: Weidenfeld & Nicolson, 2011).

Montgomery, James D., "A Formalization and Test of the Religious Economies Model," *American Sociological Review*, 68 (2003): 782–809.

Moore, R. Laurence, *Selling God: American Religion in the Marketplace of Culture* (New York, Oxford: Oxford University Press, 1994).

Mottner, Sandra, "Marketing and religion," in W. Wymer, and A. Sargeant (eds), *The Routledge Companion to Nonprofit Marketing*, 92–107 (2007).

Muhamad, Nazlida, "The Constructs Mediating Religions' Influence on Buyers and Consumers," *Journal of Islamic Marketing*, 1 (2) (2010): 124–35.

Muhamad, Nazlida, and D. Mizerski, "Muslim Religious Commitment Related to Intention to Purchase Taboo Products," *Journal of Business and Policy Research*, 3 (2007): 74–85.

Muniz, Albert M. Jr., and T.C. O'Guinn, "Brand Community," *The Journal of Consumer Research*, 27 (4) (2001): 412–32.

Muniz, Albert. M. Jr., and H. Jensen-Schau, "Religiosity in the Abandoned Apple Newton Brand Community," *Journal of Consumer Research*, 31 (4) (2005), 737–47.

Murken, Sebastian, "'Mein Wille geschehe …'. Religionspsychologische Überlegungen zum Verhältnis von Religion und Wunscherfüllung," *Zeitschrift für Religionswissenschaft*, 17 (2009): 165–87.

National Opinion Research Center. *General social survey*, December 2, 2009. Available from http://www.norc.org/GSS+Website/ (accessed January 31, 2013).

Need, Ariana, and N.D. De Graaf, "'Losing My Religion': A Dynamic Analysis of Leaving the Church in the Netherlands," *European Sociological Review*, 12 (1) (1996): 87–99.

Negus, Keith, *Popular Music in Theory: An Introduction* (Cambridge: Polity, 1996).

Nelson, Robert H., *Economics as Religion: From Samuelson to Chicago and Beyond* (University Park, PA: Pennsylvania University Press, 2001).

Neumeier, Marty, *The Brand Gap: How to Bridge the Distance Between Business Strategy and Design: A Whiteboard Overview* (London: New Riders; Pearson Education, 2006).

Niebuhr, H. Richard, *The Social Sources of Denominationalism* (New York: Heny Holt and Co., 1929).

Norris, Pippa, and R. Inglehart, *Sacred and Secular. Religion and Politics Worldwide* (Cambridge: Cambridge University Press, 2004).

Nunnally, Jum C., *Psychometric Theory*. 2nd ed. (New York; London: McGraw-Hill, 1978).

Oliver, Richard L., "Whence Consumer Loyalty?," *Journal of Marketing*, 63 (5) (1999): 33–44.

Olson, Daniel V.A., "Variations in Strictness and Religious Commitment Within and Among Five Denominations," *Journal for the Scientific Study of Religion*, 40 (4) (2001): 757–64.

Olson, Daniel V.A., "Free and Cheap Riding in Strict, Conservative Churches," *Journal for the Scientific Study of Religion*, 44 (2) (2005): 123–42.

Otteson, James R., *Adam Smith's Marketplace of Life* (Cambridge: 2002).

Pace, Enzo (2008), "Salvation Goods, the Gift economy, and Charismatic Concern," in Jörg Stolz (ed.), *Salvation Goods and Religious Markets*, 149–70 (Bern: Peter Lang, 2008).

Packaged Facts. Packaged Facts. http://www.packagedfacts.com (accessed January 31, 2013).

Palmer, Susan. J., *Aliens Adored. Raël's UFO Religion* (New Brunswick: Rutgers University Press, 2004).

Park, Jerry Z., and J. Baker, "What Would Jesus Buy: American Consumption of Religious and Spiritual Material Goods," *Journal for the Scientific Study of Religion*, 46 (4) (2007): 501–17.

Peterson, M. Nils, and J.G. Liu, "Impacts of Religion on Environmental Worldviews: The Teton Valley case," *Society & Natural Resources*, 21 (8) (2008): 704–18.

Pew Forum on Religion and Public Life, U.S. religious landscape survey. Washington DC: Pew Research Center, 2008.

Pickering, William S.F., *Durkheims' Sociology of Religion. Themes and Theories* (London: Routledge and Kegan Paul, 1984).

Pine, B. Joseph II, and J.H. Gilmore, *The Experience Economy, Updated Edition* (Boston, MA: Harvard Business School Press, 2011).

Piore, Michael J., "Qualitative Research: Does it Fit in Economics?," *European Management Review*, 3 (2006): (17–23).

Plötner, Olaf, *Das Vertrauen des Kunden* (Wiesbaden: 1994).

Podsakoff, Philip M., S.B. MacKenzie, J.Y. Lee, and N.P. Podsakoff, "Common Method Biases in Behavioral Research: A Critical Review of the Literature and Recommended Remedies," *Journal of Applied Psychology*, 88 (5) (2003): 879–903.

Polanyi, Karl, *The Great Transformation: The Political and Economic Origins of Our Time* (Boston: Beacon Press, 2001).

Pollack, Detlef, and G. Pickel, "Religious Individualization or Secularization? Testing Hypotheses of Religious Change," *British Journal of Sociology*, 58 (4) (2007): 603–32.

Popielarz, Pamela A., and J. Miller McPherson, "On the Edge or In Between: Niche Position, Niche Overlap, and the Duration of Voluntary Association Memberships," *American Journal of Sociology*, 3 (1995): 698–720.

Porter, Michael E., "Changing Patterns of International Competition," *California Management Review*, 28 (2) (1986): 9–39.

Prothero, Andrea, S. Dobscha, J. Freund, W.E. Kilbourne, M.G. Luchs, L.K. Ozanne, and J. Thogersen, "Sustainable Consumption: Opportunities For Consumer Research and Public Policy," *Journal of Public Policy & Marketing*, 30 (1) (2011): 31–8.

Rademacher, Stefan, "'Makler': Akteure der Esoterik-Kultur als Einflussfaktoren auf neue religiöse Gemeinschaften," in Dorothea Lüdekens and Raphael Waltert (eds): *Fluide Religion. Neue religiöse Bewegungen im Wandel. Theoretische und empirische Systematisierungen* (Bielefeld: 2010).

Rhodes, Ron, *The Complete Guide to Christian Denominations* (Eugene, OR: Harvest House Pub, 2005).

Richardson H, *The Credence Good Problem and the Organization of Health Care Markets* (Department of Economics, Texas: mimeo, 1999).

Riches, Tanya, *Shout to the Lord! Music and Change at Hillsong: 1996–2007* (Masters thesis, Sydney College of Divinity, 2010).

Riches, Tanya, and T. Wagner "The Evolution of Hillsong Music: from Australian Pentecostal Congregation into Global Brand," *Australian Journal of Communication*, 39 (1) (2012): 17–36.

Richter, Rudolf, and E.G. Furubotn, *Institutionenökonomik. Eine Einführung und kritische Würdigung* (Tübingen, 2010).

Riggins, Stephen H., *Ethnic Minority Media: An International Perspective* (London: Sage Publications, 1992).

Ritzer, George, *The McDonaldization of Society*, 6th ed. (London: Sage Publications, 2010).

Robbins, Joel, "The Globalization of Pentecostal and Charismatic Christianity," *Annual Review of Anthropology*, 33 (2004): 117–43.

Robertson, Roland, "Glocalization: Time-Space and Homogeneity-Heterogeneity," in Mike Featherstone, Scott Lash and Roland Robertson (eds), *Global Modernities*," 25–44 (London: Sage, 1995).

Rommen, Timothy, *Mek Some Noise: Gospel Music and the Ethics of Style in Trinidad* (Berkley, CA: University of California Press, 2007).

Roof, Wade C., "Multiple Religious Switching: A Research Note," *Journal for the Scientific Study of Religion*, 28 (4) (1989): 530–35.

Roof, Wade C., *Spiritual Marketplace, Baby Boomers and the Remaking of American Religion* (Princeton: Princeton University Press, 1999).

Rouget, Gilbert, *Music and Trance: A Theory of the Relations Between Music and Possession* (Chicago: University of Chicago Press, 1985).

Roy, Olivier, *La Sainte Ignorance. Le temps de la religion sans culture* (Paris: Seuil, 2008).

Rudy, David. R., and A.L. Greil, "Is Alcoholics Anomymous a Religious Organization? Meditations on Marginality," *Sociological Analysis*, 50 (1) (1988): 41–51.

Ruiter, Stijn, and N.D. De Graaf, "National Context, Religiosity, and Volunteering: Results from 53 Countries," *American Sociological Review*, 71 (2) (2006), 191–210.

Russell, Philip A., "Musical Tastes and Society," in David J. Hargreaves and Adrian C. North (eds), *The Social Psychology of Music*, 141–55 (Oxford: Oxford University Press, 1997).

Russell-Bennett, Rebekah, J.R. McColl-Kennedy, and L.V. Coote, "Involvement, Satisfaction, and Brand Loyalty in a Small Business Services Setting," *Journal of Business Research*, 60 (12) (2007): 1253–60.

Ryder, Norman B., "The Cohort as a Concept in the Study of Social Change," in William M. Mason, and Stephen E. Fienberg (eds), *Cohort Analysis in Social Research*, 9–44 (New York: Springer, 1985).

Salzbrunn, Monika, "The Occupation of Public Space through Religious and Political Events: How Senegalese Migrants Became a Part of Harlem, New York," *Journal of Religion in Africa*, 34 (4) (2004): 468–92.

Sandikzi, Ozlem, and G. Ger, "Veiling in Style: How Does a Stigmatized Practice Become Fashionable?," *Journal of Consumer Research*, 37 (1) (2010): 15–36.

Santos, Jessica, and B.P. Mathews, "Quality in religious services," *International Journal of Nonprofit and Voluntary Sector Marketing*, 6 (3) (2001): 278–88.

Sargeant, Kimon H., *Seeker Churches: Promoting Traditional Religion in a Nontraditional Way* (New Brunswick, NJ: Rutgers University Press, 2000).

Sarre, Philip, "Towards Global Environmental Values: Lessons from Western and Eastern Experience," *Environmental Values*, 4 (2) (1995): 115–27.

Scheitle, Christopher P., "Organizational Niches and Religious Markets: Uniting Two Literatures," *Interdisciplinary Journal of Research on Religion*, (3) (2007): www.religjournal.com.

Schiffman, Leon G., and L.L. Kanuk. 2009. *Consumer Behavior*, 9th ed. (Harlow: Pearson Education, 2009).

Schmidtchen Dieter, "Ökonomik des Vertrauens," in: H. Hof (ed.), *Recht und Verhalten: Verhaltensgrundlagen des Rechts—zum Beispiel Vertrauen*, 129–63 (Baden-Baden: 1994).

Schumpeter, Joseph, *Can Capitalism Survive? Creative Destruction and the Future of the Global Economy* (New York: Harper Perennial, 2009).

Schutz, Alfred, "The Problem of Rationality in the Social World," *Economica*, 5 (1943): 130–49.

Schwartz, Shalom H., "Universals in the Content and Structure of Values: Theoretical Advances and Empirical Tests in 20 Countries," *Advances in Experimental Social Psychology*, 25 (1) (1992): 1–66.

Schwarz, Peter, *Management dans les organisations sans but lucratif. Administrations et entreprises publiques, associations, sociétés, partis politiques, églises, oeuvres sociales* (Bern: Banque poéulaire Suisse, 1986).

Scott, David W., and D.A. Stout, "Religion on *TIME*: Personal Spiritual Quests and Religious Institutions on the Cover of a Popular News Magazine," *Journal of Magazine and New Media Research*, 8 (1) (2006): 1–17.

Sengers, Erik, "Marketing in Dutch Mainline Congregations: What Religious Organizations Offer and How They Do It," *Journal of Contemporary Religion*, 25 (1) (2009): 21–35.

Shachar, Ron, T. Erdem, K.M. Cutright, and G.J. Fitzsimons, "Brands: The Opiate of the Nonreligious Masses," *Marketing Science*, 30 (1) (2011): 92–110.

Shachar, Ron, T. Erdem, G.J. Fitzsimons, and K.M. Cutright, "Brands: The Opiate of the Non-Religious Masses?," *Advances in Consumer Research*, 36 (2009): Working Paper No 26/2007 (December), Henry Crown Institute of Business Research, Tel Aviv University.—Full working paper at: http://server1.tepper. cmu.edu/Seminars/docs/Religiosity%20and%20brand%20relianceWcover. pdf (accessed March 10, 2011).

Sheehan, Brendan, *The Economics of Abundance. Affluent Consumption and the Global Economy* (Cheltenham: Edward Elgar, 2010).

Shimp, Terence A., and S. Sharma, "Consumer Ethnocentrism: Construction and Validation of the CETSCALE"; *Journal of Marketing Research*, 24 (1987): 280–89.

Siala, Haytham, R.M. O'Keefe, and K.S. Hone, "The Impact of Religious Affiliation on Trust in the Context of Electronic Commerce," *Interacting with Computers*, 16 (1) (2004): 7–27.

Sigrist, Christoph, *Citykirche im Aufwind. Nicht Griesgram, sondern Lust, Zärtlichkeit und Freude soll die Kirche verbreiten!* (Berg am Irchel: KiK-Verlag, 2000).

Simonnot, Philippe, *Économie du droit, tome 2: Les personnes et les choses* (Paris: Les Belles lettres, 2004).

Simonnot, Philippe, *Les Papes, l'Eglise et l'argent: Histoire Economique du Christianisme des Origines à nos Jours* (Paris: Bayard, 2005).

Simonnot, Philippe, *Le Marché de Dieu. Économie du judaïsme, du christianisme et de l'islam* (Paris: Denoël, 2008).

Smidt, Corwin, S. Crawford, M. Deckman, D. Gray, D. Hofrenning, L. Olson, S. Steiner, and B. Weston, "The Political Attitudes and Activities of Mainline Protestant Clergy in the Election of 2000: A Study of Six Denominations," *Journal for the Scientific Study of Religion*, 42 (4) (2003): 515–32.

Smith, Christian, *American Evangelicalism: Embattled and Thriving* (Chicago: University of Chicago Press, 1998).

Smith, Christian, and R. Faris, "Socioeconomic Inequality in the American Religious System: An Update and Assessment," *Journal for the Scientific Study of Religion*, 44 (2005): 95–104.

Smith, Tom W., "Classifying Protestant Denominations," *Review of Religious Research*, 31 (3) (1990): 225–45.

Solomon, Michael R., G. Bamossy, S. Askegaard, and M.K. Hogg, *Consumer Behaviour: A European Perspective,* 3rd ed. (Harlow: Financial Times/ Prentice Hall, 2007).

Spence, Michael, "Signaling in Retrospect and the Informational Structure of Markets," *American Economic Review*, 92 (3) (2002): 434–59.

Srinivasan, Srini S., R. Anderson, and K. Ponnavolu, "Customer Loyalty in E-commerce: An Exploration of its Antecedents and Consequences," *Journal of Retailing*, 78 (1) (2002): 41–50.

Stahl, Geoff, "'It's Like Canada Reduced': Setting the Scene in Montreal," in Andy Bennett and Keith Kahn-Harris (eds), *After Subculture: Critical Studies in Contemporary Youth Culture*, 51–64 (New York: Palgrave Macmillan, 2004).

Stark, Rodney, "German and German-American Religiousness," *Journal for the Scientific Study of Religion*, 36 (1997): 182–93.

Stark, Rodney, "Secularization, R.I.P.," *Sociology of Religion*, 60 (3) (1999): 249–73.

Stark, Rodney, and W.S. Bainbridge, *A Theory of Religion* (New York: Peter Lang, 1987).

Stark, Rodney, R. Finke, and L.R. Iannaccone, "Pluralism and Piety: England and Wales 1851," *Journal for the Scientific Study of Religion*, 34 (1995): 431–44.

Stark, Rodney, and R. Finke, *Acts of Faith. Explaining the Human Side of Religion* (Berkeley: University of California Press, 2000).

Stark, Rodney, and C.Y. Glock, *American Piety: The Nature of Religious Commitment* (Berkeley & Los Angeles: University of California Press, 1968).

Stark, Rodney, and L.R. Iannaccone, "A Supply-Side Reinterpretation of the 'Secularization of Europe,'" *Journal for the Scientific Study of Religion*, 33 (3) (1994): 230–52.

Stark, Rodney and L.R. Iannaccone, "Truth and the Status of Religion in Britain Today: a Reply to Bruce," *Journal for the Scientific Study of Religion*, 34 (1995): 516–19.

Stark, Rodney, L.R. Iannaccone, and R. Finke, "Religion, Science and Rationality," *The American Economic Review*, 86 (2) (1996): 433–7.

Steensland, Brian, L.D. Robinson, W.B. Wilcox, J.Z. Park, M.D. Regnerus, and R.D. Woodberry, "The measure of American religion: Toward improving the state of the art," *Social Forces*, 79 (1) (2000): 291–318.

Stolowy, Hervé, A. Haller, and V. Klockhaus, "Accounting for Brands in France and Germany Compared with IAS 38 (Intangible Assets): An Illustration of the Difficulty of International Harmonization," *The International Journal of Accounting*, 36 (2) (2001): 147–67.

Stolz, Jörg, "Salvation Goods and Religious Markets: Integrating Rational Choice and Weberian Perspectives," *Social Compass*, 53 (1) (2006): 13–32.

Stolz, Jörg, "La théorie du choix rationnel et la sociologie des religions. Critiques et propositions," in J.-P. Bastian (ed.), *Pluralisation religieuse et logique de marché*, 61–78 (Bern: Peter Lang, 2007).

Stolz, Jörg, *Salvation Goods and Religious Markets: Theory and Applications* (Bern: Peter Lang, 2008).

Stolz, Jörg, "Salvation Goods and Religious Markets: Integrating Rational Choice and Weberian Perspectives," in Stolz, Jörg (ed.), *Salvation Goods and Religious Markets*, 51–80 (Bern: Peter Lang, 2008).

Stolz, Jörg, "Secularization Theory and Rational Choice. An Integration of Micro- and Macro-Theories of Secularization Using the Example of Switzerland," in D. Pollack, and D.V.A. Olson (eds), *The Role of Religion in Modern Societies*, 249–70 (New York: Routledge, 2008).

Stolz, Jörg, "Gods and Social Mechanisms. New Perspectives for an Explanatory Sociology of Religion," in M. Cherkaoui, and P. Hamilton (eds), *Raymond Boudon. A Life in Sociology. Essays in Honour of Raymond Boudon. Volume 3*, 171–88 (Oxford: The Bardwell Press, 2009).

Stolz, Jörg, "Explaining Religiosity: Towards a Unified Theoretical Model," *British Journal of Sociology*, 60 (2) (2009a): 345–76.

Stolz, Jörg, "A Silent Battle. Theorizing the Effects of Competition between Churches and Secular Institutions," *Review of Religious Research*, 51 (2010): 253–76.

Stolz, Jörg, and E. Ballif, *Die Zukunft der Reformierten. Gesellschaftliche Megatrends—kirchliche Reaktionen* (Zürich: TVZ, 2010).

Stolz, Jörg, and O. Favre, "The Evangelical Milieu: Defining Criteria and Reproduction across the Generations," *Social Compass*, 52 (2) (2005): 169–83.

Stolz, Jörg, J. Könemann, M. Schneuwly Purdie, T. Englberger, and M. Krüggeler, *Religion und Spiritualität in der Ich-Gesellschaft. Vier Gestalten des (Un-) Glaubens* (Zürich: TVZ/NZN, 2012)

Storm, Ingrid, "Halfway to Heaven: Four Types of Fuzzy Fidelity in Europe," *Journal for the Scientific Study of Religion*, 48 (4) (2009): 702–18.

Straw, Will, "Systems of Articulation, Logics of Change: Communities and Scenes in Popular Music," *Cultural Studies*, 5 (3) (1991): 368–88.

Stremersch, Stefan, and G.J. Tellis, "Strategic Bundling of Products and Prices: A New Synthesis for Marketing," *The Journal of Marketing*, 66 (1) (2002): 55–72.

Sylvan, Robin, *Traces of the Spirit: The Religious Dimensions of Popular Music* (New York: New York University Press, 2002).

Szymanski, David M., and R.T. Hise, "E-satisfaction: An Initial Examination," *Journal of Retailing*, 76 (3) (2000): 309–22.

Tabachnick, Barbara G., and L.S. Fidell, *Using Multivariate Statistics*, 5th ed. (London: Pearson/Allyn & Bacon, 2007).

Targos, William, "International Branding," in Susannah Hart and John Murphy, *Brands: The New Wealth Creators*, 123–34 (London: Palgrave, 1998).

Taylor, Steven A., K. Celuch, and S. Goodwin, "The Importance of Brand Equity to Customer Loyalty," *Journal of Product and Brand Management*, 13 (4) (2004): 217–27.

Thornley Primitive Methodist Chapel, *Quarterly Membership Return*, 1886, Durham Record Office: M/Th 6 (37–48).

Twitchell, James. B., *Adcult USA. The Triumph of Advertising in American Culture* (New York: Columbia University Press, 1996).

Twitchell, James B., *Branded Nation: The Marketing of Megachurch* (College Inc. and Museumworld: Simon and Schuster, 2005).

Twitchell, James B., *Shopping for God: How Christianity Went from In Your Heart to In Your Face* (New York: Simon & Schuster, 2007).

Usunier, Jean-Claude, and J.A. Lee, *Marketing Across Cultures. Fifth Edition* (New Jersey: Prentice Hall, 2009).

Usunier, Jean-Claude, and J. Shaner, "Using Linguistics for Creating Better International Brand Names," *Journal of Marketing Communications*, 8 (2002): 211–28.

Veyne, Paul, *Quand notre monde est devenu chrétien* (312–94) (Paris: Albin Michel, 2007).

Vivien, Alain, *Les Sectes en France: expressions de la liberté morale ou facteurs de manipulations? Rapport au Premier ministre* (Paris: La Documentation française, 1985).

Voas, David, "Intermarriage and the Demography of Secularization," *The British Journal of Sociology*, 54 (1) (2003): 83–108.

Voas, David, "The Rise and Fall of Fuzzy Fidelity in Europe," *European Sociological Review*, 25 (2) (2009): 155–68.

Voas, David, and S. Bruce, "The Spiritual Revolution: Another False Dawn for the Sacred," in Kieran Flanagan, and P. Jupp (eds), *A Sociology of Spirituality*, 43–62 (Aldershot: Ashgate, 2007).

Voas, David, and A. Crockett, "Religion in Britain: Neither Believing nor Belonging, *Sociology*, 39 (1) (2005): 11–28.

Voas, David, D.V.A. Olson, and A. Crockett, "Religious Pluralism and Participation: Why Previous Research is Wrong," *American Sociological Review*, 67 (2) (2002): 212–30.

Vokurka Robert J., and S.W. McDaniel, "A Taxonomy of Church Marketing Strategy Types," *Review of Religious Research*, 46 (2) (2004): 132–49.

Vokurka, Robert J., S.W. McDaniel, and N. Cooper, "Church Marketing Communication Methods," *Services Marketing Quarterly*, 24 (1) (2002): 17–32.

Wagner, Tom, Forthcoming. *Branding, Music and Transcendence: Hearing the "Hillsong Sound,"* PhD Dissertation: Royal Holloway, University of London.

Wallis, Roy, and S. Bruce, "Accounting for Action: Defending the Common-sense Heresy," *Sociology*, 17 (1983): 102–11.

Wallis, Roy, and S. Bruce, "Secularization: The Orthodox Model," in S. Bruce (ed.), *The sociology of religion*, 693–715 (Aldershot: Elgar, 1995).

Warner, R. Stephen, "Work in Progress toward a New Paradigm for the Sociological Study of Religion in the United States," *American Journal of Sociology*, 98 (5) (1993): 1044–93.

Webb, Marion S., W.B. Joseph, K. Schimmel, and C. Moberg, "Church Marketing: Strategies for Retaining and Attracting Members," *Journal of Professional Services Marketing*, 17 (2) (1998): 1–16.

Weber, Max, *The Protestant Ethic and the Spirit of Capitalism* (London: Unwin, 1971).

Weber, Max, *Economy and Society. An Outline of Interpretive Sociology* (Berkeley: University of California Press (1978 [1920])).

Weber, Max, *Wirtschaft und Gesellschaft* (Tübingen: J.C.B. Mohr (1985 [1922])).

Welling, Michael, *Ökonomik der Marke. Ein Beitrag Zum Theorienpluralismus in der Markenforschung* (Wiesbaden: 2006).

West, Stephen G., J.F. Finch, and P.J. Curran, "Structural Equation Models with Nonnormal Variables: Problems and Remedies," *Structural Equation Modeling* (1995).

White, Lynn Jr., "The Historical Roots of our Environmental Crisis," *Science*, 155 (1967): 1203–7.

Wolkomir, Michelle, M. Futreal, E. Woodrum, and T. Hoban, "Denominational Subcultures of Environmentalism," *Review of Religious Research*, 38 (4) (1997): 325–43.

Woodrum, Eric, and M.J. Wolkomir, "Religious Effects on Environmentalism," *Sociological Spectrum*, 17 (2) (1997): 223–34.

Wooldridge, Jeffrey M., *Econometric Analysis of Cross Section and Panel Data* (Cambridge: MIT Press, 2002).

Wrenn, Bruce, "Can (Should) Religion be Marketed?," *Quarterly Review. A Journal of Theological Resources for Ministry*, 14 (2) (1994): 117–34.

Yim, Chi Kin, and P.K. Kannan, "Consumer Behavioral Loyalty: A Segmentation Model and Analysis," *Journal of Business Research*, 44 (1999): 75–92.

Young, Lawrence A., *Rational Choice Theory and Religion* (London: Routledge, 1997).

Index of Authors

Index of Subjects

For Product Safety Concerns and Information please contact our EU
representative GPSR@taylorandfrancis.com
Taylor & Francis Verlag GmbH, Kaufingerstraße 24, 80331 München, Germany